The Ties That Divide

The Ties That Divide

Ethnic Politics, Foreign Policy, and
International Conflict

Stephen M. Saideman

COLUMBIA UNIVERSITY PRESS   NEW YORK

Columbia University Press
Publishers Since 1893
New York, Chichester, West Sussex
Copyright © 2001 Columbia University Press

Library of Congress Cataloging-in-Publication Data

Saideman, Stephen M.
    The ties that divide: ethnic politics, foreign
policy, and international conflict / Stephen M.
Saideman.
        p. cm.
    Includes bibliographical references and index.
    ISBN 0–231–12228–4 (cloth : alk. paper) —
ISBN 0–231–12229–2 (pbk. : alk. paper)
    1. Ethnic relations—Political aspects.   2. World
politics—1945–   3. International relations.
4. Culture conflict.   5. Developing countries—
Ethnic relations.   I. Title.

D883 .S15 2001
327—dc21
                                    00–047502

c   10   9   8   7   6   5   4   3   2   1
p   10   9   8   7   6   5   4   3   2   1

To Beulah, Kathy, and Jessica

Contents

Acknowledgments   *ix*

1. The Problem: Why Do States Take Sides in Ethnic Conflicts?   1

2. Explaining the International Relations of Ethnic Conflict   12

3. Understanding the Congo Crisis, 1960–1963   36

4. Religious Ties and the Nigerian Civil War, 1967–1970   70

5. The International Relations of Yugoslavia's Demise, 1991–1995   103

6. Quantitative Analyses of Ethnic Conflict's International
   Relations   154

   Appendix to Chapter 6   *200*

7. Findings, Future Directions and Policy Dilemmas   203

   Notes   *223*

   References   *249*

   Index   *269*

Acknowledgments

This project began as my dissertation, which I started shortly before the disintegration of Yugoslavia. The initial hope of the dissertation was to help understand what might happen if the Soviet Union and Yugoslavia collapsed. Ironically, I am not too late—as I revised the penultimate version, the Western countries intervened in Kosovo, breaking up *de facto*, if not *de jure*, the rump Yugoslav state. Further, the former Soviet Union is still disintegrating as the Chechnya conflict continues. In the time it has taken for me to complete this book, I have benefited from the assistance of many people.

The first debts I would like to acknowledge are to those who fostered the dissertation from which this book has sprung. The Institute on Global Conflict and Cooperation's Dissertation Fellowship funded my initial work on this project. Several people at IGCC, including the former directors, John Ruggie and Susan Shirk, as well as Sue Greer, Bettina Halverson, Jennifer Pournelle, and Kat Archibald, patiently answered my questions, and helped me in more ways than I can remember.

I am grateful to those who provided me with data and helped me analyze this data. Ted Robert Gurr, Anne Pitsch, Deepa Khosa, and The Center for International Development and Conflict Management at the University of Maryland have generously given me access to the Minorities at Risk Dataset, including raw data they collected. They also provided substantial assistance in using the dataset. Chapter six simply would not exist without their help. I am grateful to Douglas Van Belle, as he helped me develop my indicators for relative power that I used to code countries in chapters 3–5 and for the quantitative analyses in chapter 6. James Fearon provided crucial assistance in improving one of the indicators for linguistic differentials. My colleagues, past and present, at Texas Tech—particularly Ellen Anderson, Craig Emmert, Cherie Maestas, David Lanoue, and Grant Neeley—provided advice concerning the quantitative analyses. Michael Tomz helped me overcome some problems I had using the CLARIFY software.

I owe a great deal to those who have read this book in its previous drafts. I have asked many folks for a great deal of help, and received more than I asked or deserved. Obviously, my greatest debt is to Miles Kahler, who served as the chair of my dissertation committee. Over the years and particularly at the beginning, he provided insightful criticisms and helpful suggestions draft after draft. He constantly pushed me to clarify my points and to adjust my claims. Lisa Martin has often left me speechless as she consistently provided thorough and thoughtful comments more quickly than I had any right to expect. That she has always responded so insightfully and so quickly over the years has given me an ideal to which I aspire. Peter Cowhey provided penetrating comments on the early drafts. Conversations with Arend Lijphart, David Laitin, and Philip Roeder have greatly informed my understanding of ethnic politics. David Lake, Peter Gourevitch, and anonymous reviewers at *International Organization* gave me some very constructive criticism for my article published there, which summarizes much of this book, sharpening my argument. Columbia University Press's reviewers gave me very helpful ideas for improving this book. I am also indebted to Patrick James, Will Moore, and Jack Snyder for reading the penultimate draft and providing very helpful suggestions. Conversations with John Barkdull, Cherie Steele, and John Tuman were quite valuable in improving my thinking. I presented pieces of early versions of this book at a variety of conferences, and benefited from the comments from both panelists and discussants. In particular, I am grateful to David Lake, Tony Onyisi, and M. J. Peterson for their comments on my work at various conferences.

I benefited greatly from the IGCC project on the Spread and Management of Ethnic Conflict. This project began just after I finished my dissertation, so it greatly informed my revisions. While my contribution to that project is not directly related to this book, the conversations provoked by the project and the interaction with the participants stimulated my thinking. Discussions with James Fearon, George Kenney, Timur Kuran, David Lake and Donald Rothchild were especially beneficial.

I am particularly obliged to my colleagues from graduate school at UC, San Diego. Many read drafts, commented on my presentations, pushed me to improve my work, and suggested sources from other fields. Special thanks go to: David Auerswald, Deborah Avant, Brian Sala, Hendrik Spruyt, Stephen Swindle, and Michael Tierney. UCSD provided a truly supportive intellectual community—I have not been able to find anything close to it in my journeys since then.

Oberlin played as nearly as much of a role as UCSD. Isebill Gruhn and Ben Schiff were particularly important as they interested me in this line of work. Further, the students at Oberlin inspired me to think harder and more critically about my assumptions and about the world around me.

I am indebted to my co-authors: R. William (Bill) Ayres, Beth K. Dougherty, and David Lanoue. While our various projects are not directly related to this book, their contributions have informed my work, as well as relieving my workload. For that, I will always be grateful.

Cari McDonald helped corral the last bits of information I needed for this book and thanks to the Texas Tech College of Arts and Sciences for funding her research assistance. J.W. Justice and Young Choul-Kim provided valuable research during the final stages, and I owe them and the Carnegie Corporation of New York a debt for their assistance. Of course, the statements made and views expressed are solely the responsibility of the author, and not of the Carnegie Corporation.

The staff people within various Political Science Departments also made my work much easier. Christine Vaz, in particular, answered my questions, aided me in my battles against the UC bureaucracy, and generally made life easier. Kathy Klingenberg, Mary Quisenberry, Joan Brunn, Judy Lyman and Deb Morrison also helped me greatly in San Diego, as did Candace Smith did in Vermont. Dora Rodriguez and Donna Barnes, as well as some work study students, have been wonderful during my years at Texas Tech. I would also like to thank the anonymous folks in Texas Tech's Library Express department as they have quickly accessed and delivered a variety of resources.

Among the staff at Columbia University Press I would like to thank Kate Wittenberg, Senior Executive Editor, who not only tolerated all of my questions, but was also very quick to respond. She made the process much easier than I had expected. James Burger and James Short were also quite helpful in the editorial process. Leslie Bialler made the gruesome processes toward the end—copy-editing, indexing, proofing—far less painful than I would have imagined, and his good humor was always welcome, as well. Creative

Director Linda Secondari and designer Lisa Hamm were very helpful with the final stages of production, as were Judy Zielinski and David Espinosa at Impressions Book and Journal Services, Inc.

The comments and suggestions that I have received from all of these sources have significantly enhanced this book. However, the remaining flaws are my own responsibility, as I can be nearly as stubborn as my daughter, and, like her, I have not always listened.

My greatest debts are to my family. My mother, Beulah, sparked my interest in international relations long ago, unintentionally setting me out on this path. My daughter, Jessica, has often inspired me to work harder— to finish up so I can get home and play with her. I owe my wife, Katherine, for financial support during my graduate school years, for her editorial skills, which significantly improved my writing, and her emotional support during the many career swings. It is to these three women in my life (ok, two women and a big, big girl) that this book is dedicated.

Stephen M. Saideman
December 2000

The Ties That Divide

1 The Problem: Why Do States Take Sides in Ethnic Conflicts?

After the Cold War ended and the nearly unanimous effort to defeat Iraq during the Gulf War, scholars, policymakers and publics expected that countries would able to cooperate to manage crises and conflicts around the world. The European Community, as it transformed into the European Union, tried to develop a common foreign policy, hoping to play an important role in post–Cold War international relations. Yugoslavia's wars dashed these hopes because European states could not agree on how to handle them. Germany's efforts to recognize and support Slovenia and Croatia frustrated Britain and France. Russia's support of Serbia, and, by extension, the Bosnian Serbs, limited what the United States could do. Greece's policies toward Macedonia increased regional instability. Albania's support of the Kosovar Albanians increased the power and will of the Kosovo Liberation army, which, in part, caused Serbia to react violently, bringing NATO into a new war. Because the international community failed to cooperate effectively during the Bosnian conflict, analysts fear that unfortunate precedents have been set and that we need to develop new understandings of ethnic conflict so that we can manage future conflicts.[1]

Previous efforts to understand the international relations of ethnic conflict failed to help predict the dynamics surrounding Yugoslavia's demise. Therefore, analysts have argued that things have changed, so that the various institutions and norms that constrained states before are no longer as relevant.[2] There are two problems with this argument: first, it assumes that the old conventional wisdom was correct in explaining the past; and, second, as a result, it implies that past ethnic conflicts are not useful for understanding today's. Briefly, the conventional wisdom argues that in the past the mutual vulnerability of states to ethnic conflict inhibited their foreign policies, restricting support for secessionist movements and creating the Organization of African Unity and a norm of territorial integrity.[3] Now, it is argued, the norms these states developed have broken down, threatening the stability of boundaries in Africa and perhaps elsewhere. As this book will show, more states, including many that were vulnerable to separatism, supported secessionist movements even in Africa than usually suggested, but that we can still learn from the past to understand today's conflicts.

The purpose of the book is to address these difficulties. To be clear, the focus of this book is on the foreign policies of states toward ethnic conflict—the support they give to an ethnic group or the state it is battling—and not directly on the outcomes of these disputes. While the policies of external actors matter a great deal in shaping their outcome,[4] this study concentrates on the causes of these policies rather than their consequences. By asking why states take sides in ethnic conflicts, especially secessionist crises, past and present, I hope to show why the old conventional wisdom is wrong not only for today's conflicts but for yesterday's as well. In addition, I hope to demonstrate that the international dynamics of current ethnic conflicts are similar to those of the past. The answer this book poses is that the domestic political concerns of leaders, as determined by the interaction of ethnic ties and political competition, cause states to take one side or another (or both) of ethnic conflicts elsewhere. Consequently, getting states to cooperate over such disputes is much more difficult than generally argued.

In this chapter, I suggest why this question is important for both policy and academic debates, sketch out briefly the potential answers, and then present a brief outline of the book.

Relevance For Policymakers

Leaders throughout Europe, North America, and even the Middle East have focused their attention on the Yugoslav conflict, expending considerable political, military, economic, and diplomatic resources. Obviously, they must think the conflict is important. There are many reasons why policymakers cared about the Yugoslav conflict. There are the humanitarian concerns, as the conflict has produced atrocities reminiscent of Nazi war crimes.

Refugee flows have caused resentment and conflict in Germany and elsewhere. Economic sanctions have disrupted economies within the region, particularly hurting Macedonia and Romania. During the Bosnian war, leaders feared that the conflict might spread to Macedonia, perhaps causing a new war between Turkey and Greece. Many also argued that, as the first conflict after the end of the Cold War, the Yugoslavia conflict might set unfortunate precedents, encouraging demagogic politicians elsewhere to play the ethnic card. Finally, many politicians cared about the conflict because their supporters did. These same reasons also drew the attention of many states to ethnic conflicts in Rwanda, Chechnya, Sri Lanka, and Nagorno-Karabakh, among others.

Clearly, ethnic conflicts pose grave threats to the lives, livelihoods, and well being of everyone involved. Many articles and books have documented the costs of ethnic conflict imposed upon civilians as well as combatants. Ethnic cleansing has now entered our vocabulary, referring to the forced expulsion of members of an ethnic group to purify the region for another one. The strategy includes using artillery, selective executions, rape and other forms of terror to "encourage" civilians of the targeted ethnic group to flee. Many have documented the horrors committed in the name of ethnic nationalism in Bosnia.[5] When journalists reveal particular atrocities, leaders and publics in other countries are likely to desire an end to the conflict.

Since the early 1980s, ethnic conflicts have generated more refugees than any other kind of phenomena, natural or man-made, short of interstate war.[6] Refugee flows draw international attention and cause states to seek an end to the conflicts that spawn such movements for humanitarian, economic, and security reasons. When people flee a conflict, they usually suffer a great deal in the process, again causing outside actors to seek an end to the suffering. Refugees also impose costs on the countries to which they flee, since the host countries have to pay for food, shelter, clothing, and more. This is particularly troublesome since the poorest countries tend to bear the most severe burdens,[7] as the recent plight of Albania and Macedonia illustrates. Refugees cause economic dislocations as they compete for jobs and scarce goods.[8] The problem of civilians fleeing ethnic conflicts now affects more developed countries as nearly a million people fled to Western Europe from Yugoslavia.[9] Refugees may also threaten the security of countries. They can disturb the internal political balance of the host state by changing its ethnic composition. Refugees may also challenge the sovereignty of a country by controlling the territory they inhabit.[10] They may also increase tensions and conflict with the state from which they fled. To end the flow and return the refugees, the conflict that caused them has to end.

Refugee flows are not the only dynamic causing economic problems. States frequently rely on economic sanctions to compel various combatants to negotiate. While the debate about whether this strategy works is a lively one, there is much less controversy about the costs the sanctioning states must bear.[11] While economic sanctions against Serbia and Montenegro (the rump Yugoslavia) have had little impact on the economies of the United States and other major powers, they have cost Romania and other neighbors of Yugoslavia quite dearly.[12] Although sanctions are supposed to end a conflict, over time the desire develops to end the war so that the sanctions can stop.

Perhaps the most important reason why leaders care about ethnic conflict is the threat such conflicts pose to international peace and stability. "Saying the threat of ethnic violence today is 'no less serious than the threat of nuclear war was yesterday,' the Russian Foreign Minister today called for expanded United Nations peacemaking and peacekeeping, especially in the troubled republics of the former Soviet Union."[13] In his first speech at the United Nations, President Bill Clinton considered regional ethnic conflict to be one of the three most important sources of international instability.

The wars of Yugoslavia's disintegration provided the international community with a dramatic example of how ethnic conflict can promote regional instability. These conflicts remind us of other crises in the history of the region, highlighting the enduring relevance of ethnic conflict for international politics. Conflict between the Serbs and their neighbors occurred at the turn of the last century, leading to the assassination of Austria's Archduke Ferdinand by a Serbian irredentist, an event that triggered the First World War. While the Croatian and Bosnian conflicts remained within the boundaries of "Yugoslavia," the war in Kosovo threatened the stability of Macedonia, as well as increasing the likelihood of war among Albania, Bulgaria, Greece, Serbia, and Turkey. Separatist conflicts have spawned other wars, including the Ethiopia-Somalia war of 1977–1978 and the Indo-Pakistan war of 1971.

Ethnic conflicts may also spread to cause ethnic tensions to rise within other states. This chapter has thus far focused on some of the direct mechanisms through which ethnic conflict may diffuse—refugees and international intervention, but ethnic conflict may also indirectly cause more conflict elsewhere through demonstration effects and learning—contagion.[14]

Because of these consequences, which are likely to hurt many countries, analysts generally assume that the priority is to end such conflicts and to prevent a crisis from becoming an ethnic war. Barbara Walter argues that outside states need to mediate and provide credible security guarantees so that the combatants will agree to stop fighting.[15] Frank Harvey, among others, has argued that states need to make credible threats to compel the actors to stop fighting and to deter future fighting.[16] Jarat Chopra and Thomas Weiss argue that international organizations should subcontract to major powers to intervene in ethnic conflicts.[17] Chaim Kaufmann has argued that the best of all the bad solutions is to partition states that have deep ethnic conflicts, and that the international community should intervene on behalf of the weaker side.[18] A group of scholars, led by John Davies and Ted Gurr, has considered early warning systems so that states can act preventively.[19] Stedman takes more seriously the problem of getting domestic actors to cooperate, but he, too, overlooks the difficulty of getting states to cooperate.[20] The flaw in these approaches is that decisionmakers may actually care more about who wins and who loses. They may prefer the conflict to continue, rather than have their preferred combatant lose. If this is the case, then the problem of international cooperation is less about which mechanism is best for enforcing peace agreements,[21] and more about getting states to cooperate despite their disagreements.

Therefore, it is crucial that we examine whether and why states take sides in ethnic conflicts. It is logically prior to considering which mechanism should the international community use to deal with a conflict, since there needs to be some agreement among the relevant states for nearly any mechanism to work. This book evaluates explanations for why a state might choose to support one side or another—an ethnic group or its host state, because this question has been overlooked in the rush to develop conflict management tools to deal with such crises. Again, the Yugoslav conflict is quite instructive. Much frustration existed within the domestic politics of all of the states in the Contact Group (Great Britain, France, Germany, Russia, and the United States), as states failed to agree on solutions to the conflict. There was much criticism of President Clinton's inability to follow through on his campaign promises and other statements to do more for Bosnia. Perhaps the most important obstacles to American foreign policy toward Yugoslavia were the opposition of American allies, France and Britain, and sensitivity toward President Yeltsin's plight. The nationalists within Russia demanded support for their fellow Slavs, the Serbs, and criticized both the West and Yeltsin for failing to defend the Serbs.[22] I address the problem of cooperating over the Kosovo conflict in the concluding chapter.

It is important to realize that the Yugoslav experience is not unique. There have been other secessionist conflicts where states disagreed about whom they should support and about the mandate of international organizations. Rather than just trying to derive lessons from the most recent conflict, we need to compare the Yugoslav conflict to other similar conflicts to determine which patterns and dynamics are common to ethnic conflict in general. This book, by comparing the Congo Crisis of 1960–63 to the Nigerian Civil War and to the wars of Yugoslavia's disintegration, will provide some insights about how states react to such conflicts. Policymakers should not be surprised when states disagree, particularly when the leaders of various states depend on constituents who have ethnic ties to different sides of a conflict. By considering the three most likely explanations of the international relations of ethnic conflict—vulnerability, realism, and ethnic politics, I hope to clarify what policymakers should expect when ethnic crises develop in other states and what can be done to get states to cooperate to manage them.

Implications for Theory

This book also will have important implications for foreign policy analysis and international relations theory as it relates to the likelihood and consequences of international cooperation. Specifically, there are at least three different debates to which this book may relate: (1) diversionary theories of war—under what conditions will leaders use foreign policy for domestic political purposes; (2) preference formation—determining interests is essential for understanding international relations;[23] and (3) the relevance of international norms and international organizations—do international norms and organizations constrain the behavior of states, and if so, how and under what conditions?

The recent movie *Wag the Dog* and the coincidence of Clinton's impeachment with the use of force against Iraq have made the diversionary theory of war perhaps the most widely discussed hypothesis in public debates of all of foreign policy analysis. The essence of the argument is that external conflict tends to cause groups to become more united,[24] so politicians, intuitively understanding this, will engage in aggressive foreign policies when they want to increase unity at home.[25] The diversionary debate continues as analysts produce contradictory findings. This book hopes to refine the diversionary debate in two ways. First, it would address issues other than war or militarized interstate disputes by focusing on policies toward ethnic conflicts. Second, this book will suggest that the choice of target for a diversionary foreign policy is not random, but depends crucially on the domestic political challenges facing leaders.

This book relates to a second debate—what are the sources of states' preferences? Systemic theories have assumed that states seek to survive or maximize their power (variants of realism), or seek to maximize the welfare of their citizens (neoliberal institutionalism). Instead of focusing on what states, or their leaders, want, these approaches focus on how the structure of the situation encourages conflict or cooperation. Recently, scholars have focused more attention on how domestic politics might shape what leaders, and, therefore, states might desire. Andrew Moravcsik argues that liberalism, as opposed to neoliberal institutionalism, focuses on what individuals desire, how these desires are aggregated, and then the pattern of interests among states determines international outcomes.[26] Because this study compares argument based on domestic sources of preferences to the conventional wisdom based on neoliberal institutionalism,[27] this book should illustrate some of the distinctions that Moravcsik has drawn, and suggest the explanatory power of a preference-focused theory.

Third, the conventional wisdom of the international relations of ethnic conflict places much emphasis on the roles played by international organizations and norms.[28] By considering the limits of the conventional wisdom, this book might have implications for the growing debate about the impact of international norms. Specifically, under what conditions do norms trump domestic political incentives and vice versa? To be clear about the potential implications of this study for theoretical debates, I need to sketch out the rival arguments.

Competing Explanations

Rarely has any of the work on the international relations of ethnic conflict tested competing theories, so it has been hard to conclude which arguments provide the best explanations.[29] While I delineate the theories in the second chapter, it is important to spell out the arguments now so that the plan of the book makes sense.

Ethnic Politics

Chapter 2 develops an explanation based on the interaction between ethnic ties and political competition, asserting that domestic political concerns drive the foreign policies of states toward ethnic conflicts. Starting with the assumption that the desire to gain and maintain political office motivates politicians,[30] the argument follows that politicians care about the interests of their supporters. When it comes to ethnic conflicts in other states, the constituents of politicians are most likely to care about the plight of those with whom they share ethnic ties. Therefore, as long as politicians care about maintaining the support of these constituents, decisionmakers will support the combatants in ethnic conflicts elsewhere that share some sort of ethnic bond with their constituents. While all politicians must care somewhat about their supporters' desires, those facing competition will be more motivated to please their constituents. Thus, we should expect when a leader relies on supporters who have ties to a secessionist movement that the state's policy should be supportive of that movement. When the constituents in one state have ties to a state from which a group is trying to secede (a host state), then the first state will assist the second state. Leaders who face little competition may not be as attentive to their followers' desires, but leaders who face strong competition will certainly give assistance to those with whom their supporters share ethnic ties.[31] In sum, ethnic ties and political competition are the variables driving this argument.

Vulnerability

The conventional wisdom, focusing originally on Africa, has argued that ethnic divisions inhibit states from supporting separatist movements. This vulnerability also causes decisionmakers to strengthen the norm of territorial integrity by building international institutions—such as Organization of African Unity.[32] Separatism is a serious threat because most African states face serious racial, religious, tribal, and/or linguistic divisions. Leaders fear that once some group successfully questions one tenuous, artificial African boundary, then all the boundaries would be subject to challenges.

Although scholars developed the vulnerability argument to explain Africa's international relations, it has been applied to more current problems in other regions. Radmila Nakarada argues that "if the territorial integrity of Yugoslavia is compromised in the name of self-determination, then the ensuing secessions . . . will have an external domino effect. The Yugoslav precedent will reach other dissatisfied minorities (Basque, Corsica, Sardinia, Northern Ireland, Southern Tyrol, etc.) whose aspirations for independence will be encouraged. The supreme danger is that once a precedent is set, no European borders can escape re-examination."[33]

The vulnerability argument predicts that states facing their own ethnic conflicts will not support secessionists in other states for fear of encouraging either the breakdown in international norms or a direct backlash by the host state of the assisted separatists. The argument does not make specific predictions about states that are not vulnerable to secessionism. The vulnerability argument also stresses the roles played by international norms (the norm of territorial integrity) and international organizations, particularly the Organization of African Unity. By focusing on two African conflicts—the Congo and Nigeria, this book directly addresses the vulnerability argument on its home ground. If vulnerability fails to explain the behavior of African states, and if norms and international organizations do not constrain states, we should not be surprised when the vulnerability argument creates false expectations during Yugoslavia's wars.

Security Maximization

Realists expect that the international relations of ethnic conflict are similar to the behavior of states in other issue areas.[34] Therefore, relative power and security concerns should motivate states as they react to ethnic conflicts in other states. Since balancing is "the most central pattern" in international relations for realists,[35] we ought to expect that states will tend to support the weaker states and assist separatist movements in the stronger, more threatening states. That is, states will take sides depending on whether the state in question is a threat. In chapter 2, I will extend Stephen Walt's argument[36] about why states join alliances to develop realist predictions for the states' foreign policies toward ethnic conflicts. Specifically, I will develop an ad-

justed realist account focusing on relative power, offensive capabilities, proximity, and perceived intentions to develop realist expectations of the international relations of ethnic conflict.

Plan of the Book

This study develops competing explanations of the behavior of countries
toward ethnic conflicts, and then tests them through qualitative and quantitative analyses. Chapter 2 develops the competing explanations and presents the research design. First, the chapter delineates the vulnerability and
realist explanations, and derives testable hypotheses from these arguments.
Then, the chapter lays out a theory of how ethnic politics may affect foreign
policy, by focusing on the interests of politicians and of their constituents. I
draw some distinctions between how political competition combines with
ethnic politics versus more simplistic approaches that focus on the power of
nationalism.[37] In the remainder of chapter 2, I discuss the research design,
justifying the selection of the cases to be studied in chapters 3, 4, and 5, and
explaining the selection of the data to be used in chapter 6's quantitative
analyses.

Chapters 3, 4 and 5 examine how states reacted to three different secessionist crises.[38] Chapter 3 examines the international relations of the Congo
Crisis from 1960–1963. I review how the crisis started, and then present the
ethnic politics of the Katangan separatist movement, since this significantly
shaped how states perceived the conflict. Specifically, I discuss how states
perceived the essentially tribal conflict as a dispute between white colonists
and their allies on one side and black nationalists on the other. Then, the
chapter briefly assesses the United Nations' armed intervention. By focusing
on Katanga's most energetic supporters, its most hostile enemies, and some
states that were more ambivalent, I apply the competing arguments to the
behavior of more than a dozen countries.

Chapter 4 considers the behavior of outside actors toward Nigeria's civil
war of 1967–1970. Again, the chapter begins with a discussion of the origins
of the conflict. The focus of the discussion is on how the conflict became
one of religion: the predominantly Christian Ibos versus the predominantly
Muslim Hausa-Fulani. The religious definition of the conflict influenced
how outsiders reacted to the conflict, with much more disagreement among
African countries than usually presented.

Chapter 5 applies the competing theories to the international relations of Yugoslavia's demise. I discuss the conflict's origins briefly, as the ethnic dynamics within Yugoslavia influenced outside actors. Because so much has been written about Yugoslavia, the discussion of the actions of various international organizations will be brief. Instead, to explain the ambivalence, confusions, and failed efforts of international organizations, the rest of the chapter will consider why states disagreed so much about what to do and whom to support. Because there are so many potential separatists to support, this chapter is structured differently, focusing first on the most puzzling behavior of outsider actors. Then, I analyze the other significant actors.

Chapter 6 presents a variety of quantitative analyses. First, I present a variety of cross-tabulations to examine the performance of the competing arguments in chapters 3, 4 and 5. Second, the chapter presents some trends in the international relations of ethnic conflict in the 1990s to consider whether the fears of vulnerability theorists have been realized. Third, I present analyses of the attributes of ethnic groups to see what causes groups to receive support—focusing on both breadth and intensity of assistance. Fourth, the chapter presents analyses focusing on states' characteristics to determine which kinds of states are more likely to support ethnic groups elsewhere.

Chapter 7 compares the findings of the case studies and the statistical analyses to determine what causes states to support particular ethnic groups. Then, I briefly discuss the 1999 Kosovo conflict to show that ethnic politics still impedes international cooperation in the Balkans. Next, I draw the book's implications for the roles of norms, international organizations, domestic politics, and security concerns in the foreign policies of states toward ethnic conflicts. Finally, I consider this book's implications for policy debates and potential directions for future research.

2 Explaining the International Relations of Ethnic Conflict

Why do states support some ethnic groups but not others? Why do states support some states resisting secessionism, i.e., host states, but not all? The conventional wisdom is that states that are vulnerable to ethnic conflict are inhibited from supporting separatists in other states, and that this weakness will cause states to develop and then respect international organizations and norms. This argument has at least two significant flaws: it fails to explain why a state would support a secessionist movement and some do; and, many vulnerable states have supported separatist movements, as case studies in the subsequent chapters demonstrate. A likely alternative argument would be that the search for security motivates states, so a state will consider whether supporting a particular separatist movement is likely to improve its security. The neorealist focus on balancing behavior suggests that a state will support secessionist movements in those host states that threaten it, and oppose separatists in its allies. This book proposes a different argument, focusing on domestic politics. I develop a theory of ethnic politics and foreign policy, arguing that the interaction of ethnicity and domestic political competition produce incentives for politicians to support one side or another of ethnic conflicts in other states. According to this argument, the existence of ethnic ties between decisionmakers' supporters and the combatants in conflicts in other states will greatly determine the foreign policies of states. Consequently, this chapter presents competing explanations based on, respectively, international norms and organizations, security, and domestic politics. After discussing each approach, the last section of this chapter presents the book's research design.

The Conventional Wisdom: Vulnerability Inhibits States

"The greatest deterrent to territorial revisionism has been the fear of open-ing a Pandora's box. If any one boundary is seriously questioned, why not all the boundaries in Western Africa?"[1] This is the heart of conventional understandings of Africa's boundary politics and beyond. Saadia Touval stresses the vulnerability of African states to separatism to explain why they have not supported secessionist movements. "Since most states are vulner-able to external incitement to secession, it was obvious to the majority of states that reciprocal respect for boundaries, and mutual abstinence from irredentism,[2] would be to their advantage."[3] Touval goes on to argue that Somalia was the exception that proved the rule. Somalia's relative invulner-ability to ethnic conflict, due to its homogeneity, explains its exceptional irredentism.[4] While the rise of clan conflict in the early 1990s and the de facto secession of Somaliland (northern Somalia) demonstrate that Somalia is currently vulnerable to ethnic conflict, an examination of its history in-dicates that secessionism and ethnic conflict have plagued Somalia since independence in 1960.[5]

Robert Jackson and Carl Rosberg argue that the norms of international society preserve African states lacking the empirical requisites of statehood.[6] Empirical statehood, as defined by Max Weber and others, requires cen-tralized control of the means of force and an ability to exercise control of a territory. Jackson and Rosberg assert that most sub-Saharan states have lacked these attributes at one time or another without ceasing to exist. Instead, the juridical nature of statehood explains why such states have continued to exist and remained intact. The argument stresses international society, which sup-ports the rights of states, including the right to noninterference and territorial integrity. Consequently, they argue that African states and outside actors have been unwilling to support separatist movements, because of the inter-national society's prohibition against changing existing boundaries.[7]

Jackson and Rosberg's application of Grotian theory contains keen insights into the nature of sovereignty, but one of their central points is problematic.[8] Jackson and Rosberg assert that "there is a *common interest* in the support of international rules and institutions and state jurisdictions in the African region that derives from the *common vulnerability of states* and the insecurity of statesmen."[9] Thus, they make one very important, but very questionable assertion: that vulnerability to ethnic conflict and separatism presents African leaders with similar opportunities and constraints. Astri

Suhrke and Lela Garner Noble argue, "This may well be too facile an assumption."[10]

Rather than basing his argument on Grotian theory, Jeffrey Herbst applies Robert Keohane's neoliberal institutionalism to explain why African states have been able to maintain their boundaries, developing a vulnerability argument similar to Jackson and Rosberg's.[11] He compares the formation of African boundaries by the colonial powers to the newly independent African states' recognition of those boundaries.[12] He argues that politicians in both situations faced similar interests and obstacles: the motivation to avoid war and the problems of defining boundaries in a continent without clear dividing demographic, ethnographic or topographic formations. Herbst argues that both the Berlin Conference of 1885 and the Organization of African Unity [OAU] designed simple decision rules to overcome the problems of administration and weak institutionalization. After decolonization, African leaders found control over the capital city of a territory, surrounded by colonial boundaries, to be sufficient.[13]

Herbst's argument offers an excellent explanation of why African states chose particular rules and institutions. However, his analysis of African leaders' motivation to cooperate is flawed. He argues that African states were too weak institutionally to exert control over territory within their own boundaries, not to mention administering territories beyond the existing borders. Therefore, they were not interested in expansion. In addition, the costs and uncertainties of war were too great, especially the possible "echo effects" of other states also forcing changes in their boundaries.[14]

While African leaders did seek to avoid war, this did not necessarily inhibit them from supporting secessionist movements in other African states. Herbst seems to consider only Somali-like irredentist invasions as boundary changing behavior or violations of territorial integrity rather than support for secessionist movements, such as diplomatic recognition or the provision of military equipment. Yet aiding secessionist movements in other states would not require the material or institutional resources needed for war nor would it necessarily engender the grave costs that war may entail.

To buttress his argument, Herbst uses the notion of *specific reciprocity*, as developed by Robert Keohane.[15] "The reciprocal agreement followed by the independent African states is the same as that followed by the European colonialists: one nation will not attack or be attacked as long as minimal domestic administrative presence is demonstrated."[16] The behavior of each African state is contingent on the behavior of the other states: each will cooperate as long as the others cooperate. However, "specific reciprocity is not a sure-fire recipe for promoting cooperation."[17] Specific reciprocity can lead to either cooperation or mutual recrimination. The interesting question is why cooperation develops, as in Africa generally, rather than a feud, as in South Asia between Pakistan and India; specific reciprocity cannot predict which outcome will occur or explain why.

The difficulty lies in one of the main assumptions of specific reciprocity: "the extent to which the players have interests in common."[18] Assuming common interests begs the most important and interesting question: why do particular states have common interests and are willing to cooperate, while others do not? Herbst, like Jackson and Rosberg, argues that all African leaders confront a similar threat, Balkanization, and that this threat gave these leaders a common incentive to cooperate.[19]

Still, even if we assume that states have common interests, they must solve a collective action problem, as Herbst admits. "However, in the case of the state system that protects African boundaries, the large number of states is not a problem, because each state still feels at risk from secession, conquest, or some other boundary change."[20] Although elites face many threats, for Herbst, vulnerability to secession overrides the collective action problem. "Since all countries are at risk from disgruntled minority groups, there is a general sense that all states gain crucial protection from the current system."[21]

Herbst's approach does not adequately solve the problem that he seeks to address. Why do states still cooperate despite the temptation to free ride? Given the logic of collective action,[22] vulnerability is not sufficient for explaining cooperation; the existence of common interest is insufficient for explaining cooperation—the temptation to free ride continues to exist. The move that Herbst and others make is that there is no free riding because a single violation of the boundary regime may undermine the entire system. "Precisely because all parties know that once African boundaries begin to change there would be an indefinite period of chaos, the grave danger of not cooperating is clear to all."[23] Thus, since any boundary change, such as a successful secession, would reverberate throughout Africa,[24] no country would have any interest in supporting such behavior.

In these arguments, analysts treat vulnerability to ethnic conflict in general and secessionism specifically as a sufficient condition for explaining why a state would not support a separatist movement. Yet, vulnerability fails to explain why a state would want to support a secessionist movement, suggesting only that a state that was invulnerable to secessionism could do so if it wanted. Because states do help secessionists, the vulnerability argument only accounts for one value of the dependent variable. Further, mutual vulnerability does not necessarily mean that states will pursue identical solutions to shared problems, for vulnerability may present different politicians with varying interests. Vulnerability by itself says very little about how leaders choose to deal with their fragile positions and divided states. Leaders may opt for external aggression to unify a divided society,[25] or they may opt to acquiesce, depending on the nature of the internal conflict they face and their political interests.[26] The third flaw in vulnerability thinking is that mutual vulnerability may cause states to try to engage in preemptive behavior—one state may support separatists in a neighbor since the nearby state may do so. Thus, rather than deterring states from supporting secessionists, vulnerability may compel fearful states to support such groups.[27] This is similar to the problem faced by Herbst—reciprocity predicts that states respond in kind, but fails to address why mutual cooperation rather than mutual recrimination is the expected outcome. The fourth major problem with vulnerability arguments is that states under attack by secessionist movements have supported similar groups in other states, which the next four chapters prove.

Despite the vulnerability argument's weaknesses, it remains popular today as analysts apply it beyond the African context. Radmila Nakarada refers to Pandora's Box, arguing that the disintegration of Yugoslavia might threaten to cause ethnic conflict throughout Western Europe[28] while others argued that it might spread to the Soviet Union.[29]

The heart of the vulnerability argument is that vulnerable states do not support separatist movements, and they actively support the creation and maintenance of international organizations and norms to maintain existing boundaries at the expense of self-determination. From these arguments, particularly those of Jackson and Rosberg and Herbst, we can derive the following testable hypotheses:

V1. *States that are vulnerable to ethnic conflict and separatism are less likely to support secessionist movements.*

V2. *The existence and specification of international norms prohibiting assistance to secessionists decreases the likelihood of states supporting secession.*

V3. *The involvement of international organizations trying to limit external support to secessionist movements should reduce the likelihood of such support.*

V4. *A state sharing a history of cooperation with a host state will not support separatists within the host state.*

V5. *A state sharing a history of conflict with a host state is more likely to support separatism within the host state.*

The first three can be derived from either Jackson and Rosberg or Herbst as each assert the importance of vulnerability, norms, and international organizations. The latter two are logical implications of Herbst's application of specific reciprocity.

Table 2.1 summarizes the most important predictions of the vulnerability argument.

In sum, the vulnerability approach predicts that states vulnerable to secessionism will support host states and oppose secessionists. The vulnerability assumption by itself makes no predictions about the behavior of invulnerable states. However, the larger arguments associated with the vulnerability assumption suggest that international norms and international organizations may constrain even invulnerable states.

Realism and the International Relations of Ethnic Conflict

Alexis Heraclides argues that states support secessionist movements abroad to improve their international political positions. "Most important among instrumental motives and instrumental restraints were considerations

TABLE 2.1 The Vulnerability Argument's Predictions

	State is Vulnerable to Secessionism		Existence of International Norms, Involvement of International Organizations	
Predicted Policy:	Yes	No	Yes	No
State Supports Secessionists	No	Indeterminate	No	Indeterminate
State Supports Host State	Yes	Indeterminate	Yes	Indeterminate

of an international political nature, namely the international political con-
figuration of the region, strategic gains, position of allies, great and middle
powers and friends, and relations with the state (government) threatened by
secession."[30] Unfortunately, Heraclides does not develop a theory or a model
of international political interests and secession.[31] Indeed, no realist or Neorealist has applied their approach directly to the international relations of
secession.[32] We can apply realism by extending its logic to this issue area.
The problem, of course, is that realism is not a single approach, but a set of
approaches, with contrasting assumptions and conclusions. Specifically, defensive realism asserts that states balance power or threats; while offensive
realism suggests that states engage in predatory behavior.[33] Since defensive
realism is the more widely accepted realist theory of foreign policy,[34] the
case studies will test the essential argument of defensive realism—that states
balance threats,[35] while the quantitative analyses will evaluate both defensive
and offensive realism. In this section, I extend the balance of threat argument
to develop testable hypotheses for the international relations of ethnic conflict, and then I briefly discuss the implications of offensive realism.

A. Balancing Threats by Supporting Ethnic Conflict

The essence of realism is that states seek to maintain their security in a
dangerous world. For defensive realists, this means that states will respond
to threats through the creation of alliances. Stephen Walt asserts that states
will generally ally to balance against the greatest external threats.[36] For this
book, I extend Walt's approach, suggesting that there is an additional way to
balance threats: supporting efforts, particularly those of secessionist movements, to weaken one's adversary by promoting its dissolution. States can
improve their relative position and security by abetting efforts that would
reduce the aggregate power of their adversaries and the threats they pose.
The most general hypothesis that can be derived from the realist viewpoint,
then, is that *when threatened by another state, states will support secessionist
movements in that state* (in addition to, or instead of forming alliances).

The most important aspect of Walt's approach is the perception of threats.
Walt considers the most important variables affecting "the level of threat that
states may pose: aggregate power, geographical proximity, offensive power,
and aggressive intentions."[37] The latter three components are Walt's inno-
vation, and he adds them to the core of the traditional and Neorealist balance

of power model,[38] which concentrates on the relative capabilities of states. The greater a state's power is, holding all else constant, the more threatening it is. *The stronger a state is, the more likely others will support secessionist movements within it.*

Likewise, when a state increases its offensive capability, it poses a greater danger to other states. While Walt's notion of offensive capability is very traditional with his focus on the relative advantage of the offense or defense, he considers offensive power as "the ability to threaten the sovereignty or territorial integrity of another state at an acceptable cost."[39] Recently, he has expanded his notion of offensive capability to include ideological subversion.[40] His approach therefore might be stretched further to consider the ability to support a secessionist movement, i.e., the ability to threaten the territorial integrity of a state, as an offensive capability. *A state able to support secession then will pose a severe threat, causing others to support secession within that state.* The problem here is that this will not vary much among states, since all states can grant diplomatic recognition, and nearly all states are capable of giving other forms of assistance.

The third aspect of threat, geographic proximity, is clear—the closer an adversary is, the greater the threat is poses. States will respond more strongly if the potential adversary is nearby than if it is far away, often resulting in checkerboard patterns of alignment.[41] Obviously, for this project, geographic proximity plays a role as it allows states to provide assistance such as arms and equipment to separatist movements more effectively. One would expect that states would react most strongly to the activities of and crises within their neighbors, as opposed to states on another continent.[42] Therefore, *states will be more likely to support secession in their neighbors than elsewhere.*

The fourth, and most complicated, component of threat, is perceived intentions. "States that are viewed as aggressive are likely to provoke others to balance against them."[43] Of course, a state with aggressive intentions is more threatening than a state without such aims. The focus on perceived intentions raises two difficult issues. How do states perceive intentions? Why does a state develop particular intentions? For Walt's work, the question of how states perceive different threats is problematic. "Perceptions of intent are likely to play an especially crucial role in alliance choices. . . . One cannot determine a priori, however, which sources of threat will be most important in any given case; one can only say that all of them are likely to play a role."[44] This difficulty leaves Walt's work with a significant hole. He cannot predict the alignment of states if he cannot suggest how states will generally perceive intentions or weigh the different components of threat.

Walt's argument also leaves open the question of why states develop aggressive intentions.[45] Why be hostile if this will cause counter-balancing alliances, as Walt argues? Regardless of this problem, it does produce the following hypothesis: *a state perceived as willing to use the ability to disrupt the territorial integrity of other states will provoke increased support by other states for secessionist movements within its own territory.*[46] Briefly put, where Walt would expect alliance formation, this book expects support for separatists attacking the perceived adversary. States support secessionist movements in those states that threaten them.

Walt does an excellent job of explaining why states react as they do to perceived threats, but he does not really develop a theory of threat formation or perception. One source of this weakness is Walt's interest in avoiding the inclusion of domestic politics in his argument. Steven David explicitly incorporates domestic politics in his theory of omni-balancing.[47] For David, leaders are concerned about both domestic and international threats, and often choose to ally externally with whatever states are likely to help them in their domestic battles. This book goes further than David's: arguing that leaders are primarily worried about domestic politics, causing them to engage in foreign policies that can run strongly against their country's security concerns.

By explaining states' foreign policy preferences, derived from elites' interests, the theory of ethnic politics and foreign policy may aid in comprehending why some threats are perceived as such and why some states develop "hostile" or "aggressive" intentions. Ethnic politics cannot explain all the adversarial relationships in the world. However, when considering relations toward separatists and the desire to support the enemy of one's adversary, the definition of enemies and threats may be better understood if ethnic rivalries within and between states are taken into account.

B. Maximizing Power and Predatory States

Recently, scholars have engaged in a lively intra-realism debate about whether states pursue power or security. Those arguing that states maximize power consider themselves offensive realists.[48] Schweller argues that "What triggers security dilemmas under anarchy is the possibility of predatory states."[49] States that seek power are the cause of insecurity, Schweller asserts. Labs goes further, suggesting that all states are opportunistic, and will expand power if they can do so with relative little cost.[50] For this study, Labs makes an important prediction: "Stronger states are more likely to purse expansion than weak states, because, all other things being equal, they are more able to do so."[51] This suggests *that stronger states will support secessionists in weaker states*, and this will hold true not only for great powers, but also for weak states, as they prey upon even weaker states.[52] Further, weaker states may be deterred from supporting ethnic groups in stronger states since such states are more dangerous. Thus, offensive realism predicts the very opposite of defensive realism's predictions.

The difficulty we face in the case studies is that a secessionist group may get support from states that are stronger than the host state as well as those that are weaker. Without a good theory of why some states may be predatory and others not, it will be hard to conclude that either realist variant is on target. Ultimately, it may be hard to tell whether power and security issues matter at all. The quantitative analysis should provide more conclusive results about which variant of realism better explains the international relations of ethnic conflict.

In sum, realist accounts produce the following testable hypotheses:

R1. *When threatened by another state, states will be more likely to support secessionist movements in that state.*

R2. *The stronger a state is, the more likely others will support secessionist movements within it.*

R3. *States are more likely to support secessionists in a state able to support secession.*

R4. *States will be more likely to support secession in their neighbors than elsewhere.*

R5. *States supporting secession are more likely to encounter much opposition internationally, and their secessionist movements will get more support.*

R6. *Stronger states are more likely to support secessionists in weaker states* (offensive realism).

Table 2.2 summarizes the most important realist prediction for the case study. States will respond to threats by supporting secessionists, but if a host state poses no threat, then predictions become less clear. As the case studies

TABLE 2.2 Defensive Realism and Expected Foreign Policies

Predicted Policy:	Host State:	
	Is Threatening	Not a Threat
State Supports Secessionists	Yes	No
State Supports Host State	No	Indeterminate

reveal, figuring out how to combine the various components of threat consistently is a difficult task.

Ethnic Ties, Political Competition and Foreign Policy

Ethnic politics does not always inhibit foreign policy as the vulnerability arguments asserts, but serves as a critical dynamic compelling some politicians to support secession elsewhere while constraining others.[53] The theory of ethnic politics and foreign policy builds upon a few basic assumptions and deductions about the motivations of politicians, the interests of their supporters, and their influence upon foreign policy. First, politicians care primarily about gaining and maintaining office, the prerequisite for most other goals attainable through politics.[54]

Second, each politician requires the support of others to gain and maintain political offices—the supporters forming the politician's constituency. How the constituency supports a decisionmaker varies, depending on the regime type and on existing political institutions. In a democracy, the constituency's support primarily comes through voting, though campaign contributions also matter. In an authoritarian regime, the leaders' constituencies generally consist of those who control the means of repression, such as the officer corps of the military as well as the security apparatus. Regardless of the particular support mechanisms, incumbent politicians care most about preventing these supporters from leaving their coalition, i.e., exiting.[55] The degree to which the politician is threatened—the intensity of political competition—depends on existing political institutions, particularly as these institutions affect the alternatives available to potential defectors. For instance, if there is only one party, or if existing parties are unable to exert influence due to the particular electoral system, then the politician does not need to be as concerned about the loss of some constituents.

Third, ethnic identities influence the preferences of potential and existing constituents, and, therefore, who might wish to exit and why.[56] Ethnic groups are "collective groups whose membership is largely determined by real or putative ancestral inherited ties, and who perceive these ties as systematically affecting their place and fate in the political and socioeconomic structures of their state and society."[57] These ties usually are related to race, kinship (tribe or clan), religion, and language. There is a long-running debate about whether ethnic identity is a given in society (primordial) or created by politicians as they see fit. I follow the moderate position: multiple ethnic identities frequently co-exist, and the political context determines the salience of particular identities.[58]

From these assumptions, we can deduce that the ethnic ties of potential and existing constituents to external actors influence politicians' preferences. If ethnic identity influences individuals' preferences toward domestic policies, these same identities should influence constituents' preferences toward foreign policies. Scholars have found that ethnic ties influence states' behavior. Davis and Moore find that the existence of ethnic ties between an advantaged group in one state and a nonadvantaged group in a second state increases the probability of interstate conflict.[59] Henderson finds that, since 1820, the existence of religious differences between states increases the probability of war.[60] Carment and James find that ethnic conflicts are different from other kinds of conflicts.[61] Consequently, we have some reason to believe our deduction that ethnicity plays some role in the foreign policy decision making process.

Why does ethnicity matter for foreign policy? First, ethnic identity, by its nature, creates feelings of loyalty, interest, and fears of extinction.[62] International boundaries do not cause members of ethnic groups to ignore the condition of those who are similar to themselves—their ethnic kin.[63] Constituents will care most about those with whom they share ethnic ties, or those with whom a history of ethnic enmity exists. Ethnic enmity matters as much as ethnic ties, because ethnicity is partially an attempt to define who one is by who one is not.[64] Second, ethnic ties influence foreign policymaking because support for ethnic kin abroad can be a litmus test for a politician's sincerity on ethnic issues at home. Politicians lack credibility if they take symbolic stands on ethnic issues, but do not follow up when an ethnically charged foreign event develops.

Politicians care about the ethnic composition of their supporters, as this may determine who might exit and over what issues. Thus, politicians avoid certain issues and embrace others to prevent their supporters from exiting and to attract their competitors' constituents. For instance, if a politician needs Muslims for political support, then the role of religion in the state will be a prominent area of interest for both the politician and his/her supporters. If a politician's supporters are predominantly African-American, then the constituency of that politician will prefer policies benefiting African-Americans. The ethnic identities of potential defectors not only restrain politicians, but they can also provide opportunities.

Politicians can use the circumstances of ethnic kin to emphasize certain ethnic identities at the expense of other identities and other issues. When constituents become focused on economic problems or on a particularly problematic ethnic identity, a politician can use a foreign event to increase the salience of a specific ethnic identity domestically, creating unity—at least for the short term.[65] Consequently, if ethnic ties determine the foreign policy preferences of constituents, then such ties also influence the politician's foreign policy choices—both as constraint and opportunity. The constituents may compel the politician to follow a particular foreign policy, the politician may anticipate their demands, or the politician may use foreign policy to emphasize particular identities and de-emphasize others. To be clear, the theory here does not specify whether politicians are manipulating the public or are being pushed by public opinion. Ethnic politics can produce top-down or bottom-up dynamics. While one dynamic may produce different policies than the other, it may be hard to distinguish the two in practice.[66] Therefore, I do not develop these distinctions here. Either way, if the politician can influence foreign policy, the existence of ethnic ties and antagonisms between the politician's supporters and external actors will shape the state's foreign policy.

Table 2.3 presents the predictions that a focus on the ethnic ties provides. Specifically, states will assist the side with which the ruling politicians' constituency shares ethnic ties. Because constituents care about those with whom they share ethnic ties, they prefer for their state to take sides in ethnic conflicts elsewhere, supporting the side with which they have ethnic ties. Politicians, because they need support and fear its loss, take the preferences of their supporters seriously, and push for policies assisting the ethnic kin of their constituents. Ethnic enmity will work in ethnic politics like realism does in international relations insofar as the enemy of my enemy is my

TABLE 2.3 Ethnic Ties and Expected Foreign Policies

Predicted Policy:	Ruling Politician's Constituency Has Ethnic Ties With:		
	Secessionists	Both	Host State
State Supports Secessionists	Yes	Yes/No*	No
State Supports Host State	No	Yes/No*	Yes

* If constituency has ties to both sides of an ethnic conflict, the state is likely either to support both sides (ambivalence) or neither (neutrality).

friend. A politician's constituents want not only to support their ethnic kin, but also to oppose those with whom they share a history of ethnic enmity. Ethnic enmities cause politicians not only to oppose those actors with whom ethnic enmity exists, but also to support ethnic groups fighting the ethnic adversary of their constituents.

A. Heterogeneity and Competition

One complication is that the constituencies of politicians are not always homogenous. The constituency of a politician may consist of multiple ethnic groups, with each having ties to different sides of ethnic conflicts in other countries. For instance, a hypothetical politician's constituency consists of both Muslims and Jews. When dealing with conflicts between these two religious groups in other states, that politician has a hard time choosing which side to support. The politician prefers to avoid taking a position on the conflict—neutrality. The politician may also try to satisfy both groups by supporting both sides of the conflict—ambivalence. Alternatively, politicians depending upon multiple ethnic groups for support may develop non-ethnic ideologies to bind their constituents together and to deemphasize the role of ethnicity in politics. Civic nationalisms may have less clear implications for foreign policies than ethnic nationalisms, as the content of the particular civic nationalism varies from state to state.[67] The content matters as it shapes the definition of friends, enemies, and acceptable policies. For instance, Indian nationalism requires an independent, anti-colonial foreign policy.[68]

Because political competition drives this process, we should expect behavior to vary as competition varies among states.[69] Generally, all politicians should care about their supporters, even if they face relatively less competition because all politicians are "running scared."[70] That is, more support means more power, and although the defection of supporters may not mean the immediate loss of power, their departure generally leaves politicians weaker than if they had not defected. Still, politicians facing less competition are somewhat more autonomous than those who must worry very much about the defection of a few supporters. Hence, while ethnic ties should influence the foreign policies of all states having such ties, the states most likely to develop policies that run counter to the ties of the leader's constituents are those where competition is relatively less intense. In other words, we should expect all politicians facing high competition to support the side with which they have ethnic ties, and we should expect *most, but not all*, politicians feeling less competitive pressures to behave similarly.

The role of competition here separates this theory of ethnic politics and foreign policy from approaches focusing purely on the power of nationalism without considering how ethnicity plays out through the political process.[71] Such approaches assume that all countries with a given ethnic identity will give support to ethnic kin elsewhere because of the emotional bonds of their citizens. However, these arguments ignore the political process. Leaders facing less competition or cross-pressures may be less interested in supporting the population's ethnic kin.[72]

For ethnic ties to matter in political competition, the most likely folks to exit one politician's constituency and enter another's have to possess an identifiable ethnic character. If a politician has to worry about the Socialist Party exiting and they have no ethnic appeal, the threat of exit is unlikely to produce an ethnic foreign policy. However, if a party or group of important constituents can be identified by its ethnicity, particularly if it makes ethnic demands, then ethnic ties come into play.

B. Perceiving Ethnic Ties and Enmities

Because ethnicity is a perceptual, rather than objective, phenomenon, the crucial question becomes: why are ethnic ties or enmities perceived in each particular case? Whether some ethnic bonds are more important depends on the political and social contexts. It is difficult to predict a priori which ethnic ties will be perceived as more salient than others. For the case studies, three factors help to explain why some ethnic identities are perceived as being important and at stake, while others are not: the combatants' ethnic composition; the secessionists' strategies; and the particular group's history.[73]

The ethnic composition of the secessionists and of their host state are the most obvious factors influencing the perception of ethnic ties between the secessionists and the constituencies of elites in other states. If a secessionist movement is religiously homogeneous, and the movement is seceding from a state of consisting of members of another religion, then religion will most likely be perceived to be the salient ethnic division of the conflict. However, a secessionist movement is rarely homogeneous and often multiple kinds of ethnic identities may be salient. Which of these identities influences the perceptions of outsiders depends on other factors.

Some secessionist movements will try to define themselves in certain ways, thus shaping the perceptions of themselves and their adversaries. As politicians within states seek to emphasize particular identities, so do leaders of secessionist movements to gain more support from those inhabiting the secessionist region. Because international support is so critical to the success of secessionist movements, these efforts to emphasize ethnicity may be aimed at both domestic and international audiences.[74] A politician seeking the support of a racially homogenous but linguistically heterogeneous region will seek to define the conflict as one of race rather than language. The policies that this politician might follow would then influence the perceptions of those in other countries. Further, to increase international support, leaders of secessionist movements may emphasize wider identities, such as race or religion, rather than language or kinship. Consequently, politicians leading secessionist movements may follow policies and make statements that cause the constituents of politicians elsewhere to perceive a particular ethnic identity to be at stake.

Past behavior influences current perceptions. The past behavior of the secessionist movement will influence which ethnic identities are perceived by outsiders to characterize the conflict. If the groups leading the secessionist movement have emphasized a particular identity in the past or have engaged in conflict with other ethnic groups previous to this conflict, then that will affect which ethnic identities and enmities are perceived. If a leader of a secessionist movement has criticized a particular religion in the past, members of that religious group will feel ethnic enmity whether they live in the secessionist region or not. The conflict may become perceived as a religious conflict. History is not a very parsimonious variable, but the interactions of the past certainly influence present-day perceptions.

The theory of ethnic politics and foreign policy focuses our attention toward the ethnic identities of the combatants in each conflict. From the various assumptions and deductions, the theory makes the following predictions:

Ela. *States are more likely to support actors with which important constituents share ethnic ties.*

Elb. *States are more likely to oppose those actors with whom the decisionmakers' constituents have a history of ethnic enmity.*

Elc. *States are more likely to be neutral or ambivalent toward those conflicts where decisionmakers' supporters have ties to both sides.*

E2. *Leaders facing less competition are more likely to act contrary to what ethnic ties would suggest.*

E3. *Ethnic groups are likely to define themselves by broader identities to maximize their domestic and international support.*

Before moving on, some clarifications are required. First, this approach does not suggest that supporting secessionism is without costs. Indeed, one of the argument's implications is that politicians' domestic interests may cause them to engage in foreign policies that hurt their country by undermining the national interests. Supporting secession may alienate valuable allies, offend potential trading partners, and perhaps even cause the direct backlash that vulnerability theorists predict. Because this approach begins with politicians rationally pursuing power and position, these other interests may matter and may dissuade politicians to pursue ethnically based foreign policies if politicians calculate that the supporters they gain through such policies offset the number of constituents who exit. Still, the basic prediction holds—that ethnic politics will trump other interests.

Second, obviously, an approach based on ethnic ties cannot explain the policies of countries lacking ethnic ties or enmities between one's own constituency and the combatants, other than to say that states without ethnic ties are less likely to support secessionist groups. This is similar to the vulnerability argument's weakness—it cannot explain the behavior of states that are not vulnerable to ethnic conflict. While this may seem to be a glaring weakness, it is not that damaging. Ethnic conflict is present in most states, and is the central focus of politics in more than a few. According to one analysis of ethnic conflict, 112 out of 149 (75%) states contain minorities at risk.[75] While this does not mean that ethnic politics, as discussed above, dominates the political scene in each of these states, these figures are suggestive. Ethnic conflict is not restricted to one portion of the world. The region with the fewest ethnic groups at risk in the MAR dataset is northern Africa and the Middle East, not a part of the world usually considered free from ethnic politics. According to Gurr and Haxton, 71 percent of the advanced, industrialized states contain minorities at risk, so ethnic politics should apply to first world countries as well as third world countries.[76]

Even so, there will be some cases where this approach may not apply as politicians will not be constrained by ethnic politics nor will there be opportunities for ethnicity to be manipulated for political gain. This is a limitation of the theory. However, the broader assumptions upon which this theory is based, that the content and structure of domestic politics matters for foreign policies toward secessionist movements, may still aid in explaining the policies of these countries. Also, the other factors emphasized by the other theories (international norms and organizations, the pursuit of security, the temptation to engage in predation) may come into play more strongly when ethnic ties are absent.

Research Design

How do we test these various claims? To determine whether ethnic politics, vulnerability, or security influence the international relations of ethnic conflict, I perform both qualitative and quantitative analyses. I study particular cases of secessionist conflicts to assess the reactions of a variety of countries to the same conflict. In addition, I apply a variety of quantitative techniques to consider whether the findings in the case studies apply more broadly.

A. Selection of Cases

I chose to study how states reacted to particular secessionist crises, rather than to a variety of ethnic conflicts. This project is largely aimed at overturning the conventional wisdom, and the conventional wisdom focuses on secessionist conflicts. Thus, it is a much fairer test of the vulnerability argument than if we focused our attention on ethnic conflicts for which the vulnerability argument says little, such as rebellions or genocides. Further, by focusing only on secessionist crises, we can engage in most similar comparisons, which allow us to hold many things constant and focus our attention on the few factors that vary—the ones that might have a causal impact.[77] For policy relevance, we need to consider the international relations of secessionist crises since these conflicts have provoked strong reactions in many states, and have repeatedly challenged the abilities of international organizations to manage them. While the United Nations and others have been concerned with Rwanda, more attention has been paid to, and more resources expended upon, Chechnya, the wars in Yugoslavia, and, more recently, the conflict between Kosovo's Albanians and Serbia.

If we focus on secessionist crises, the question then becomes which ones and why? Since I am challenging the conventional wisdom, it makes sense to examine it on its home turf—Africa, where the vulnerability approach is most likely to work.[78] If the vulnerability approach fails to explain the international politics of African secessionist crises, we must seriously question the veracity of its claims. Rather than choosing randomly among all secessionist conflicts,[79] I chose to study two African secessionist crises: the Congo Crisis of 1960–1963 and the Nigerian Civil War of 1967–1970. Each crisis should provide strong support for the conventional wisdom, and analysts have cited each as doing so.[80]

During the Congo Crisis, African states should have behaved as the vulnerability argument predicts. First, they were most vulnerable to separatism shortly after decolonization. There was still some question as to whether the boundaries created by the colonial powers would be respected, and this was not resolved until 1964 with the Organization of African Unity's declaration recognizing the colonial boundaries as legitimate. Further, since many African states became independent shortly before or during the Congo Crisis, they had not really consolidated their regimes. Given the uncertainty about boundaries and the basic weakness of African regimes, if vulnerability inhibits states from supporting separatism, African states should not have supported Katanga.

Second, the Congo Crisis is a most likely case for the vulnerability argument, and relatively least likely case for the ethnic politics approach, because the intervention of the United Nations should have deterred states from supporting Katanga. The conventional wisdom asserts that international organizations help to define the international norms and inhibit states from supporting secession.[81] The United Nations intervened more directly and more forcefully in the Congo Crisis than in any other secessionist crisis to date. Therefore, arguments focusing on the role of international organizations should do well here, and those that deemphasize international organizations, like the theory of ethnic ties and foreign policy, should not provide as accurate predictions or as good explanations. Likewise, the tribal cleavages that spurred this conflict suggest that the conflict would have a relatively narrow appeal beyond the Congo. Because, at first glance, such a conflict is unlikely to matter to the constituents of leaders elsewhere, an ethnic politics argument might be at a disadvantage in this case.

Likewise, the Nigerian Civil war is also a most likely case for the vulnerability argument. African states were still as vulnerable to separatism as they were a few years earlier. The Organization of African Unity was strongly involved, trying to deter others from intervening in the conflict. Most importantly, the war took place only three years after African states approved a resolution that affirmed the legitimacy of the colonial boundaries and the norm of territorial integrity. If the vulnerability arguments are correct, then African states should not have supported the Biafran separatists. I also chose the Nigerian Civil War because this case facilitates a most similar comparison. The secessionists and the host states of each conflict share many common attributes, which helps to isolate the variations that might cause behavior. Both Katanga and Biafra were mineral-rich regions, so the economic values of the seceding regions were similar.[82] Both the Congo and Nigeria, at the time of the conflicts, were potentially the most powerful states in the region. The Cold War continued through both conflicts, so we can control for ideological competition and great power interest in Africa, which could potentially influence the superpowers' allies. What does vary between the two cases are the ethnic identities at stake. For the Congo Crisis, tribal and racial identities are relevant, while during the Nigerian Civil War, tribal and religious identities were at stake, so the case selection assures variance in the key independent variable of ethnic ties—tribe, race, and religion.

Why then study the international politics of Yugoslavia's disintegration? Studying this conflict helps to disarm two potential criticisms: that the theory of ethnic politics and foreign policy only applies to the third world or to a particular period. Some non-African states played important roles in the African secessionist crises, and ethnic ties influenced their policies. Still, analyzing the Yugoslav conflict should provide stronger evidence as to whether ethnic ties are still relevant and whether they influence institution-alized democracies and regimes making the transition to democracy. The Yugoslav conflict should be a hard test for the ethnic ties approach because European states had many other interests at stake. Among them are: building a common European foreign policy; reforming the economies of the former Soviet empire; developing institutions to govern European security; and set-ting precedents in the post-Cold War era. Finally, the Yugoslav conflict is an interesting anomaly. Given the web of economic and security institutions in Europe, many certainly expected a greater degree of cooperation than actually occurred.

Other secessionist crises occurred during the 1990s, so why did I choose to study Yugoslavia rather than Chechnya, East Timor, or Somaliland, to name just a few? Yugoslavia, despite (or because of) all of its complexities, is probably more similar to the Congo Crisis than other conflicts in the past decade. Like the Congo, Yugoslavia and later Bosnia faced the possibility of disintegration. Further, both conflicts challenged international organiza-tions as they intervened and threatened to set new and dangerous precedents. Just as the Congo Crisis shaped reactions of states and organizations to the Nigerian Civil War and other subsequent secessionist disputes, the disinte-gration of Yugoslavia has and will shape how countries react to separatist conflicts in Russia, in the successor states to Yugoslavia, in Indonesia, and elsewhere.

B. Selection of Observations

Studying these three secessionist crises allows us to analyze more than three observations, because each case breaks down into a number of obser-vations: each country's policy toward the conflict.[83] Thus, the number of observations grows to between thirteen to eighteen per crisis, totaling forty-six. The important methodological question then becomes by what criteria did I choose the observations. To make sure the dependent variable varies, I chose from the possible universe of observations the major actors in each conflict: those strongly supporting the secessionist movement and those strongly supporting the host state. While scholars have criticized picking observations based on the dependent variable,[84] it is necessary here since the previous approaches ignored the significant variation in the behavior of states—that some states supported the separatist movements. The risk in choosing cases according to the dependent variable is that one can truncate the range of the independent variables. To compensate partially for this, I also chose contiguous states that were neutral or supported both sides during the conflicts. Realist arguments make assertions about proximity—closeness breeds fear as nearby states can cause more damage. Vulnerability arguments suggest that spillover and backlashes are likely, and these are probably more likely to affect neighbors of conflict than those far away. Further, studying neighboring states in all three cases provides a common basis for comparison.

While I did study countries having no ethnic ties to the combatants,[85] I do not discuss them at length since the ethnic politics argument says nothing about states that have no ethnic ties. Such states may support host states or separatists, but ethnic ties will not explain nor predict their behavior. Instead, the other explanations may have more leverage when ethnic ties do not exist. States may feel the constraints of vulnerability if they do not have a dog in the fight. Likewise, security threats may shape a state's policies when politicians are not pushed by their constituents.

C. Coding the Observations

I determine whether ethnic ties exist by considering the existing literature on the domestic politics of each country to establish the essential constituencies for the reigning politicians and to determine the constituency's ethnic composition. If the constituency is homogeneous, coding is simple—do the members of the constituency share the same race, religion, language, or kinship (tribe or clan) as the secessionist movement or the host state? Since the secessionist movement and its host may each have multiple ethnic identities, and since ethnic identity is partly perceptual in nature, perceptions of the conflict will influence the perception of ethnic ties. If the constituency is not homogeneous, the focus is then on considering the ethnic ties of each ethnic group in the constituency. Ethnic ties will exist if any group of constituents has a shared ethnic identity as one of the combatants in the secessionist conflict. Ethnic enmity is said to exist if the literature on the countries in question refers to a history of ethnic conflict between the relevant groups.

The core notion of political competition here stresses whether supporters can leave one politician's constituency and throw their support to another, and whether such a change can influence the balance of power within that polity. By this definition, competition can exist and be more intense in an authoritarian regime than in a democracy. While I cannot readily specify exact rules for how competitive all political systems will be, there are some general dynamics to consider. Politicians in military regimes or new democracies are likely to face more competition when the military is fragmented or has a history of frequent coups d'etat. In authoritarian systems where the government controls the secret police and there is significant fear about informers, reigning politicians can worry less about whether some members of the military are disgruntled. Politicians in democracies face greater pressure if the electoral system means that a few votes change who governs or if the ruling party depends upon coalition partners to govern. Officials in democracies will feel less pressure if the electoral system guarantees them roughly the same share of seats in each election. For the case studies, the question will be—can the relevant constituency threaten the power of decision makers? As long as we determine competitiveness of the political system apart from using the outcomes of interest, we can avoid tautology.

A state is vulnerable to secessionism if:

(a) a secessionist movement actually tried to secede in recent history (the previous ten years);
(b) members of a group have organized with the goal of independence; or
(c) area studies experts view particular regions to be potentially secessionist.[86]

The last distinction should not be problematic as the vulnerability approach focuses on fears of separatism, rather than ongoing or past secessionist wars.

Coding threat is somewhat less straightforward. Relative power is the most simple to code once an indicator of power is created. In chapter 6, I discuss the creation of relative power indicators from Correlates of War data. For the case studies, I use this indicator to code each potential supporter's power relative to the host state as stronger or weaker. I then code whether the host state or secessionist group threatens the potential support, based on the ability for either the host or the secessionists to support ethnic groups within the potential supporter and on the perceived intentions of each.

Finally, I code the dependent variable as support for a particular side if a state gives either material assistance in the forms of arms, equipment, and/ or money, or diplomatic assistance in the forms of recognition; votes in favor of that side in international organizations; or interceding with other states on the behalf of that side.

D. The Quantitative Analyses

Chapter 6 will use a variety of statistical techniques to test hypotheses derived from the three competing arguments. Specifically, I will use the Minorities at Risk [MAR] dataset and raw data from the MAR project to determine which theories best capture the international relations of ethnic conflict in the 1990s. The dataset includes information about nearly all ethnic conflicts in the world.[87] Therefore, it should help us determine whether the findings from the case studies apply beyond secessionist crises and are relevant today.

The analyses will be of four kinds. First, I use simple cross-tabulations to consider how the competing arguments performed in the case studies. Second, basic trends in numbers and level of support throughout the 1990s will test whether arguments about precedents,[88] demonstration effects, and the like are accurate. Third, I test whether various characteristics of ethnic groups influence the level and breadth of support groups receive. In particular, I will consider the influence of the identities of groups; the existence, behavior, and power of their kin; groups' degree of separatism; and the relative power of their host states. Fourth, I test whether various features of potential supporters cause them to give more or less support to ethnic groups in conflict. Again, to test the competing arguments, these analyses will consider: the major identities of states' populations and the leadership, the vulnerability of states to separatism and ethnic conflict, and the relative power of potential supporters. To be clear, the nature of the data makes it hard to test the ethnic ties approach, so these analyses will tend to focus more attention on how well the other arguments hold up.

The concluding chapter will compare the three case studies and consider how the qualitative and quantitative findings relate to each other. I then briefly examine the Kosovo conflict as it raises questions both about the Yugoslav case study and about the timeliness of this book. I conclude by reflecting on the implications of this research for ongoing policy and theoretical debates.

3   Understanding the Congo Crisis, 1960–1963[1]

Katanga's attempted secession from the Congo needs to be analyzed in any study of the international politics of separatism. As the first secessionist crisis following decolonization in Africa, it influenced future expectations and understandings about the nature of secession and its international consequences.[2] Even more importantly, the United Nations intervened in the crisis with troops, who, after some hesitation, fought and defeated the separatists. The Congo Crisis thus serves as a test case of the influence of international institutions on secessionism, since the armed forces of an international organization defeated a secessionist movement. As the Cold War seriously influenced how states responded to this crisis, a study of the Katangan secession may also reveal whether the domestic political interests of elites influenced behavior more than security concerns. Many states were involved on either side during the Congo Crisis, so there is a significant variation in the dependent variable: policies toward the secessionists. Thus, the Congo Crisis serves as a crucial case. This study finds that while East-West rivalry may have shaped superpower interests, the conflict itself was a tribal dispute that became viewed as a racial one.

The approaches developed in chapter 2 produce varying predictions and explanations for the politics of the Congo Crisis. Vulnerability arguments stressing the effects of international cooperation would expect very few states to support the secessionist movement, Katanga, because of the strong role played by the United Nations, and those states that do support Katanga would be those less vulnerable to secessionism. The United Nations is important for vulnerability theorists as it represents both a set of norms governing boundary-maintenance (though not as explicitly as the Organization of African Unity), and a solution to the transaction costs of defining boundaries, cheating, and punishment for cheaters.

Realists, focusing on the support of secession for balancing threats, would suggest that states threatened by Katanga would support the Congo, and those threatened by the Congo would support Katanga. Neighboring states will be more likely to support Katanga as they feel the threat posed by the Congo more severely, according to this approach. Whichever side is perceived to be the lesser threat to others' territorial integrity will gain support. Those who are seen as likely supporters of boundary-changing efforts will encourage counterbalancing efforts.

The theory of ethnic politics and foreign policy predicts that those leaders depending upon the support of ethnic groups with ties to Katanga or enmity toward the Congo would support Katanga, and those relying on constituents with ties to the Congo or enmity against Katanga would support the Congo. Because most perceived the crisis as a racial conflict, leaders depending upon black supporters or on those hostile to whites would support the Congo, and leaders depending on white supporters would assist the Katangans. Politicians depending on support from both blacks and whites would be ambivalent or neutral during this crisis.

The Crisis Begins

On June 30, 1960, the Congo became independent, even though the Belgians had scarcely begun the task of preparing the state for its new status.[3] Although the Belgians had not intended to free the Congo so quickly, France's painful experience with decolonization intimidated Belgian decision makers.[4] As a result, they shortened a four-year plan for independence to six months. Fears of instability were quickly realized as units of the Force Publique, the Congo's armed forces, began to mutiny shortly after independence, on July 5. Events quickly escalated, despite the efforts of President Joseph Kasavubu and Prime Minister Patrice Lumumba to settle the crisis, culminating in the declaration of Katangan independence, by the province's President, Moise Tshombe, on July 11.

Katanga, containing the richest mines of the Congo, had been a site of separatist sentiment before independence, but Belgian opposition deterred the movement.[5] "The mutiny of the Force Publique, and the resulting chaos combined with Lumumba's refusal to call in Belgian troops, changed the situation completely. Those Europeans who had opposed secession now saw it as the only way of effectively restoring law and order and safeguarding Belgian investment in Katanga."[6]

Tshombe strategically positioned Katanga as a bastion against the spread of communism in central Africa, seeking aid from Belgium and other Western states.[7] Belgian troops based in Katanga acted to maintain order within that province, while Belgium sent reinforcements. These troops also took action within the rest of the Congo to safeguard the lives of Europeans.

On July 12, the crisis became internationalized as officials within the Congolese government, including the Deputy Prime Minister, asked the United States Ambassador for American troops to help restore law and order. Upon learning about the appeal for American troops, Kasavubu and Lumumba called for United Nations assistance to "prevent aggression and to restore the internal situation;" and asked for troops from neutral nations rather than the U.S.[8]

On July 14, the UN Security Council met to discuss the crisis. The Secretary-General, Dag Hammarskjold, argued that "the United Nations accede to the request of the Government of the Congo," and he recommended sending military and technical assistance.[9] As the only African state on the Security Council, Tunisia proposed a resolution calling for withdrawal of Belgian troops and authorizing the Secretary-General to follow his own recommendations. Passed with eight votes in favor and the abstentions of Great Britain, France, and Taiwan, the resolution provided the Secretary-General with a vague mandate, and each participant came away with a different understanding of the resolution. Regardless of the conflicting interpretations, the resolution clearly authorized the Secretary-General to take action in the Congo, involving the UN in one of its most controversial and complicated endeavors.

The Ethnic Politics of Katanga

Due to the internal and external politics of Katanga, both before and after its declaration of secession, supporters and detractors alike perceived the Katangan separatists as friendly to and perhaps manipulated by white European settlers, Belgium, and the white minority regimes of Southern Africa. The Katangan secession was perceived by many as a neocolonial plot to divide the richest African state, and to weaken the position of Patrice Lumumba, one of the most outspoken and influential Black Nationalist leaders. This crisis came to be defined in different, though related ways: as a racial struggle between black Africa on the one hand and white Western powers and white minority regimes on the other, and as an important battle between neocolonialism and the newly decolonized states of the third world. The Congo Crisis therefore had both racial and ideological implications, influencing the domestic political benefits and costs elites faced as they reacted to this conflict.

The Confederation des Associations Tribales due Katanga, also known as Conakat, led the secessionists. From its very beginning's, Conakat received support from the white settlers living in Katanga. Conakat's political allies during the pre-independence period were Union pour la Colonisation and of the Reassemblement Katangaise, [Ucol], formed by Belgians to encourage colonization of the Congo, and the Union Katangaise, the political party of the more extremist settlers.[10]

"Conakat became progressively more involved in the publication of political programs strongly inspired by the views of the Ucol and the Union Katangaise and in direct cooperation with the leaders of these organizations."[11] In exchange for material and technical support, Conakat pushed at the pre-independence negotiations for provisions very favorable to white settlers, including the limitation of universal suffrage for the election of the lower chamber of the national assembly; the right of Belgian residents of the Congo to be eligible for both voting and political office; and legal qualifications that would have prevented Patrice Lumumba from running for office.[12]

As a result of Conakat's close ties to the settlers, the Balubakat Party, which represented the Baluba tribe in Katanga, left the Conakat coalition, leaving the Lunda tribe as the dominant group among the coalition's remaining supporters.[13] This split became crucial in the elections of May 1960, for both the national and provincial legislatures that would shape Katangan and Congolese politics in the post-independence period. While the elections left Balubakat with a small plurality in votes in the Katanga province, Conakat gained a small majority in seats. The *Loi Fundamentale*, the transitional constitution legislated by the Belgian parliament and influenced by Congolese-Belgian negotiations, ensured that provincial cabinet positions would be elected by a majority, which Conakat had. However, it also required that two-thirds of the provincial assembly vote for a legitimate quorum. Because the Balubakat controlled slightly more than one-third of the seats, they could block the formation of a provincial government in Katanga as long as they abstained from voting. The colonial Vice-Governor intervened and persuaded the Belgian parliament to change this provision, allowing the Conakat to form a cabinet consisting solely of Conakat Party members.[14] The new Katangan provincial government's first move was to prepare for secession from the new, nationalist state of the Congo.

In the first days of post-independence period, events and decisions strongly signaled how significantly white settlers influenced Katanga and the government of Belgium. Many of the important administrative positions were held by white European settlers and former Belgian colonial officials. The behavior of the Belgians, particularly that of the army, was very different in Katanga than elsewhere in the Congo, making it clear that Belgium was supporting the secessionist movement in Katanga.

Because of the close ties between Conakat and the white settlers in Katanga, and the post-independence efforts by Belgium and white settlers to support Katanga's secessionist bid, outsiders quickly perceived Katanga as a supporter of white interests in the Congo, with many arguing that Rhodesia's white minority regime and Belgium were pulling the strings of their Katangan puppets. The tribal conflicts between the Lunda and the Baluba received little attention from any of the external actors,[15] including the UN, and even Tshombe himself did not emphasize the tribal sources of conflict within Katanga and between Katanga and the Congo. Instead, he positioned himself as an anti-communist, rather than an oppressed minority, thus facilitating the definition by others of the conflict as a racial one and as one between Pan-Africanism and Neo-imperialism.

Many quickly viewed the secessionist crisis to be part of a larger racial conflict between the white colonial powers, Belgium, France, Great Britain, and the white minority regimes of southern Africa, the Federation of Rhodesia and Nyasaland and South Africa on one side; and the Black Nationalist states of Africa on the other. Indeed, the secession was the first open conflict between neocolonialism and the nationalist, nonaligned movement in Africa.[16] The issues of race and neocolonialism would play an important role in the decisions made by elites and the policies their states followed as they dealt with the crisis in the Congo.

Supporters of the Katangan Secessionist Movement

Although no state gave formal recognition to Katanga, some states provided other forms of assistance, allowing Tshombe's regime to last three years and to weather two offensives by the United Nations before being defeated by the third. The most important supporters of the separatists were Belgium, the former colonial power; the Federation of Rhodesia and Nyasaland, the white-minority regime neighboring Katanga; and Congo-Brazzaville.

Belgium

"The decisive aid, ensuring the very existence of the regime in July 1960, was that which the Belgian soldiers gave to Katanga on the eve of, and just after, the proclamation of independence. Without it, the Katangan state would not have been able to exist."[17] Belgian troops established order in Katanga after the post-independence uprisings, and Belgian officials urged the European inhabitants of Katanga to stay in the province to continue to run the administrative apparatus of the province-state.[18] The orders of Belgian troops in Katanga were different from those given to Belgian troops in the rest of the Congo: to expel Congolese troops loyal to the central government.[19]

Belgian officers trained and led the Katangan gendarmerie, until the UN removed most of them. The gendarmerie played a crucial role in preventing the Congolese armed forces from defeating Katanga's secession at the outset. Major Guy Weber, who was responsible for the establishment of order in Katanga, and was later military adviser to Tshombe, reported directly to Brussels.[20] Another Belgian officer organized the gendarmerie. Belgium gave Katanga arms and facilitated the recruitment of mercenaries.[21] Belgians also served as political advisers to Tshombe and his regime.[22]

Belgium's policies changed toward the end of 1962, as it became more reluctant to support Tshombe's duplicity and more interested in ending the crisis. To understand Belgium's policies, both the inconsistencies and the changes, one must examine the dynamics of Belgium's domestic politics during this time. It has been argued quite forcefully that economic interests solely motivated Belgium's policies in the Congo, particularly in Katanga, but these analysts cannot explain why Belgian voters embraced Tshombe and his cause.[23] While the economic significance of Katanga was clear, it is less obvious why economically motivated Belgian politicians would support Katanga rather than build bridges with Lumumba and Kasavubu.[24]

At the outset of the crisis, Belgium was governed by a weak coalition of the Christian Democratic Party (the Christian Democratic Party) and the Liberal Party.[25] The main party in opposition was the Socialist Party. Analysts have argued that inconsistencies in Belgian policy, such as the policy of nonrecognition of Katanga, enacted simultaneously with the provision of aid to the secessionists, were the result of this weak and divided government.[26] While the Socialists declared that troops should not be sent to the Congo and that Katanga should not be recognized because such an action would alienate world opinion, the Liberals pushed for recognition of Katanga. The Christian Democrats sought to compromise between the two positions by giving arms, equipment, and other forms of support to Katanga, but refusing to give diplomatic recognition. A new government formed in spring 1961 as the result of new elections, leading to a coalition between the Socialist Party and the Christian Democrats. This government had stronger support, with Paul-Henri Spaak, Belgium's most distinguished diplomat and former Secretary-General of NATO, serving as the Foreign Minister. While constrained by public opinion, this government was said to have a greater interest in resolving the crisis and a greater ability to do so. Considering Belgium's ethnic politics may help to explain the behavior of the different parties.

Specifically, rising linguistic conflict within Belgium may aid in understanding the interests of Belgian politicians at this time. Linguistic division "was to become the dominant political issue of the 1960s and 1970s, breaking up the old party structure and making the state almost ungovernable."[27] While the cultural differences between Flanders (the Flemish-speaking region) and Wallonia (the French-speaking region) had existed for a long time and were exacerbated by the Nazi occupation during the Second World War, "the 1960s were a watershed in Belgian politics."[28] Flanders was undergoing an industrial revolution while Wallonia's mining and industry were in decline.[29] Changes in the economic balance of power can spark increased nationalism,[30] and this occurred in Belgium as Flemish nationalism became more assertive and Walloon nationalism became more strident, with open conflict finally breaking out during the winter strikes of 1960–1961.[31] The rise of linguistic conflict was problematic for each of Belgium's three major parties as each consisted of Flemish and Walloon wings. While each party tried to avoid it, the linguistic issue eventually split the three parties into six, each dividing into Flemish and Walloon versions. The Christian Democrats split in 1964, the Liberals in 1972, and the Socialists were the last to divide in 1978.[32]

According to the logic of ethnic politics, since each of the three major parties had linguistically heterogeneous constituencies, all three would try to avoid using linguistic divisions as a political tool to avoid dividing their supporters. Consequently, each party would prefer to emphasize policies that stressed some common bond among members of their constituency, such as attachment to the Belgian state—civic nationalism. If politicians could overcome linguistic divides by mobilizing their followers through Belgian nationalism, they might prevent, or at least delay, the breakup of their supporting coalitions. The Liberal Party, due to its conservative background, and the Christian Democratic Party, due to its ties to the monarchy, relied on Belgian nationalism. The Socialist Party, due to its class and ideological appeals, relied on Belgian nationalism the least.

Events in the Congo provided Belgian elites with many opportunities to stress Belgian nationalism.[33] The Congo's Independence Day, June 30, 1960, triggered Belgian nationalism when Lumumba responded to King Baudouin's paternalistic speech with a tirade against Belgium's colonial policies.[34] The Belgian press and people reacted very strongly against Lumumba, increasing Belgian nationalism.[35] Because this sentiment was aimed directly against Lumumba, it favored Tshombe.

> In Belgium, public opinion reacted sharply in favour of Katanga. Most Belgians were smarting at the accusations of aggression and were furious that the world had not shown more understanding of Belgian motives. . . . Tshombe's statement requesting Belgian help and showing that he believed in Belgian good faith came as a welcome solace and the majority of Belgians thought the government should do everything possible to help him.[36]

By supporting Tshombe, Belgian politicians rode the wave of Belgian popular opinion as they defended Belgium from the attacks of radical Black Nationalists like Lumumba. Although Belgium was splitting along linguistic cleavages, supporting Katanga was a policy upon which Flemings and Walloons could agree, as the conflict in the Congo was one of race, not language.[37] Indeed, Belgian politicians were so constrained by the pro-Katanga sentiment and Belgian nationalism that the government had to oppose the UN resolutions of September 1960.[38] Otherwise, the government might have collapsed, as Belgian civic nationalism was the glue that temporarily held the multi-linguistic parties together.

Belgium's policies were expected to change when a more stable government entered in 1961, with foreign policy being made by Socialist and career diplomat Paul-Henri Spaak. In his memoir, he admits, "For me, the Katangan situation was most difficult. I was fundamentally and profoundly opposed to secession."[39] If Spaak was so opposed to secession, why did the Christian Democrats agree to appoint him Foreign Minister? As Spaak had served as NATO's Secretary-General and in many other important diplomatic positions, he was seen as one of the few national, as opposed to regional, factional, or ethnic, politicians. In a time of increasing ethnic conflict at home, it made sense to appoint a Foreign Minister who was seen as being Belgian, rather than as Walloon or Flemish.

Another important question: if Spaak opposed Katanga's secession, why did Belgium continue to support Katanga after his appointment? Even though the Socialist Party was less constrained by Belgian nationalism, they still could not afford to offend Belgian nationalists or its coalition partner. When Spaak took measures to meet UN demands, such as to repatriate Guy Weber and other Belgians serving in Katanga's internal security forces and gendarmerie, he met much opposition.

Even Spaak resorted to nationalism and ethnic politics when he needed to fend off attacks made by domestic opponents. He denounced the November 1961 UN resolution, directly aimed against the Katangan secession, by calling it "a bid to hunt down the white man."[40] In December 1961, the UN offensive caused great resentment and violence in Belgium. Spaak addressed a joint session of the Belgian parliament, blasting the United Nations for acting "out of proportion" and using "intolerable" means. This speech was approved unanimously by the parliament, with the exception of the Communist Party.[41]

Belgian nationalism eventually decreased, as politicians and voters refocused on economic issues and linguistic problems. Tshombe's double-dealings, where he agreed to various negotiations and then later rescinded his compromises, also wore out public sentiment. Consequently, Spaak was more free to adhere to UN resolutions, to support U.S. and UN policy initiatives. He was able to eventually blame Tshombe and his European advisers for prolonging the crisis.[42]

Vulnerability theorists cannot account for Belgium's behavior. First, Belgium supported a secessionist movement precisely when separatist sentiment in Belgium was rising. This is precisely the opposite of what vulnerability implies, according to the conventional wisdom. Second, the United Nations was strongly engaged in this conflict, and its membership aimed many of the resolutions directly against Belgium's policies, but the initial Belgium response was to defy the UN. The reciprocity hypotheses receive some support as Belgium engaged in conflict with actors with whom it had a history of conflict and engaged in cooperation with actors with whom it had a history of cooperation. However, this begs the question of why such histories existed. In sum, the vulnerability approach cannot explain Belgium's behavior.

Realism provides a better, but still relatively weak, account for Belgian policy. The Congo could not pose a direct threat to Belgium's security because of distance as well as the Congo's weakness. However, one could argue that the Congo posed a threat to Belgium's interests in the region. It is not clear how great a threat this would be since Rwanda and Burundi became independent in 1962, greatly reducing Belgium's interests in the region. Obviously, a hostile government in the Congo threatened Belgian access to minerals in Katanga. Assisting the Katangans clearly had economic benefits. Realists must, then, answer two questions. Could Belgium have protected its access by supporting the Congo's government? Would supporting Katanga threaten Belgium's security? Regarding the former question, Belgium could either have appeased Lumumba or worked against him to create a Congolese government more friendly to Belgium interests,[43] instead of supporting Katanga. Concerning the latter question, given the tremendous opposition Belgium faced from much of the world, supporting Katanga did pose some real risks. Belgium placed its most important ally in a difficult position, as the U.S. was competing for influence in Africa. Once it was clear that Katanga was opposed by most of the world, Belgium should have abandoned it to save political capital for other, more important, issues.

Belgian's politicians could support Katanga because the conflict in the Congo was of a different ethnic tie—race—than the one polarizing Belgian society—language. In this time of intensifying divisions at home, the Congo Crisis presented an opportunity to take pro-Belgian nationalist positions that was too good to ignore. Belgian nationalism does not necessarily indicate which foreign policies leaders mobilizing Belgian nationalism ought to follow. However, after Lumumba attacked Belgium and its King, giving support to Lumumba's enemies was the foreign policy most likely to mobilize Belgian nationalism and unite the multi-linguistic constituencies of Belgian elites. Although the narrow predictions of ethnic ties do not predict Belgium's behavior, the dynamics of ethnic politics provide a better explanation of Belgian foreign policy than does vulnerability to secession or security maximization.

The Federation of Rhodesia and Nyasaland

The Federation of Rhodesia and Nyasaland's support of Tshombe's separatist regime was almost as important as Belgium's. Mercenaries moved through Northern Rhodesia to Katanga.[44] Smugglers ran arms and supplies across the border, including the fighter aircraft that attacked UN troops during the first two rounds of UN action. Katangan minerals were transported across Rhodesia for sale elsewhere, providing Tshombe with the hard currency necessary for the purchase of more arms, equipment, and mercenaries.[45] When the United Nations sought to place observers on the Federation's side of the border to block aid for Katanga, Prime Minister Roy Welensky refused.

Why did a political entity that itself would disintegrate less than a year after Tshombe's defeat make such efforts? It was precisely the fear of Black Nationalism and of Communism that motivated the policies of Welensky's government. At this time, Welensky was negotiating the transition of parts of the Federation to black majority rule. While he was reluctant to do so, the rise of Black Nationalism, the opposition of the world community, and the pressure of the British government forced the white rulers of the Federation to accommodate some demands of the Federation's black majority.

Rhodesia's white leaders perceived Lumumba and his followers in the Congo to be helping the Black Nationalists and Communists within the Federation. Welensky argued that: "To our mind the security of Southern Africa from Communism [i.e., Black Nationalism] requires that Katanga be recognised *de facto* by as many countries as possible. Such recognition would strengthen Tshombe's hand enormously."[46] Since Katanga covered a large part of the border between the Federation and the Congo, it was seen as a buffer zone that would prevent the unstable areas of the Federation from being subjected to radical influences, such as Lumumba's brand of Black Nationalism and radical ideology.[47] Support for Katanga was seen as a measure to prevent the spread of ethnic instability from reaching Northern Rhodesia and to contain communism.

At the same time, the events in the Congo distracted attention away from the disturbances occurring within the Federation. "For the moment . . . ,

Northern Rhodesia was driven from everyone's minds by the Congo."[48] Opposing UN efforts and blasting Britain's policies toward the Congo and Katanga as being "gutless" enabled Welensky to mobilize white Rhodesians in support of his regime, at a time when there was increasing opposition to his handling of Black Nationalism within the Federation.[49] Welensky's United Federal Party was being attacked by the Rhodesian Front, a more right wing, white supremacist party, for allowing Black Nationalist violence to occur in the Federation.[50] Indeed, to ensure Welensky's domestic political position, "It was felt that the Federal Government had to mount an anti-Pan-Africanist campaign."[51] Part of this campaign was Federation support for Tshombe, who was seen as both friendly to white interests and a target of the Pan-African movement. The logic of both realism and ethnic enmity apply: the enemy of my enemy is my friend. Because Tshombe was the enemy of the Pan-African movement, which opposed white rule in Rhodesia, he was perceived to be a friend of Rhodesia's white leaders.

The Federation of Rhodesia and Nyasaland is a case where racially homogeneous parties competed with each other for the support of one racial group, the whites, as each party sought to portray itself as the best defender of white interests, and a secessionist movement existed within a neighboring state that seemed to favor white interests. Because he faced parties attempting to outbid him, Welensky assisted the movement most supportive of white interests in central Africa—the Katangan separatists.

Admittedly, it is hard to disentangle realist accounts from ethnic political explanations in this case. Clearly, balancing power by itself would not predict the Federation's policy since the Congo was only potentially powerful, and focusing on power alone would cause the Federation to worry more about South Africa than the Congo. However, the Congo, led by Lumumba, presented a security threat to the Federation since it possessed the ability, as a neighboring state, and apparently the intent to destabilize the Federation by supporting opposition groups. Thus, the adjusted realist argument predicts the same outcome as ethnic politics, once the ethnic definition of enemy and friend are taken into account—that the ability of the Congo to threaten the Federation depended crucially on the role of race in both polities.

Finally, neither vulnerability nor the demands of international organizations inhibited the Federation of Rhodesia and Nyasaland. The Federation was extremely vulnerable to separatism and ethnic conflict as Black Nationalism and secession were increasing at the time of the Congo Crisis. Rather than inhibiting the Federation's foreign policy, this situation caused the country to develop a very aggressive foreign policy—to support secession nearby to reduce its own separatist threat. Likewise, defying the United Nations was good politics at home. Clearly, the racial conflict within the Federation and the competition for white votes drove the country's foreign policy to be aggressive, rather than acquiescent.

Congo-Brazzaville

Congo-Brazzaville's foreign policy toward this conflict is very anomalous. "Congo-Brazzaville was virtually the only one [black African-ruled country] that faithfully defended to the very end the secessionist policy of Moise Tshombe."[52] Congo-Brazzaville, indeed, was the only African state ruled by black Africans to support Katanga's secession. President Abbe Fulbert Youlou's crucial support of Tshombe took many forms. The ports and airports of Congo-Brazzaville were used for the shipping of arms and equipment to the separatists in the Congo. Youlou gave diplomatic support, as he called upon the non-African states to pull their troops out of the UN force during the first round of attacks.[53]

The conflictual relationship between the two Congos has many roots, as do the motivations for Youlou's support of Tshombe. Much has been made of French encouragement of Youlou and of his French advisers.[54] However, assertions of French dominance do not address the crucial differences between the policies and politics of Congo-Brazzaville and those of other former French colonies. Youlou was dependent upon the French, but this dependence was a consequence of Youlou's political strategies, not a cause.

Youlou's party and his rule depended on an ethnic group that was a minority in Congo-Brazzaville, and ethnic conflict was a serious problem as the state became independent. Because of the weakness of his regime, Youlou needed both to pacify the opposition and divert attention from domestic problems. Youlou followed a strategy different from that of other African states, and from those predicted by the theory of ethnic politics and foreign policy. Rather than build a national identity and party through the mobilization of Black Nationalism and Pan-Africanism, as in Guinea or Ghana (to be discussed below), Youlou sought to lessen ethnic opposition through two different methods: a dam-building project that would ensure greater employment, and by bribing ethnic groups with funds solicited from abroad.

"All the country's hopes for improving the economic situation had centered on construction of the Kouilou dam and on the industrialization of Pointe Noire. Youlou, for his part, had staked his whole political future on carrying out this project."[55] By employing his country's youth, Youlou hoped to limit the influence of the state's radical movements. The dam project became a symbol of economic independence for Congo-Brazzaville, even greater than political independence from France. Ironically, funding the dam required greater compromises of Congo-Brazzaville's sovereignty and foreign policy.

During his election campaign, Youlou revealed that he had received 100 million Congolese Francs from France to aid in the building of the dam. He traveled abroad to gain aid, and one of the greatest sources of finances in Africa was Tshombe's regime. In exchange for economic assistance to build the dam, Youlou provided Katanga with the logistical support necessary for the maintenance of the secession. "So great was his [Youlou's] obsession with the Kouilou dam that it affected his political judgment . . . , and his determination to build the dam became a factor in his alignment with Moise Tshombe."[56]

Youlou also sought funds to pay off ethnic groups directly, relying on foreign sources of money. He traded his foreign policies for the funds necessary to pay off his constituents.[57] In exchange for supporting Katanga, Youlou received enough financial aid to keep the domestic ethnic groups relatively satisfied. Only after the collapse of Katanga did Youlou seek to build a one-party system and civic nationalisms like Sekou Touré of Guinea or Kwame Nkrumah of Ghana to manage domestic ethnic conflict. It was too late for such an attempt, however, as ethnic unrest and civil strife of all kinds escalated until Youlou was overthrown.[58]

Oddly enough, Youlou and Kasavubu, the President of Congo-Leopoldville, shared the same tribal background, coming from the Bakongo, a large kinship group whose territory crossed the boundaries of the two states. Though Youlou provided Kasavubu with assistance in his actions against Lumumba, he continued to support Tshombe's efforts against Kasavubu's government.[59]

Given the ethnic conflict facing Youlou, he should have supported the Congo against the Katanga separatists, if vulnerability inhibits foreign policy. As a small, weak state, it should be surprising that Congo-Brazzaville resisted the will of the United Nations. Despite the constraints of vulnerability and international opposition, Congo-Brazzaville was one of Katanga's most aggressive supporters.

Realist hypotheses receive more support. Because the Congo was both stronger and a neighbor of Congo-Brazzaville, Youlou's policies support two realist hypotheses: that weaker states will support secessionist movements in stronger states, and that neighbors are more likely to support secessionists than other states. Further, given Congo-Brazzaville's Western leanings and dependence on the French, one could argue that Lumumba was as threatening to Youlou as he was to Welensky.

The logic of ethnic politics predicts that Youlou would have supported the Congo in its efforts to maintain its territorial integrity because of shared racial and tribal ties of his constituency with the Congo's government. Although Congo-Brazzaville's behavior contradicts the theory, its behavior still indicates that politicians are generally motivated by the ethnically defined interests of their supporters when making foreign policy decisions. The theory of ethnic politics and foreign policy could not predict Youlou's policies because it fails to take into account an alternative way to deal with ethnic conflict—buying it off.

Other Supporters of Secession

The patterns of politics and policies of these states are not unique. Elites with similar ethnic constituencies and strategies followed identical policies. In South Africa, as in the Federation of Rhodesia and Nyasaland, political competition was between different white parties, with several competing to be better white supremacists than each other.[60] Like Welensky, white South African elites viewed Lumumba as a threat who would increase the influence and power of Black Nationalism in Southern Africa, and perceived Tshombe as a supporter of white interests and security.[61] Consequently, South Africa also gave significant assistance to the Katangans.

Defenders of the Congo's Territorial Integrity

A number of countries supported efforts to maintain the Congo's territorial integrity. This support usually came in three forms: financial assistance to the United Nations, contribution of soldiers to the UN force, and diplomatic efforts, mostly at the UN, to end Katanga's secession.

Ghana

Kwame Nkrumah, Ghana's leader, played an important role both before and during the Congo crisis. Lumumba considered himself to be Nkrumah's protégé, and followed policies and strategies in the Congo that had worked for Nkrumah in Ghana.[62] Nkrumah built a mass party on a radical, pan-African ideology, attempting to overcome ethnic divides, and Lumumba sought to imitate him by building the Mouvement Nationale Congolais, a mass-based party, focused on pan-Africanism as a bridge between ethnic groups.

During the crisis, Nkrumah was probably the most active African leader seeking an end to the secession, aiming to keep the Congo united and Lumumba in power. Ghanaian troops were among the first to arrive in the Congo as members of ONUC, and Ghana's contribution to ONUC was among the largest, despite its own small armed forces.[63] Nkrumah sought to influence the UN mandate by pushing for a more active role, and for inter-vention on the side of Lumumba, "as non-interference in the internal affairs of the Congo, is no longer tenable."[64] After Lumumba's death, Nkrumah continued to push for a UN role in the crisis, arguing that a withdrawal would aid Lumumba's enemies.[65]

An examination of Ghana's domestic politics, including Nkrumah's role in efforts to unify the state, may aid in understanding his foreign policies toward the Congo. In 1956, the Nkrumah's Convention People's Party ran as the only party seeking a nation-wide base of support. The opposition parties were based on deeply divided regional and ethnic groups. After win-ning this election with a Pan-African campaign, Nkrumah embarked on a set of policies to eliminate ethnically based challenges to his rule.[66] As the government shifted from a multiparty democracy to the personal rule of one individual, Nkrumah sought to build a national identity while reducing the salience of alternate identities.

"Of Ghana's regimes, Nkrumah's Convention People's Party (CPP) lasted the longest and had the most articulated policy on the subject of ethnicity."[67] This policy tried to build a Ghanaian civic identity at the expense of regional and ethnic divides. Two instruments that Nkrumah used to build this civic identity are of particular interest: ideology and his own popularity. The civic nationalism centered on his ideology and the role of Nkrumah and Ghana in that ideology.[68] Nkrumah's ideology stressed Ghana's historical role a leader of all Africa, with a mission to build a union of African states and to oppose neo-imperialism.[69] Nkrumah referred to the glories of the ancient Ghana empire, and stressed the fact that Ghana was the first of the colonized African states to become independent, in 1957. Nkrumah went so far in his support of a radical vision of pan-African as to include an article in Ghana's 1960 constitution that provided for the surrender of sovereignty for " 'the furtherance of African unity.' "[70]

Nkrumah sought to use his popularity to increase support for his regime. He played a very strong role in the decolonization of Ghana, making him a national hero, so that Nkrumah became identified as a symbol of Ghanaian nationalism and a force for unity within Ghana.[71] Nkrumah's foreign policy continually emphasized his role as leader of the Pan-African movement. By leading conferences, speaking at the UN, and meeting with Lumumba, Nkrumah was able to use his foreign policy to improve his own political position and image at home.[72] Thus, foreign policy was a key part of Nkrumah's attempts to build a civic Ghanaian identity at the expense of more divisive ethnic ties.

A politician's effort to develop a civic nationalism does not require a particular foreign policy. However, the content of Nkrumah's and Ghana's civic nationalism, Pan-African ideology, compelled Ghana to act decisively during the Congo Crisis. Ghanaians believed that "the Katanga secession was simply a case of neo-colonialism at work,"[73] providing Nkrumah with an important opportunity to emphasize his position as leader of Pan-Africanism and the relevance of his ideology for both domestic and international politics.

Because his support came from multiple ethnic groups though a single racial group, and his opposition relied on ethnic divisions, including active secessionism, Nkrumah developed a thorough strategy of domestic and foreign policies designed to de-emphasize ethnicity and to develop a civic nationalism. This civic nationalism may not have mattered for foreign policy during the Congo Crisis had this conflict been characterized by religious or linguistic conflict, rather than racial enmity and a battle against neocolonialism. Pan-Africanism mattered in this crisis because of the particular definition of this conflict and perception of Katanga. Consequently, when faced with a conflict perceived to be between Pan-Africanism and Black Nationalism on one side and neo-imperialism and white minority rule on the other, Nkrumah predictably became the most ardent supporter of the Congo's territorial integrity.

In this case, vulnerability and ethnic ties produce the same prediction. As Ghana faced its own separatists, it energetically fought Katanga. Further, reciprocity arguments suggest that Ghana would support the Congo, since the leaders of the two countries had a good relationship and had worked well together in the past. Therefore, this observation by itself cannot tell us much about whether vulnerability or ethnic ties provides better predictions.

To make a realist prediction, we need to understand what threat the Congo posed to Ghana. In terms of relative power, Ghana could be considered weaker than the Congo in 1960. The Congo posed no real offensive threat to Ghana, because the Congo lacked both the capability and the perceived intention to disrupt Ghana's ethnic politics. Therefore, the Congo did not seriously threaten Ghana, so we should not expect Ghana to support Katanga. One could argue that Katanga endangered Ghana because of its alliance with white colonial interests and its opposition to Pan-Africanism. However, in terms of relative power, offensive capability, and proximity, Katanga could not seriously threaten Ghana. Given that the various components of threat point in different directions, realists cannot make a clear prediction in this case.

By itself, Ghana is suggestive, as its ethnic politics and resulting civic nationalisms produce policies predicted by both ethnic ties and vulnerability arguments, and the case also illustrates the difficulty of applying realism.

Nigeria

Nigeria's support of the Congo's central government was extensive. Not only was Nigeria's contribution of troops to the UN operation in the Congo the third largest,[74] but Nigeria also paid all assessments as well as making voluntary contributions, providing food and an air base for transporting UN troops and equipment.[75] The total cost of Nigeria's contribution was over $44 million, a huge amount for a newly independent state.[76] Nigerian personnel also played an important role at the UN. "The Nigerian delegation took a strong stand against the secession of Katanga, arguing that the end of secession was one of the sine qua non conditions for a viable and stable Congo republic."[77] Not only was Jaja Wachuku, Nigeria's UN representative, very assertive within the General Assembly and Security Council debates, but he also was named chair of the UN Conciliation Commission seeking solutions to the conflict.

Why was Nigeria so enthusiastic in its support of the Congo's territorial integrity? It is easy to say with hindsight that Nigeria realized that it was vulnerable to secession, and therefore sought to prevent separatists elsewhere from seceding. However, other aspects of Nigeria's domestic politics influenced Nigeria's foreign policy as much or more than its vulnerability to secession. Nigeria's policies were so assertive in this crisis because it was one of the few issues that held together its own ruling coalition.[78] Nigeria's three major parties each represented each of the three largest tribal groups. The National Council of Nigeria and the Cameroons [NCNC] represented mostly Ibos, the Action Group [AG] represented the Yorubas, and the Northern People's Congress [NPC]'s constituency was made up of Muslim Hausa/Fulani.[79] During the campaign of 1959, foreign policy became a prominent issue, with each party supporting Pan-Africanism, while differing on other issues. After the election, no party had a majority, leaving the NPC holding the largest number of seats and forming a coalition with the NCNC.

Prime Minister Sir Abubakar Tawafa Balewa of the NPC and Jaja Wachuku, the Minister of Economic Development, the head of the Nigerian delegation at the UN, and of the NCNC, shaped Nigerian foreign policy.

> The moderate to conservative diplomacy which . . . typified the foreign policy of the Balewa government also reflected the need to maintain a viable coalition in Lagos. Given the severe internal strains and constant readjustments that had to be made to sustain such a coalition, the prime minister usually sought to avoid becoming embroiled in world issues that might have afforded his domestic opposition an opportunity to stir up debate.[80]

Wachuku consistently pushed Abubakar for a more aggressive policy against Katanga. As the public sought a harsher policy as well, Nigeria's policy toward Katanga grew more aggressive, and Nigeria took the lead along with Ethiopia in the efforts to end the Katangan secession.[81] The government consciously sought to use policy in the Congo to build consensus at home by publicizing the efforts of the Nigerian forces donated to the UN force.[82] Nigerian efforts in the Congo were very successful domestically in that "its participation in the Congo mission tended to divert critical attention from indigenous currents that proved to be dysfunctional to political stability in Nigeria."[83]

The logic of ethnic politics can explain Nigeria's foreign policy at this time. Each of the two most significant foreign policymakers, Balewa and Wachuku, were supported by tribally homogeneous constituencies. Along racial lines, however, each represented only a portion of a single racial group:

black Nigerians. Because each man required the support of the other's party to maintain their coalition, they had a common interest in emphasizing the ethnic ties binding their two tribally oriented constituencies. Thus, when the Katangans attempted to secede, and were perceived to be influenced or controlled by white settlers, Balewa and Wachuku could agree to support the Congo's efforts to maintain its territorial integrity.[84]

Vulnerability theorists also could point to Nigeria's foreign policy as supportive of their arguments. Nigeria fought a secessionist war only a few years after the Congo Crisis, so one could argue that Nigeria fought Katanga to deter its own potential separatists. Realists would consider Nigeria to be quite similar to Ghana: the Congo posed a threat to neither of them, and Katanga might have had nasty intentions but could not really threaten either state directly. Consequently, this case, like Ghana, supports both ethnic ties and vulnerability claims, but does not weaken nor strengthen the realist case.

Other Supporters of the Congo

Several other states played an important role in defending the territorial integrity of the Congo, especially Guinea and India. In Guinea, Sekou Toure faced ethnic political problems that were very similar to those confronting Nkrumah in Ghana. Toure followed an ethnic-political strategy that was almost identical to Nkrumah's, resulting in similar foreign policies.[85]

The Indian National Congress Party also had to deal with the sticky problem of keeping a multiethnic party together.[86] As in Ghana and Guinea, the best political strategy was to build a civic nationalism.[87] By building ties to the state, it was hoped that ethnic divisions could be overcome. The pursuit of an activist nonaligned, anticolonialist foreign policy was seen as one way to build Indian nationalism.[88] Again, because the Congo Crisis was perceived to be caused by neocolonialists, the content of India's civic nationalism, anticolonialism, had relevance for this crisis. Indian elites could take strong positions on the Congo Crisis, highlighting India's civic nationalism at the expense of more divisive ethnic identities.

Ethiopia, Morocco, and Tunisia played very similar roles. They were among the first to contribute troops, and their contributions were among the largest in the early going, each numbering more than 2,500.[89] Tunisia, as the only African state on the UN Security Council for much of the crisis, authored many resolutions in favor of the Congo and against Katanga. Ethiopia, as a supporter of the United Nations, and a state facing its own border and separatist problems, actively supported ONUC and criticized those who attacked the United Nations. Morocco aligned itself with the more radical African states, such as Ghana and Guinea, and gave strong support to Lumumba and his successors. Morocco and Ethiopia support both the ethnic ties argument and the vulnerability hypothesis as they were both vulnerable to separatism, and ruled by leaders who depended upon supporters having enmity with Katanga.[90] Tunisia did not face separatism itself, but its leaders also relied on those who despised the Katangans and their allies.[91] Realism cannot really capture these states' behavior as they did not really face a threat from either the Congo or Katanga.

The Congo Crisis was defined as a conflict between Black Nationalism and Pan-Africanism on one side and white-minority rule and neo-imperialism on the other. This enabled leaders in most African states to act decisively, because each elite could build support at home by using the crisis to emphasize Black Nationalism, anticolonialism and/or civic nationalism.[92] While civic nationalisms, as developed by several politicians seeking to downplay ethnicity, do not necessarily imply particular foreign policies, the content of these civic nationalisms mattered for this crisis. Pan-Africanism, Black Nationalism, and anticolonialism indicated support for the Congo, because of the perception of Katanga as a white-dominated movement with a tainted history.

Ambivalent and Neutral Actors

While many states took a strong stand on one side of the conflict, some countries were less certain in their support. These states either followed ambivalent policies or tried to stay neutral. The interests and actions of these states need to be analyzed so that comparisons can be made between those states that are strongly involved and those that are not.

United States

American foreign policy in the Congo was inconsistent and often contradictory. During the first few months of the conflict, the U.S. simultaneously supported UN efforts and tried to develop a more pro-Western government in the Congo. The U.S. supported all resolutions sponsored by the Afro-Asian states, and footed a disproportionate amount of the UN bill.[93] American transport planes flew most of the UN troops into the Congo, and the U.S. provided other forms of logistical support as well. However, during August and September of 1960, the U.S. encouraged Kasavubu and, later, Mobutu to dismiss Lumumba and take power.[94] Even after Lumumba was removed from power and placed under arrest, the U.S. sought to eliminate him. Katanga was, at first, regarded in the U.S. as possible insurance against the whole of the Congo becoming communist, and the White House gave some thought to recognizing it. However, the U.S. was reluctant to alienate the rest of Africa.[95]

After Lumumba's death and the new U.S. administration took office, American policy became more consistent. The U.S. supported the formation of a new regime through the Congolese Parliament, with a pro-Western leader, Cyrille Adoula, at its helm. Meanwhile, American support for ending Katanga's secession increased, including the use of force by ONUC. The UN mandate was expanded as the U.S. backed each resolution, and the U.S. gave logistical support for all three UN offensives.

David Gibbs argues that early in the crisis the financial ties of the individuals within the Eisenhower administration were closely tied to Belgian interests in Africa, while officials within the Kennedy administration had divergent preferences: some had ties to Belgian interests and others had investments in companies seeking to replace Belgian firms in Katanga.[96] Gibbs contends that Kennedy's policy was more inconsistent, as a result of the different economic ties, and that Eisenhower's policies were more consistent. Gibbs is right on two sets of issues: U.S. policy was motivated by anti-communism, and the change in Presidents played a crucial role, but he fails to explain why the problem and the ensuing suggested solutions were perceived differently by each president.

Eisenhower viewed the Congo Crisis through traditional Cold War lenses: Lumumba was "radical and unstable," "a Soviet tool," and "a Communist sympathizer if not a member of the party."[97] This is not surprising, considering his background: he became President by defeating a party charged with losing China, and was elected at the height of McCarthyism. Therefore, foreign policy in Africa was seen strictly in Cold War terms. The United States " . . . could not afford to see turmoil in an area where the Communists would only be too delighted to take advantage."[98] As a result, U.S. policy was fixated on getting rid of Lumumba, who had asked for Soviet help, and the U.S. was less resolute when dealing with Tshombe, who strategically painted himself as staunchly anti-Communist.[99] Further, the desire to avoid alienating Belgium also constrained the Eisenhower administration. Until 1958, American relations with Africa were routed through the embassies of the colonial powers, and the U.S. generally deferred to their wishes.

President Kennedy signaled a completely different approach when he named his Assistant Secretary of State for African Affairs before identifying his Secretary of State, and by arguing that "We can no longer think of Africa in terms of Europe."[100] While anti-communism primarily motivated Kennedy's Congo policies, his views were more nuanced, due to his experiences and his successful campaign strategies. In July 1957, Kennedy had made a name for himself in foreign affairs when he became the first elected American official to oppose French policy in Algeria. While Democrats and Republicans immediately criticized him, Kennedy's predictions were appreciated a year later, when French President Charles De Gaulle allowed the French colonies in Africa to vote on independence. "For African visitors in Washington, Kennedy became the man to meet."[101]

Kennedy's statements on Africa were the results of his views of nationalism, and they were also a key part of his own political agenda. The Algeria speech was "in part, a bid to attract support from the party's liberal leadership."[102] Within the Democratic Party, JFK's left flank was his weakest, and he realized that he needed liberals' support to get the party's Presidential nomination. However, he was reluctant to push for civil rights in the U.S., as he feared alienating Southern voters. To get more of the liberal and black vote without losing the Southern whites, Kennedy used African issues to his advantage, making 479 references to Africa in a three month campaign. "Kennedy's handling of the Africa issue in the 1960 campaign . . . was a minor classic in *political exploitation of foreign policy*."[103]

As a result, among Kennedy's first actions as President was the establishment of a committee to explore all policy options in the Congo. From the reports of that committee, he came to see the Congo Crisis in a different light than had the previous administration, which had seen Katanga as a fall-back position—insurance against the loss of the Congo to the Communists. Instead, Kennedy saw Katanga as the cause of the Congo's instability,[104] and the moderate regime put in place in the Congo largely due to Kennedy's policies of early 1961 was threatened by its inability to handle Katanga. If Adoula could not handle Tshombe, he would lose power to more extreme elements, including Communists. Therefore, Kennedy permitted and, later, pushed for broader UN mandates for more assertive actions by ONUC.

However, Kennedy's policies were constrained by domestic opposition. The Katanga lobby in Washington, led by Sen. Thomas Dodd of Connecticut, included some of the most formidable Senators. Most of the groups supporting Katanga and opposed to Kennedy's policy in the Congo were anti-communist, anti-UN, and right-wing, including the John Birch Society and the Young Americans for Freedom.[105] The Katanga lobby "also attracted certain Southern whites who seem to have regarded Moise Tshombe as the African incarnation of Uncle Tom."[106] Having won the support of the left wing in the Democratic Party in part by using foreign policy in Africa, Kennedy faced opposition from the right wing. It is not surprising, then, that the most assertive attempts to end the Katangan secession, using American fighters and pilots, were most seriously considered after the Cuban Missile Crisis, when Kennedy's right flank was more secure.[107]

Thus, Kennedy's domestic political interests influenced his perceptions of the crisis and the forces constraining his policies. He viewed African nationalism and instability in the Congo differently from Eisenhower, as he sought to include liberals and blacks in his electoral coalition. Kennedy's actions were initially limited by the influence of the Katanga lobby, but this constraint became less important after the Cuban Missile Crisis strengthened his political position at home. The changes in policy during the crisis illustrate the difficulties a politician faces when his constituency is not only ethnically heterogeneous, but also consists of divergent ideological forces.

The alternative arguments are indeterminate. The United States did not face a severe separatist threat at the time, and severe ethnic conflict was a few years in coming. So, vulnerability cannot explain the choices of the U.S., although American interest in preserving the United Nations might. As the Soviet Union and others harshly criticized the United Nations and proposed changing the Secretary-General to a troika system, the United States needed to give greater support to the institution and to make it effective in the Congo for this international organization to survive.

Realist accounts are also indeterminate, as the contrasting policies of Eisenhower and Kennedy demonstrate. Eisenhower believed, in part, that giving support to the richest part of the Congo, Katanga, might benefit American interests by providing an island of pro-Western support in case Lumumba ruled the Congo. Kennedy perceived Katanga to be the problem. Realists would be right in arguing that the Congo was an important place

and deserving to be a Cold War battleground, but Realists could easily disagree with each other about what was the best strategy at the time.

The Central African Republic

The Central African Republic provides an interesting contrast to Congo-
Brazzaville. The Central African Republic shared many political, social, and
economic characteristics with Congo-Brazzaville, but followed different policies. Like Congo-Brazzaville, the Central African Republic was a former
French colony, and was very dependent upon the French for economic
assistance. Similarly, the newly independent government faced the problem
of tribal divisions. Most importantly, the Central African Republic's leadership depended heavily on the support of its European settlers.

President David Dacko relied on the European residents for his position.
Not only did they occupy the most important positions in the government
and the economy, but they also gave money for trucks and bribes when
Dacko needed to flood the capital with members of his own kinship group
to counter his opposition. This particular event indicates that Dacko was
dependent not only on the good will of the white settlers, but on his own
kinship group. Because of this dual dependence, and of the Europeans'
ability to direct the assembly (due to unity of the white settlers),[108] "Dacko
was not in a position to contemplate an adventurous foreign policy."[109]

The Central African Republic's foreign policy was, therefore, neutral,
though it preferred the United Nations not to intervene. As a neighbor, the
Central African Republic was very concerned with the conflict. The European settlers, in particular, were alarmed, considering themselves vulnerable
to the same sort of crisis.[110] While they may have been interested in supporting the Katangans, the other portion of Dacko's constituency, his black
kinship group, was less concerned with the welfare of the white settlers in
Katanga. Consequently, the Central African Republic opposed interference
in the Congo by the United Nations, arguing that the UN " 'should keep
its hands clean in respect of the problems of African internal politics,' "[111]
but avoided any more tangible support for the Katangan separatists. Unlike
almost any other African state, the Central African Republic's support came
from different racial groups, constraining its foreign policy.

Again, vulnerability produces no predictions about how the Central African Republic would respond since it was not vulnerable to separatism. Real-

ism suggests that the C.A.R should have responded as Congo-Brazzaville did and supported Katanga, but it did not. The two states acted differently because the leaders of each followed different strategies for handling their domestic political problems.

Ethnic Politics and the Congo Crisis

The analysis of Congo Crisis suggests that coding threat and producing the resulting predictions is much harder than distilling expectations from vulnerability or ethnic ties, and the realism's correct predictions are largely produced by the incorporation of ethnically defined threats. Vulnerability provides the fewest correct predictions and the most indeterminate expectations. On the other hand, focusing on racial politics gives us the clearest, most accurate predictions, although even this approach wrongly predicts a few cases.

Balancing Threats and the Congo Crisis

This case study reveals several difficulties in applying realism. Because threat contains several components, it is hard to tell when sufficient threats exist to cause a state to engage in "balancing" behavior, such as supporting Katanga. What should we expect of states that are not threatened by the Congo nor seriously threatened by Katanga? Further, the case reveals that states motivated by security may still have multiple options, and we need more information to predict which choice a state will make. The Congo Crisis suggests that larger security interests and competitive dynamics may matter. Finally, the expansion of offensive capability to include ethnic threats produces much of the predictive power of realism in this case.

Of the thirteen observations studied, the adjusted realist approach got four right, was indeterminate in six, and wrong in three. This case suggests that since Walt's approach does not have a method of weighing the various components of threat, it is hard to make determinate predictions, unless each component points in the same direction. "One cannot determine *a priori*, however, which sources of threat will be most important in any given case; one can say only that all of them are likely to play a role."[112] As a result,

TABLE 3.1 Applying Realism to the Congo Crisis

Country	Weaker or Stronger than the Congo*	Congo's Offensive Threat	Katanga's Threat	Neighbors of the Congo	Predicted Policy	Actual Policy
Belgium	Stronger	Moderate	Low	No	Unclear	Supported Katanga, Weakened
Federation of Rhodesia and Nyasaland	Stronger	High	Low	Yes	Support Katanga	**Supported Katanga**
South Africa	Stronger	Moderate	Low	No	Unclear	Supported Katanga
United States	Stronger	Low	Low	No	No Support for Katanga	*Ambivalence shifted to support Congo*
Central African Republic	Weaker	High	Low	Yes	Support Katanga	*Neutrality*
Ghana	Weaker	Low	Moderate	No	Unclear	Supported Congo
Guinea	Weaker	Low	Moderate	No	Unclear	Supported Congo
Ethiopia	Stronger	Low	Moderate	No	Support Congo	**Supported Congo**
Morocco	Stronger	Low	Low	No	No Support for Katanga	Supported Congo
Tunisia	Weaker	Low	Low	No	No Support for Congo	*Supported Congo*
India	Stronger	Low	Low	No	No Support for Katanga	Supported Congo
Nigeria	Stronger	Low	Moderate	No	Support Congo	**Supported Congo**
Congo-Brazzaville	Weaker	High	Low	Yes	Support Katanga	**Supported Katanga**

* This is coded by a ratio of the country's power relative to the Congo's, using measures of military and economic capabilities and population measures, as discussed in chapter six. **Bold** indicates a correct prediction. *Italics* indicate an incorrect prediction.

we cannot provide clear predictions when some of the indicators of threat point in one direction, and other indicators point in the other direction.

A state neighboring a country possessing the capability to threaten its territorial integrity is most likely to perceive a threat and react accordingly. The Congo threatened both the Federation of Rhodesia and Nyasaland and Congo-Brazzaville, so it makes sense that both supported Katanga. However, the Central African Republic is very similar to these countries, yet chose to remain neutral during the conflict.

For those states stronger than the Congo but not neighbors, it was hard to make conclusive predictions. One could expect these states not to support Katanga, as they did not need to balance against the Congo, due to the low threat they faced. We can only predict that these states would support the Congo if Katanga threatened them. Since threats motivate states, the absence of threats suggests an absence of motive. Because Katanga could become a base of white or neocolonial interests in Central Africa, it could have posed a threat to sub-Saharan African states. However, these states could have done nothing as well, since the Katangan threat was only a potential one, and not nearly as alarming as other threats.

Several states faced no significant threats, particularly India, Morocco, and Tunisia, due to their distance from the conflict, but they still chose to support the Congo. For these cases, realism is ultimately indeterminate, since realism suggests that these countries would not support Katanga, but given the absence of threat, no prediction could be made for supporting the Congo.

American behavior during this crisis neatly demonstrates a key problem — when a security threat exists, a state can respond in a variety of ways, and realism, by itself, may not provide a clear prediction. The U.S. could have defended its security interests by supporting Katanga, building a bridgehead of support in the region, or it could have changed the Congo's government to one that is friendlier to American interests. Eisenhower considered the former, but Kennedy chose the latter. Threat for realism, thus, is like vulnerability for neoliberal institutionalists — it is less determinate than the theorists suggest.

I must note that the simple predictions of table 3.1 ignore the larger geopolitical game going on, as states may not be balancing against the Congo or Katanga, but with or against Belgium, South Africa, and the other major players in the conflict. Obviously, the Congo Crisis became embroiled in the larger white-minority/black nationalist conflict and the Cold War as well.

States may have reacted to what the Federation of Rhodesia and Nyasaland was doing, rather than Tshombe's policies. Still, racial politics would influence how states reacted to the Federation as much or more than how they reacted to Tshombe and Lumumba.

Realism can account for some of the behavior of states in this case when it is expanded to include ethnically defined threats. Katanga was a threat to African states because of its perceived alliance with and dependence upon white settlers in Katanga and in the larger region. Belgium, the Federation, and South Africa considered the Congo a threat because of their ethnic divisions and because of Lumumba's stand as a Pan-Africanist and Black nationalist. If South Africa and the Federation were not white-minority regimes, the Congo would not have been a threat nor would Katanga have been an appealing ally. This is a problem for realism because the inclusion of ethnicity as a determinant of threat is a significant move away from the parsimony that realists value, and forces us to pay more attention to domestic politics.

Vulnerability and International Cooperation

Were states vulnerable to secession inhibited from aiding Katanga? The cast of countries abetting Katanga undermines the vulnerability argument. All the four states giving significant support to Katanga were vulnerable to ethnic conflict. The threat of secession was particularly strong for Belgium and the Federation of Rhodesia and Nyasaland, yet their vulnerability did not deter support for a secessionist movement in another country. Many of the Congo's supporters were vulnerable to secession, so one could argue that they wanted to maintain the Congo's territorial integrity to set a good precedent for their own situations. For three remaining observations, vulnerability could not provide a prediction since separatism was not a threat. At best, as table 3.2 below indicates, vulnerability predicts six cases correctly, gets four completely wrong, and cannot make a prediction for three others.

Since this was the first major separatist crisis of Africa's decolonization, it set precedents, rather than being shaped by them. It is hard to argue that norms of territorial integrity influenced states since the conflict between self-determination and territorial integrity was only becoming apparent at the time. This conflict was only resolved by the creation of the Organization of African Unity in 1963 and its subsequent declaration legitimizing the former

TABLE 3.2 Vulnerability and the Congo Crisis

Country	Vulnerability	Vulnerability Predictions	Actual Policy
Belgium	High	Support Congo	*Supported Katanga, Weakened*
Federation of Rhodesia and Nyasaland	High	Support Congo	*Supported Katanga*
South Africa	High	Support Congo	*Supported Katanga*
United States	Low	No Prediction	Ambivalence shifted to supported Congo
Central African Republic	Low	No Prediction	Neutrality
Ghana	High	Support Congo	**Supported Congo**
Guinea	High	Support Congo	**Supported Congo**
Ethiopia	High	Support Congo	**Supported Congo**
Morocco	High	Support Congo	**Supported Congo**
Tunisia	Low	No Prediction	**Supported Congo**
India	High	Support Congo	Supported Congo
Nigeria	High	Support Congo	**Supported Congo**
Congo-Brazzaville	High	Support Congo	*Supported Katanga*

Bold indicates a correct prediction.
Italics indicate an incorrect prediction.

colonial boundaries. Therefore, it would be unfair to say that the willingness of states to support Katanga challenged international norms since such norms were not really established.

On the other hand, any assertions about the role of international organizations are fair game since the United Nations played a very strong role here, defeating the Katangans on the battlefield. Most states did not support Katanga, and many gave help to UN efforts, particularly after the UN's effort and the institution itself were challenged after Lumumba's assassination. However, it is hard to disentangle the effect of the UN on individual states from the pre-existing preferences of states since the UN's efforts were a product of lobbying and voting by states. In other words, did the UN cause states to support the Congo or did states cause the UN to support the Congo? Because of the strident diplomacy, including threats to withdraw troops from ONUC, and these states followed through on their threats, it is clear that states drove the UN to take more and more aggressive stands against Katanga, rather than the UN's anti-Katanga policy shaping what states did. Belgium, ordinarily considered a good international citizen, resisted the United Nations, and continued to support Katanga despite active UN opposition. A pattern that was to develop and repeat itself from the 1960s until late into the 1980s was that UN opposition did not deter, inhibit, or alter the foreign policies of the white-minority regimes.

Finally, arguments about reciprocity receive support here. States that had a good prior relationship with Lumumba and the Congo gave support, while states having a bad history gave support to his enemies. This gives the vulnerability argument some support since it is based on a logic of reciprocity. The problem is that this approach begs the question of why does a history of cooperation or conflict exist. Ethnic politics addresses this question.

The Theory of Ethnic Politics and Foreign Policy and The Congo Crisis

The Congo Crisis indicates that ethnic politics influences the foreign policies of states. In this dispute, racial divisions played an extremely important role, both in the domestic politics of states and in their impact on the conflict between the newly independent states and the former colonial powers and the white-minority regimes. Out of a total of thirteen countries, ethnic ties between leaders' constituents and the combatants in the conflict predict the policies of ten countries accurately. Variations in political competition help to explain the three exceptional cases: Congo-Brazzaville, the U.S., and Belgium.

A narrow focus on ethnic ties predicts that Congo-Brazzaville would have supported the Congo and not Katanga. Still, the demands of ethnic politics shaped this country's policies, as elites sought an alternative way to deal with ethnic conflict. Because President Youlou faced less immediate political competition, he could seek alternative strategies in the short term, including buying (or at least renting) potential opponents. While the heart of the theory of ethnic politics and foreign policy argues that ethnic ties matter, leaders facing less competition will be more likely to act contrary to the ethnic ties

TABLE 3.3 Racial Politics and the Congo Crisis

Country	Racial Ties To:	Ethnic Competition	Ethnic Ties Predictions	Actual Policy
Belgium	Katanga*	High	Support Katanga	**Supported Katanga**, *Weakened*
Federation of Rhodesia and Nyasaland	Katanga	High	Support Katanga	**Supported Katanga**
South Africa	Katanga	High	Support Katanga	**Supported Katanga**
United States	Both	High	Ambivalence or Neutrality	**Ambivalence** shifted to *Supported Congo*
Central African Republic	Both	High	Ambivalence or Neutrality	**Neutrality**
Ghana	Congo	Low	Support Congo	**Supported Congo**
Guinea	Congo	Low	Support Congo	**Supported Congo**
Ethiopia	Congo	Low	Support Congo	**Supported Congo**
Morocco	Congo**	High	Support Congo	**Supported Congo**
Tunisia	Congo**	Low	Support Congo	**Supported Congo**
India	Congo**	High	Support Congo	**Supported Congo**
Nigeria	Congo	High	Support Congo	**Supported Congo**
Congo-Brazzaville	Congo	Low	Support Congo	*Supported Katanga*

Bold indicates a correct prediction.

Italics indicate an incorrect prediction.

* The Belgian case is as much about its enmity, not ethnically oriented, against the Congo.

** The Indian, Moroccan and Tunisian coding focuses more on ethnic enmity with the Katangans, which produces the same foreign policies as ethnic ties with the Congo.

of their constituents. Thus, Congo-Brazzaville's policies are not as aberrant as it might appear.

As the leader of a multiracial party, Kennedy's policies, as predicted by ethnic politics, would be ambivalent rather than increasingly hostile to the Katangans. The theory predicts that Kennedy would face opposition from his white constituents if he backed the Congo's government, and would dismay his black supporters if he did not support it. Kennedy, indeed, faced these kinds of obstacles and opposition as he developed policies toward the Congo. The Katanga lobby constrained Kennedy until his position became more secure. Though the specific expectations of the theory of ethnic politics and foreign policy do not accurately predict the more assertive policies of the U.S. toward the end of the crisis, this approach does help explain the difficulties Kennedy faced when developing policies toward Katanga and the Congo.

Explaining Belgium's foreign policy during the crisis is difficult, as ethnic politics does not provide strong predictions when the ethnic conflict within the state making foreign policy decisions is not perceived to be related to the ethnic politics of the secessionist crisis. While all of the parties in Belgium were led by and supported by whites, race is not a salient ethnicity around which Belgian politics was organized. Linguistic conflict mattered, however, and most politicians of the three major parties sought to de-emphasize language. Civic nationalism could be emphasized to downplay linguistic identity. Because of Lumumba's and Tshombe's statements concerning Belgium, it was easy for Belgian elites to support Katanga as Belgian nationalism was inflamed during the crisis. The hardest part of Belgium's policies to explain is the declining support for Katanga. One possible explanation is that when Spaak took power, his socialist party may have been less dependent on using Belgian nationalism. Having a class-based ideology may have allowed Spaak to be relatively less compelled or interested in Belgian nationalism.[113] A complementary explanation is that Belgium was worn down by the opposition of the United Nations and eventually of the United States.

Overall, this case indicates that ethnic ties and enmities greatly influence the preferences of these decisionmakers, determining which side of the conflict they assisted. However, this case study does suggest that there are other ways for politicians to deal with threatening ethnic identities and conflicts, besides mobilizing an alternative ethnic or civic nationalism.

In particular, reducing the sources of ethnic strife may be desirable. In Belgium, economic decline increased communal tensions. Policies that

ameliorate or improve a state's economic fortunes may aid in reducing ethnic conflict. Therefore, there was a greater economic interest for Belgium
to support secession in the Congo. Likewise, in the white-dominated regimes
of Rhodesia and South Africa, preventing the spread of Black Nationalism
and Communism in the Congo by assisting Katanga was seen as a necessary
policy to limit increased ethnic strife at home. In Congo-Brazzaville, Youlou
attempted to buy off ethnic conflict, but only delayed his own demise. In
each case, important domestic political imperatives, driven by ethnic politics, affected foreign policy though not always in ways predicted by the theory
of ethnic politics and foreign policy.

This case also indicates the external perceptions of a conflict are crucial.
Because the conflict in the Congo was seen as a black/white, Pan-African/
neocolonial conflict, politicians in other states, and their constituencies, had
strong preferences. If the conflict was seen purely as a struggle between
different black tribes within the Congo, most states would not have cared as
much, and the UN would not have gotten involved. The definition of this
crisis as a racial struggle and a contest between neocolonialism and the newly
independent states was a consequence of the Katangan secessionist movement's pre-independence history, the behavior of white settlers and Belgium,
and the agenda-setting efforts of various states within international fora.

Summary

A single case cannot falsify a theory, but the Congo Crisis suggests that
each approach has some value and some weaknesses. The impressive role
played by the United Nations supports the arguments made by Jackson and
Rosberg and Herbst about the influence of international organizations, but
the willingness of states vulnerable to secession undermines the fundamental
assumption guiding their works. This crisis indicates that a broad conception
of offensive capability and a focus on perceived intentions can be helpful,
though other adjusted realist variables such as geographic proximity and
aggregate power do not seem to play as strong a role as hypothesized. Finally,
the Congo Crisis indicates that there is a strong correlation between the
ethnic ties and the side supported. The next case study, the Nigerian Civil
War, should indicate whether the Congo Crisis was unique.

4   Religious Ties and the Nigerian Civil War, 1967–1970

Shortly after the Congo Crisis, Nigeria's ethnic conflict accelerated. This strife between ethnic groups developed into a secessionist war between Biafra, the Eastern region of Nigeria, largely composed of the predominantly Christian Ibo tribal group, and the Federal Military Government of Nigeria, which consisted of the Muslim Hausa-Fulani group, the religiously heterogeneous Yorubas, and many smaller tribes.

The Nigerian Civil War provides a good contrast to the Katangan secession as four years separated the two conflicts, thereby holding most variables relatively constant. Despite the short time between the two secessionist crises, and despite many similarities between Biafra and Katanga, the international politics of the Nigerian Civil War were not identical to those of the Congo Crisis. No states recognized Katanga while five states recognized Biafra. No global organization, such as the United Nations, became involved in the Nigerian Civil War, but a new regional organization, the Organization of African Unity [OAU], played an important role. In contrast to the UN's role in defeating the Katangan separatists, the Nigerian armed forces defeated Biafra. The Katangan secession increased fears of neocolonialism and white control over Black Africa. Instead, Biafra's secession resonated mostly along religious divides as the Christian Ibos of Biafra were seen as the "Jews of Africa" being oppressed by Nigeria's predominantly Muslim Northern region.

Comparing these two secessionist crises is both feasible and interesting, as there are many features common to both civil wars. Analysts perceived

the Nigerian Civil War to have confirmed the international norms and precedents set in the Congo Crisis.[1] Both secessionist regions, Katanga and
Biafra, contained the richest mineral resources in the state from which they
were seceding. As a result, the interests of outside powers were significant
in both crises. Moreover, each movement sought to secede from one of the
larger influential African states, increasing the impact these crises might have
on future events and relations in Africa. In both cases, outside aid prolonged
the crisis and increased tensions between states.

By studying a secessionist civil war occurring shortly after the Congo
Crisis, we can make comparisons between the various states involved in each
crisis. Some states followed similar policies in both crises, while other states
developed very different policies. For vulnerability arguments, the most important concerns in this case are: did vulnerability to secessionism inhibit
support for the Biafrans? Further, did the specification of boundary maintenance norms by the Organization of African Unity deter states from supporting secession? The adjusted realist framework concentrates on whom
Nigeria or Biafra threatened. If Nigeria is such a strong state relative to
others, more states will balance against it, by supporting Biafra, among other
means. Finally, the theory of ethnic politics and foreign policy predicts that
as the conflict becomes defined as a religious one, those politicians with
Christian constituents would support Biafra, and politicians relying on Muslim supporters would aid Nigeria. The only leaders going against the ethnic
ties of their constituents would be those facing less severe competition.

The Origins of Biafran Secessionism

While ethnic conflict existed before the coup d'état that ended the First
Republic of Nigeria, strife between the tribal groups increased because of
the military takeover. On January 15, 1966, a coup against the civilian government of Nigeria occurred, resulting in the deaths of the Prime Minister
as well as the governors of the Northern and Western states. Only the Eastern
governor, an Ibo, survived. The leader of the military regime, Major General
Johnson Aguiyi Ironsi, also an Ibo, proclaimed Nigeria to be a unitary state,
abolishing federal institutions established before decolonization. This led to
anti-Ibo riots in the Northern Region as fears of Ibo domination grew.

A second coup, on July 29, 1966, resulted Ironsi's death, and the ascen-
sion of Colonel Yakubu Gowon, a member of a smaller tribe. Rioting and

massacres of Ibos in the northern regions occurred afterward, leading to large flows of Ibos returning to the eastern region. General C. Odumegwu Ojukwu, appointed military governor of the Eastern Region after the first coup, was reluctant to submit to the authority of the Federal Military Government. After failed negotiations, Ojukwu declared the independence of the Republic of Biafra, which consisted of the territory of Nigeria's Eastern Region, on May 30, 1967. Fighting broke out in July 1967, and the conflict ended two and a half years later in January 1970, after a series of offensives by the Nigerian armed forces.

International intervention consisted of humanitarian efforts to aid the civilian population in Biafra, arms assistance to the secessionists by a few states and to Nigeria by several others, diplomatic recognition of Biafra by four African states, and efforts at consultation and mediation by the Organization of African Unity. Biafran diplomats exerted great efforts to internationalize the conflict, resulting in a mixed record of success. By emphasizing both religious differences as a cause of this civil war and the risk of genocide, Biafrans sought diplomatic recognition and military support for their movement. Though four African states (and Haiti)[2] recognized Biafra, and several countries provided arms, Biafra was unable to parlay these gains into broader support.

Biafra's Ethnic Politics

General Ojukwu and the other Biafran leaders engaged in ethnic politics to both domestic and international audiences. Within Biafra, emphasis on religious ties and raising fears of genocide were policies consciously devised to unite many tribes. At the international level, Biafran elites used religious ties and the potential genocide to gain assistance from states in Africa, Europe, and America.

While the Ibos were the largest ethnic group within Biafra, they accounted for only 64 percent of the Eastern Region's population.[3] Within Biafra, there were several smaller tribes with histories of tensions with the Ibos, and they were less enthusiastic about secession. A more common bond in Biafra was that of religion: 90% of the population were Christians, and most of the rest were animists. Less than 0.5% of the Biafran population were Muslims.[4] By stressing religious ties, the Ibos were seeking to get support from non-Ibo Christians, and by emphasizing the history of enslavement by Muslims, the Ibos were trying to appeal to the animists. By defining the conflict as one between Biafra and the Muslim Hausa-Fulani, rather than the whole of Nigeria, the Biafrans emphasized religious identities. Ojukwu broadcasted to Biafrans, that "the aim of the Hausa-Fulani oligarchy is to subjugate and enslave what was Southern Nigeria."[5]

The emphasis on religious persecution also aimed at the international audience, as Biafra sought to get foreign assistance. Biafrans defined themselves as the Jews of Africa, comparing their situation to that of the Jews of Europe during the holocaust and of Israel and its hostile Arab neighbors. The international community ignored both the Jews of Europe and the Christians of Biafra as they faced genocide. "Today, a similar situation is taking place in the West Coat of Africa. More than 30,000 inhabitants of what used to be Eastern Nigeria were murdered in cold blood. Pregnant women, children, unarmed *Christian* worshippers, were among the victims of the pogrom in Northern Nigeria last year."[6]

While there was some veracity to the claims of religious conflict, the Biafrans faced one significant difficulty in defining this civil war as one of religion. General Gowon, two-thirds of the Nigerian cabinet, and most of the federal army were non-Muslims. Ojukwu argued: " 'Gowon claims to be a "Christian and a son of a Methodist Minister" a claim calculated to impress foreign churchmen and press correspondents who do not know that he is in reality the leader of a Muslim jihad directed towards the annihilation of Biafrans and the islamization of Biafra.' "[7]

Biafran appeals to religious ties had important consequences. It influenced the perceptions of many non-state actors, as well as the domestic politics of some of most important countries involved in this crisis. Many nongovernmental humanitarian organizations became involved in the civil war as they sought to provide humanitarian aid to the Biafrans. Most prominent among these groups were those affiliated with Protestant and Catholic Churches[8] including Nordchurchaid, World Council of Churches, and Caritas.

These groups helped Biafra in two ways. First, besides providing needed goods, they paid Biafrans for services rendered with foreign exchange. "The most decisive and reliable source of funds that could be used to purchase military equipment abroad was the foreign exchange component in the vast, privately administered, humanitarian relief effort."[9] Thus, Biafra could buy arms on the open market, since few states were willing to give away weapons. Second, humanitarian relief flights provided cover for the airlift of arms from

Gabon, the Ivory Coast, and various Portuguese colonies. When Nigeria allowed day flights of humanitarian supplies, if inspected by government officials for contraband, Biafra refused to admit planes that had undergone this procedure. By forcing the relief planes to fly at night, Biafra was able to deter Nigeria from shooting down all incoming night flights.[10] Religious appeals and assertions of genocide aimed against Christians by the Muslim north also influenced the positions of many states toward Biafra and Nigeria.[11] This strategy was a double-edged sword, as it encouraged some states to support Biafra, while it alienated many others, pushing them into Nigeria's camp.

Biafra's Supporters

Unlike the Katangan crisis, where almost all the supporters of the secessionist movement could be classified as white-ruled regimes, the states assisting Biafra do not fit into any neat categories. Indeed, Biafra's supporters were very strange bedfellows, including: radical Anglophone states and conservative Francophone states of East and West Africa; France, the People's Republic of China [PRC], Israel, and the white-minority regimes of Southern Africa. Because both Tanzania, a leader of radical Black Nationalism, and South Africa, a white-ruled regime, supported Biafra, race cannot explain the international politics of this conflict. Likewise, as the Ivory Coast, one of the most conservative and anti-communist African states, and the PRC assisted the secessionists, the communist/anti-communist conflict cannot explain the policies of states toward this crisis. By assessing the ethnic political opportunities, constraints, and strategies that elites face in the countries supporting Biafra, we understand better why ethnic groups receive support.

Tanzania

As the first state to grant recognition to Biafra, Tanzania played a very influential role in internationalizing the Nigerian Civil War. No state had recognized Katanga, and none had recognized Biafra in eleven months between the declaration of secession and Tanzania's announcement. An important precedent was set, increasing the willingness of other states to recognize Biafra, as the three other African states to give diplomatic recognition did so within a month of Tanzania. Tanzania's efforts went beyond recognition of Biafra. Tanzanian officials lobbied other states to recognize Biafra, including Zambia, whose President, Kenneth Kaunda, was a close friend of Tanzania's President Julius Nyerere. Tanzania also voted against various OAU resolutions supporting the Federal Military Government. More importantly, after giving the Biafrans a chance to meet representatives of the People's Republic of China, Tanzania apparently gave significant material support to the Biafran armed forces as Nyerere permitted his state to become a "staging point for arms from China."[12]

Why did Tanzania, led by Nyerere, give diplomatic recognition and other forms of assistance to Biafra? Nyerere's policies are especially puzzling. Tanzania was the initiator of the Organization of African Unity resolution sanctifying the existing boundaries,[13] and Nyerere had made many statements before the crisis affirming the territorial integrity of African states and the norm of nonintervention.[14] Nyerere rejected the religious dimension of the conflict, and asserted that self-determination "is an issue of life and death,"[15] and that Biafra's secession was necessary to increase the Ibos' security.[16] Many scholars have argued that Nyerere was following his principles when Tanzanian officials asserted "Only by this act of recognition can we remain true to our conviction that the purpose of society and of all political organization, is the service of man."[17] Nyerere's humanitarian principles can only serve as a partial explanation of Tanzania's behavior. Why was he able to act on his beliefs? Not all leaders can follow their principles as most leaders are constrained by their own political constituencies and strategies (as the case of Senghor of Senegal illustrates below). There are several reasons, other than humanitarian interests, that can help in explaining Nyerere's support of Biafra.

Due to Tanzania's political and social structures, Nyerere faced fewer constraints than other leaders. Before independence, Nyerere organized a mass-based party, the Tanganyika African National Union [TANU] aimed at achieving independence and developing a Tanganyikan national identity to overcome the many tribal ties in the society. TANU was so successful in gathering support that political competition between parties became meaningless, leading to Nyerere's development of a one-party state, with intraparty competition. Nyerere sought a one-party system as he believed that multiparty systems created divisions and cannot foster so broad civic nationalism as a single-party system can.[18]

The rules governing elections and intraparty competition minimized the incentives politicians had to mobilize religious or tribal ties to gain power. "Participation is made possible but so structured as not to mobilize cultural pluralism. The election does not offer incentives or provide opportunities for aggregative communal coalition."[19] Because each election at every level was between two candidates approved by TANU party committees, and because of the structure of the constituencies and the electoral system, politicians had little incentive or ability to gain support by emphasizing ethnicity. Besides electoral incentives, references to ethnic divisions were to be banned from political competition. Part of the instructions given to the body assigned to develop the one-party system included prohibitions against discrimination based on race, tribe, color, or religion. " 'There shall be no propagation of group hatred, nor of any policy which would have the effect of arousing feelings of disrespect for any race, tribe, sex, or religion.' "[20] The result of this mass-based, non-ethnic political structure was that Nyerere was not compelled nor constrained by the ethnic composition of his constituency, especially in the realm of foreign policy.[21] Thus, Nyerere's ability to develop a foreign policy that defied the narrow predictions of all three models suggests that political competition, or its absence, is a critical factor in foreign policymaking.

There were two difficult divides confronting Nyerere in 1968: religion and the differing interests and histories of mainland Tanganyika and the island of Zanzibar. While more than 40 percent of the Tanganikan population followed traditional African religions, a growing 30 percent were Muslims, and the remaining were Christians.[22] Recognizing a secessionist movement posturing as a Christian victim of Islamic domination would seem to be a dangerous policy. Realizing this, Nyerere played down the religious nature of the war. "In spite of attempts on both sides of the quarrel to bring in religion, the conflict between Nigeria and Biafra is not a religious one."[23] Still, recognizing Biafra could have alienated the mostly Muslim island of Zanzibar, which had recently united with Tanganyika to form Tanzania in 1964. However, instead of offending the relatively new citizens of Tanzania, Nyerere sought to reassure them through his recognition of Biafra. In justifying the extension of recognition, Nyerere argued that governments "should be very solicitous of the interests of minorities, because they are the ones which need the protection of the State. If a dominant group does not act in this protective manner, then civil strife and consequent Biafras become inevitable."[24] The audience for Nyerere's statement is Zanzibar as

Tanganyikan individuals and institutions were dominant in the new United Republic of Tanzania. Nyerere also asserts that he would not resist an attempt by Zanzibar to secede.[25] Because Zanzibar did not have a shared history or culture with mainland Tanganyika,[26] and as Nyerere was a Christian mainlander, he had to reassure Zanzibar frequently as they felt insecure in a political system dominated by Nyerere and TANU.

Supporting Biafra's fight against Nigeria would not be as offensive to Zanzibaris as it would be to other Muslims, because of Zanzibar's history, where an Arab minority oppressed Africans living on Zanzibar until the 1964 revolution. Zanzibar's ruling party, the Afro-Shizari Party, won office as a "result of its ability to tap long-latent resentment of Arab social and political preeminence."[27] Since the Afro-Shizari Party continued to govern Zanzibar after it united with Tanganyika, its preferences and strategies influenced Tanzania's politics and policies. Because predominantly Muslim Zanzibaris hated Arabs, and the Biafrans were fighting a state said to be dominated by Arabs (the Fulani of the Northern Region), supporting Biafra would not necessarily alienate the newest members of Tanzania.

Still, Nyerere's policies during this crisis are an anomaly that cannot be explained by ethnic ties. Because his constituency consisted of different religious groups having ties to both sides of the Nigerian Civil War, the theory predicts that Nyerere would stay neutral or follow ambivalent policies. However, Nyerere took very assertive steps to favor Biafra. Several factors may have lessened the ethnic constraints he faced. He did try to redefine the conflict as a human rights problem, rather than a religious conflict. The institutions governing political competition in Tanzania gave Nyerere greater autonomy than had the politicians of other states. The part of his constituency having religious ties to Nigeria, the Zanzibaris, may have supported his policies because they may have perceived the Nigerian Civil War as a racial conflict between Africans and Arabs, rather than a religious dispute between Christians and Muslims. Even so, Nyerere's recognition and support of Biafra policies are "difficult to explain," as one analyst put it.[28]

Tanzania's foreign policy is even harder for the vulnerability argument to address. First, Tanzania faced a very serious threat of separatism because of the recent union of Tanganyika and Zanzibar. Second, Nyerere played an important role in specifying the norm of territorial integrity, so it is quite surprising that Tanzania recognized the first secessionist movement to come along after the OAU declaration, which legitimated the colonial boundaries. Third, the OAU, an organization that Tanzania helped to create, played a strong role in the conflict, trying to deter support for Biafra, yet Tanzania openly and aggressively followed policies that violated the OAU consensus.

Realists cannot make sense of Tanzania's support of Biafra, either. While Tanzania was less powerful than Nigeria, all other measures of threat suggest that Nigeria did not threaten Tanzania. Nigeria had no meaningful ability to disrupt Tanzania's territorial integrity. The distance separating the two states meant that Nigeria could not pose a conventional military threat. Indeed, as the white minority regimes in southern Africa posed far greater threats due to their size, proximity, and hostile intentions, it is quite puzzling that Tanzania would support efforts to divide a potential ally.

Overall, Tanzania presents quite a puzzle. Its foreign policy toward Biafra contradicts most clearly the vulnerability argument and realist accounts. Further, Nyerere's policy ran counter to what ethnic ties would suggest. He should have played a neutral or ambivalent role in this conflict since his constituents had ties to both sides. However, the political system insulated Nyerere from political competition at this time, allowing him to do what he wanted. Because of his dominance in the political system, Nyerere could redefine the conflict as a humanitarian crisis, and could emphasize the Arab/racial component of the conflict, rather than the religious dimension.

Zambia

Zambia's President, Kenneth Kaunda, an ally and friend of Nyerere, faced similar political circumstances and, like Nyerere, gave Biafra diplomatic recognition. Kaunda's justification was similar to Nyerere's: " 'You cannot reassure people who are afraid through the barrel of a gun.' "[29] Zambia also assisted the secessionists by providing some relief supplies, a couple of old cargo planes, and some foreign currency, which enabled Biafra to purchase arms from the international black market.[30] Although Nyerere seemed to make great efforts to encourage other states to recognize Biafra, the Nigerian diplomats considered Kaunda more troublesome.[31]

Many have argued that Kaunda was simply influenced by his friend, Nyerere, but there is more to Zambian foreign policy than merely following Tanzania. Like Nyerere, Kaunda faced the difficult task of uniting many different tribes as he sought to gain independence for Zambia, which was part of the Federation of Rhodesia and Nyasaland. The United National Independence Party [UNIP] was to Kaunda and Zambia what TANU was to Nyerere and Tanzania. It was a multitribal party whose leaders sought to play down tribal differences.[32]

The most important method Kaunda used to de-emphasize tribal cleavages was to develop a civic nationalism, which included the ideology of Humanism. Humanism developed out of Kaunda's Christian and pacifist beliefs, and combined Christian and traditional convictions.[33] The core belief of Zambian civic nationalism and of Humanism centers on respecting the dignity of individuals. " 'I personally do not believe in such "ions" and "isms" other than Zambianism which I would define simply as the service of man by man for the protection of all that is good in the Zambian way of life.' "[34] This ideology was not designed merely to affect domestic politics, but foreign relations as well. "Humanism is designed not only to overcome internal racial conflict, but also to advance an alternative international order in Southern Africa based on racial equality and respect."[35] After gaining power, Kaunda continued to stress Humanism and acting according to it: " 'Saying we are Humanists is not enough. Behaving like Humanists is what must be done. Humanism is our guiding light.' "[36] Therefore, Humanism shaped the policies of Kaunda and UNIP in both domestic and foreign realms.

Like Ghana's and India's civic nationalisms in the previous chapter, Zambianism's international implications are not clear unless applied to specific issues and events. Because the Biafrans portrayed themselves as Christian victims of genocide, Kaunda and his supporters felt that Humanism required an end to the bloodshed as quickly as possible, even at the cost of Nigeria's integrity. "Whereas it is our ardent desire to foster African Unity, it would be morally wrong to force anybody into Unity founded on blood and bloodshed. For unity to be meaningful and beneficial it must be based on the consent of all parties concerned, security and justice to all."[37]

Kaunda was free to follow the tenets of Humanism, as he had no Muslim constituency to offend. Unlike many African states, Zambia's Muslim population was minuscule.[38] Three-quarters of the population were followers of traditional religions, while the remaining Zambians were Christians.[39] The religious mix was somewhat different among the populace of Barotseland, a Zambian territory attempting to secede.[40] As this separatist region was predominantly Christian,[41] Kaunda's support for Biafra might have been an attempt to position himself as a good Christian, and thereby appeal to Christian separatists within his own state to support him and to remain in Zambia.

While there is little doubt that Kaunda believed in the tenets of Humanism, it is also obvious that Humanism was a political ideology, part of an effort to develop a civic nationalism and to play down tribal identities. This civic identity influenced foreign policy as opportunities arose to demonstrate the relevance of Humanism for international, as well as domestic, politics. Kaunda sought to build a multitribal party, and developed a civic nationalism to mobilize support on grounds other than tribal ties. Because his constituency consisted of few Muslims, Kaunda could support Biafra without losing much domestic support, and because the content of Zambia's civic nationalism was derived from Christian and animist doctrines, Kaunda was inclined to assist Biafra.

The rival explanations cannot account for Zambia's foreign policy. Clearly, the existence of secessionists in Barotseland suggests vulnerability to secession did not inhibit Kaunda. Otherwise, he would have supported Nigeria, given Zambia's own separatist threat. Realists cannot account for Zambia's foreign policy either. While Zambia was weaker than Nigeria, the countries were too far apart to threaten each other. On the other hand, Zambia neighbors Rhodesia, which clearly presented a superior threat. One would expect Zambia to rely on the support of other African states against southern Africa's white minority regimes, but Zambia, instead, took the same side as Rhodesia by supporting Biafra.

Ivory Coast

Nyerere and Kaunda found themselves in strange company when President Felix Houphouët-Boigny, seen as one of the most conservative leaders in Black Africa, recognized Biafra. Houphouët-Boigny's support went beyond recognition; Abidjan, capital of the Ivory Coast, served as a crucial transit point for arms from Portugal, France, and the European black market. The Ivory Coast not only gave significant financial support to Biafra,[42] but also provided arms, ammunition, and other supplies that the French would replace.[43]

Why did the Ivory Coast assist the Biafran separatists? Some argue that French President Charles de Gaulle influenced Houphouët-Boigny, but others assert that the persuasion was in the other direction — Houphouët-Boigny is said to have converted de Gaulle to the Biafrans' side.[44] This kind of argument begs the question of why Houphouët-Boigny was more susceptible to French influence than leaders of other former French colonies. Religion helps explain Houphouët-Boigny's support of Biafra: his Catholic background and that of the majority of the National Assembly; and his fear, distrust, and hatred of Islamic states.

Houphouët-Boigny was known for his astute ability to manipulate ethnic politics to minimize opposition.[45] He kept a careful balance of different tribal groups in his cabinet to ensure that no group was alienated. This is an interesting contrast to the religious composition of the National Assembly. While only eight or nine percent of the population of the Ivory Coast were Catholic,[46] more than half of the National Assembly were.[47] This was no accident as Houphouët-Boigny's party, the Parti Democratique de la Cote d'Ivoire [PDCI], was the only party represented in the Assembly because of electoral procedures that eliminated competition.[48] Support for the Biafrans, self-defined as a Christian movement, can be seen as a product of Houphouët-Boigny's use of religious identity to bind his party together, despite tribal divisions.

Houphouët-Boigny's support of a group seeking to secede from a (perceived) Muslim-dominated state fits into his traditional pattern of mobilizing latent hostility toward Muslims. Houphouët-Boigny "hated and feared communism and Pan-Arabism as the twin forces really fighting against Biafra."[49] Within Ivory Coast as well as many other African states, there is still much resentment toward Muslims due to the role they played in the slave trade. By aiding Biafra, Houphouët-Boigny could be seen as opposing Islamic domination in another state. While Christians were not a majority in the Ivory Coast, non-Muslims were. Because of his anti-Islamic postures, Houphouët-Boigny could gain the support of a large percentage of the population despite their other differences.

While ties to France may have influenced Houphouët-Boigny somewhat, the important motivations for supporting Biafra were the roles of Catholicism and Islam in domestic politics. Because his support came mostly from Catholics, and the rest from animists, and because of existing enmity against Muslims, Houphouët-Boigny could support a "Christian" secessionist movement against a "Muslim" state. Indeed, this policy could mobilize his Catholic constituency without alienating the animists. A more domestically oriented emphasis on a particular religion might alienate either group, but the two religious groups within Houphouët-Boigny's constituency shared a hostility toward Islam.

The irony of Ivorien support for Biafra is that it gave a separatist movement within the Ivory Coast, the Sanwi, a justification for its own secession. In 1969, citing France's and the Ivory Coast's assistance to the Biafrans, the

Sanwi argued that they should be allowed to separate from the Ivory Coast because their movement suffered as much as the Ibos.[50] This movement was quickly repressed. Thus, vulnerability did not deter the Ivory Coast from supporting Biafra. Neither did the OAU, although this is a bit less surprising here than in the Tanzanian case since Houphouët-Boigny did not play as important a role in creating the OAU or its resolution on territorial integrity.

Realism performs better here than the vulnerability argument. Because the Ivory Coast is close to Nigeria, and significantly weaker, supporting Nigeria's division could improve the Ivory Coast's security. A smaller Nigeria without its oil resources would not pose as much of a threat. So, either realist imperatives or ethnic politics (or both) drove Ivorien policy toward this conflict.

Gabon

Gabon's assistance to Biafra was very similar to the Ivory Coast's. Libreville, Gabon's capital, was one of the most important points in Biafra's arms pipeline, particularly for the transport of French arms.[51] Like the Ivory Coast, Gabon provided arms to the Biafrans from its own arsenal, with the expectation that the French would replenish them.[52] Gabon was also the third African country to recognize Biafra, and consistently took positions supportive of Biafra at the Organization of African Unity meeting. As Gabon's policies were similar to the Ivory Coast's, and because Gabon's President, Albert Bongo, was a close friend of Houphouët-Boigny, many of the interests argued to be behind the actions of the Ivory Coast have also been argued to be the Gabon's motivations for its policies toward Biafra. "In some ways Houphouët-Boigny has acted as a sort of super-president of Gabon. . . . There is no need to assume that Bongo's motives differed from those of Houphouët-Boigny, or to consider anything that went on in Libreville relating to Biafra was outside the control of the Ivorien President."[53] Those who follow this line of argument assert that French influenced Bongo.

While people viewed Houphouët-Boigny as influenced by France, Bongo was perceived to be even more of a lackey. "Gabon has been the *most compliant* of France's former Black African territories, adjusting automatically to French pressures. . . . The most glaring example of *Gabonese subservience to French policy recommendations was evident in Libreville's recognition of Biafra* in 1968."[54] There are two problems with arguments emphasizing

Houphouët-Boigny and France. Such assertions cannot account for why other former French colonies did not fall in line with France, nor do they take seriously domestic interests that might have motivated Bongo and Gabon. The crucial difference between Bongo and other leaders of francophone African states is that he presided over "the most Christianized of the states of the French Community in Africa."[55] In addition, the rest of the population, with the exception of about one percent, were animists.[56] Thus, Bongo was relatively unconstrained when dealing with Biafra since he did not face a sizable Muslim population. Indeed, as tribal cleavages were seen as a crucial problem that needed to be overcome,[57] shared religious background could be used to unite disparate groups.[58]

By recognizing the self-defined Christian Biafrans, Bongo could emphasize the Christian bonds his supporters shared as he tried to build an all-encompassing mass party, resulting in a single-party system.[59] Bongo supported Biafra as this policy served to emphasize religious unity, binding his constituency, rather than tribal divides.

Of the two other competing arguments, again realism outperforms vulnerability. The vulnerability argument cannot explain Gabon's foreign policy, as its leaders had to worry about a potential secessionist movement in the Haut-Ogooue region. Because of Nigeria's proximity, and because of its strength relative to Gabon, it could be considered to present a threat to Gabon. Thus, realists correctly predict Gabon's aid to Biafra. Still, ethnic politics provides a convincing explanation of why Gabon differed from nearly all of Africa in its Biafra policy.

Other Supporters of Secession

Several states outside black Africa gave significant assistance in the forms of arms, ammunition, and military supplies. Specifically, Israel, France, the People's Republic of China [PRC], Portugal, Rhodesia and South Africa all assisted Biafra. While ethnic politics was not a crucial determinant of policy in all of these states, it did play a role in many. We can consider only could the policies of France and the PRC to be completely free of ethnopolitical motives.

Among these outside actors, Biafra's definition of the conflict as Islam versus a minority religion most clearly motivated Israel. As Biafra used the themes of persecution, genocide, and their fate as the " 'Jews of Africa,' " they gained the popular support of Israeli Jews.[60] Though Israeli Jews did not have ethnic ties with the Christian Ibos, they shared a common ethnic enmity: Islam. The Israeli parliament pressured the foreign ministry to do more to aid Biafra.[61] Israel reportedly sent to Biafra Soviet equipment, captured from the Arab forces during the June War of 1967.[62] Israel also assisted Biafran efforts to buy arms from private arms dealers.[63] There was some dispute during the conflict as to whether Israel gave aid to Biafra. "This was dispelled by the mournful statement of Mr. Abba Eban, then Israeli Foreign Minister, on January 19 1970 in which he lamented the collapse of the Biafran rebellion, arguing that 'Israel had exerted itself . . . in providing aid to the former secessionist regime.' "[64]

Portugal, still a colonial power in Africa, and the white minority regimes of Rhodesia and South Africa supported Biafra as they had aided Katanga. Portugal's aid was most important as airports in Lisbon, Portuguese Guinea, and Sao Tome were used for the shipment of arms. Lisbon was also the center for Biafra's arms purchasing and pilots' training.[65] While South Africa and Rhodesia were not as well positioned geographically as Portugal and its colonies to assist Biafra, some efforts were made, including the shipment of small arms.[66]

These three supporters of Biafra shared a very distinctive attribute: the rule of white Europeans and their descendants where black Africans were in the majority. Their common domestic political situations and their similar policies toward Biafra were not coincidental.

By helping to sustain a civil war in Africa's most populous and potentially strongest country, these three white-supremacist governments undermined African unity, weakened the African liberation movements' drive against themselves (Nigeria had been one of the biggest contributors to the O.A.U.'s 'freedom fighter' funds) and nourished their own propaganda message depicting black Africa's inherent and incurable instability.[67]

It is also possible, though less likely, that each of these states may have been motivated by religious ties as each of these countries' regimes was led by Christians who relied on the support of Christians. For instance, predominantly Catholic Portugal was sympathetic to the Biafrans because of these religious ties.[68] Other motivations included financial gain, as Portugal profited from its relationship with Biafra. However, the most important attribute shared by these three states, one that motivated their policies both in Katanga and Biafra, was their interest in weakening black Africa. Does this make realism the best explanation of these states policies? Yes, but only after the ethnic definition of threat or enemy is brought into play. Without the role of race in these states, it is hard to understand why, for instance, Rhodesia and South Africa are not enemies. Vulnerability cannot account for these three states as Portugal was not vulnerable to separatism, and the other two states faced serious ethnic conflict but supported Biafra anyway.

Nigeria's Supporters

In its struggle against Biafra, Nigeria received support by many states inside and outside Africa. While British and Soviet arms assistance gave the Nigerians the ability to end the secession militarily, other forms of assistance from African states also helped. In particular, the diplomatic support of Ethiopia and of Nigeria's immediate neighbors, Niger and Cameroon, prevented the Biafrans from getting the resources they needed.

Ethiopia

The efforts of Ethiopia's Emperor, Haile Selassie I, to support Nigeria's territorial integrity have been called "Herculean."[69] As chairperson of the OAU's Consultative Committee on the Nigerian Civil War, Selassie was extraordinarily energetic in his attempts to end the conflict.[70] His aim was to end the conflict as quickly as possible while preventing Nigeria's disintegration. Although the impact of the OAU upon this crisis is debatable, Selassie's influence within the organization is clear. Not only did he push through resolutions at the OAU reaffirming support for Nigeria, but the Emperor also shaped the Consultative Mission's findings, which reaffirmed the OAU's condemnation of secession. " 'The point of our task,' the Emperor declared in summing up, 'is to end secession.' "[71]

Selassie's defense of Nigeria's territorial integrity is explained by many as the result of Ethiopia's problems with its own boundaries: Eritrean secessionists, Somali irredentism, and border disputes with Sudan. The Emperor referred to these difficulties he faced at home as he cited the possible contagion effects of a successful Biafran secession.[72] However, Ethiopia's vul-

nerability to secession cannot explain by itself why such efforts were taken
to support Nigeria. Other states facing separatism and ethnic strife supported
Biafra anyway, including Gabon, the Ivory Coast, and Zambia. Paradoxi-
cally, though they stood on opposite sides of this conflict, Ethiopia shared
some characteristics with the Ivory Coast and Gabon. All three were conservative states that had sizable Christian populations and a historical and
cultural fear of Islamic domination.[73]

Ethiopia's political elites at this time were Christians, and his bureaucrats,
cabinet officials, military officers and the like were almost entirely Christian.[74] At first glance, one would expect that the Emperor's foreign policy
would emphasize religious identity at home. Biafra would seem to the perfect opportunity to use religion to mobilize support. However, this was not
the case for several reasons. Though traditionally the Ethiopian Orthodox
Church and Christianity were unifying forces in the Ethiopian polity, as the
Empire expanded and included more Muslims, religion lost its utility for
mobilizing popular support as it began to create differences rather than
loyalty to the state.[75] Consequently, the Emperor sought to accommodate
religious differences as he called for tolerance, met with Muslim leaders,
and finally included one in his cabinet in 1966.[76] Hence, as he faced the
Nigerian Civil War, his interest was to resolve a conflict abroad before it
could inflame religious antagonisms at home.

In a similar vein, the Emperor sought to undermine the Ethiopian Orthodox Church's power. Not only was emphasizing religion a damaging
political strategy for the Emperor, but the existence of an independent authority, such as the Church, was also seen as a threat. Over time, the Emperor succeeded in weakening the Church's political strength.[77] Aiding secessionists that were proclaiming themselves Christian martyrs would be
going against this policy. "Within the boundaries of this religiously plural-
istic, ethnically and linguistically diverse political entity that is called Ethiopia, *the government has been deliberately pursuing a policy of creating an
Ethiopian national identification, a higher loyalty than that to religion or
group.*"[78]

Part of creating such a national identity was Ethiopian leadership in Africa. Traditionally, Ethiopia was isolated from the other African states, and
did not share a common history. As Ethiopia was never colonized, and only
briefly occupied by Italy, Ethiopians had not taken part in the various Pan-
African independence movements as had Nkrumah, Nyerere, Kaunda,
Sekou Touré, and even Houphouët-Boigny. By taking the lead in creating the
Organization of African Unity, with its headquarters in his capital, Emperor

Selassie radically reoriented Ethiopian foreign policy.[79] "The new emphasis on African unity also serves to broaden the horizons of loyalty of Ethiopians, who are asked to think of themselves as Africans and Ethiopians, not as Shoans, Tigreans, Eritreans or Amhara."[80] As the Emperor positioned himself as a leader within the Pan-African movement, he tried to build ties between the various ethnic groups and himself. After carefully using a Pan-African foreign policy to attempt to build an Ethiopian national identity, the Emperor would not sacrifice leadership of the OAU and the pan-African movement by supporting Biafra.

The Emperor's constituency was homogeneous along religious lines, i.e., the Christian Amhara ethnic group, suggesting support for Biafra. However, he did not face an organized ethnically defined opposition at the time of the Nigerian Civil War, so he was not forced into engaging in religiously oriented outbidding. Further, because he wanted to expand his constituency to include Muslims, support for Biafra was to be avoided. The Emperor sought to build a greater Ethiopian nationalism at the expense of religious and linguistic divides within his society. Because this new nationalism was tied to Ethiopia's position as a leader of Pan-Africanism, the Emperor was interested in supporting Nigeria and the Organization of African Unity.

In this case, vulnerability provides an accurate prediction—Ethiopia's vulnerability may have encouraged its support of Nigeria and opposition to Biafra. Clearly, Ethiopia was one of the states most vulnerable to separatism. Further, Ethiopia had played a major role in creating and maintaining both the OAU and its norms. In addition, Ethiopia and Nigeria had a positive relationship before this crisis, so one would expect that that relationship would affect Ethiopia's policies. Thus, of all the cases thus far discussed, Ethiopia best supports the vulnerability argument.

Realism, on the other hand, does not provide such a clear prediction. Ethiopia is similar to Nigeria in relative power, once we control for the size of Nigeria's population. Nigeria does not pose a significant threat to Ethiopia because of distance and perceived intentions. So, realists would predict no Ethiopian support for Biafra, but not necessarily Ethiopia's enthusiasm for Nigeria's territorial integrity.

Cameroon

Because of its location, adjacent to Biafra, Cameroon's policies were very important in this crisis. Because Cameroon could have provided the Biafrans with bases, arms, and military supplies, the Nigerian government viewed Cameroon's support to be critical, and they were not disappointed.[81] President Ahmadou Ahidjo was "among the most hostile to Biafra's existence."[82] While Cameroon allowed unarmed Biafrans to transit across Cameroon, and refugees were permitted to stay in camps,[83] Ahidjo did not allow arms and ammunition to be supplied to the Biafrans.[84] Cameroon also supported Nigeria's position at the OAU, as Ahijdo served on the Consultative Mission along with Selassie and Niger's President.

While Cameroon's proximity to Nigeria might have deterred Ahidjo from assisting the Biafrans, it is also important that his domestic political interests indicated support for Nigeria, not Biafra. As he considered the preferences of both his own party and of West Cameroon, where he had less support, Ahidjo faced significant opposition to Biafra. First, within his own party, Ahidjo could not find many eager to support Biafra. Ahidjo's political base in Northern Cameroon was, like himself, of Fulani descent.[85] That is, they belonged to an Islamic tribe, speaking the same language as Northern Nigeria's leaders. As the war came to be defined as a conflict between Northern Nigeria and the Ibos of Eastern Nigeria, Ahidjo assisted the side with whom he and his supporters shared historical, religious, linguistic, and cultural ties.[86]

Second, Biafra's Ibos were not particularly popular in West Cameroon. The Cameroons were administrated as part of Nigeria after the British gained the former German colony after the first World War. A movement grew in the 1950s in the Southern Cameroons to separate from Nigeria to join with the French colony of Cameroon. As these territories were part of the League of Nations mandates, and later fell under the jurisdiction of the United Nations Mandate system, a plebiscite was held to determine whether Northern and Southern Cameroons would be part of Nigeria or unite with Cameroon. While the Northern Cameroons voted to stay with Nigeria, the Southern Cameroons chose to become West Cameroon as part of a federation of Cameroon. Part of the pre-plebiscite campaign for unification with Cameroon involved the manipulation of hostility toward the Ibos of Eastern Nigeria. "In reality the union was less a positive joining together of two parts of the former German Kamerun . . . than a rather negative flight of the South Cameroonians from Nigeria on ethnic grounds. The Southern Cameroonians were concerned above all to *avoid Ibo* and Yoruba domination in a federal Nigeria."[87] It has even been argued that the Ibos "acted as a catalyst to the political expression of the West Cameroon 'ethnicity.' "[88] This

anti-Ibo antagonism did not wane after unification, as the small Ibo population remaining in West Cameroon dominated the local commerce, increasing resentment.[89] Indeed, the party that had campaigned for unification
with Cameroon, the Kamerun National Democratic Party, became West
Cameroon's most powerful party. Its leader, John Foncha, was both Prime
Minister of West Cameroon and the Vice President of Cameroon from independence until 1968.[90] Thus, the majority of West Cameroon opposed
aiding Biafra.

As a result of these domestic political interests—his own supporters had
ties to the Nigerian elites and his coalition partner's constituency hated the
Ibos despite some common religious ties—Ahidjo's policies were very supportive of Nigeria's territorial integrity. This case indicates that both ethnic
ties and enmities of coalition partners need to examined, and that more than
one ethnic identity may be influencing the interests and perceptions of those
involved.

Vulnerability fares much better than realism in this case. Cameroon had
to deal with separatism within its boundaries so vulnerability theorists would
be correct in predicting that Cameroon's opposition to Biafra. Realists, on
the other hand, would have failed to predict Cameroon's policies. Because
Cameroon is much weaker than Nigeria, and because of its proximity to
Nigeria, realists would have expected Cameroon to support Biafra, just as
they correctly predicted Congo-Brazzaville to support Katanga. Instead,
Cameroon opposed Biafra and significantly helped Nigeria.

Niger

Niger's position was very similar Cameroon's. President Hamani Diori
asserted that "The territorial integrity of Nigeria is the important thing, the
rest is purely domestic."[91] Although his close friend and mentor Houphouët-
Boigny supported Biafra, Diori was willing to risk this alliance as he main-
tained consistent support for the Nigerian Federal Military Government.[92]

Most analysts agree that Diori's foreign policy in this crisis was motivated
by his supporters' ethnic composition. Diori himself admitted "if Niger made
any overt move toward greater recognition [of Biafra], his people would not
let him back into the country."[93] Considering both the tribal and religious
makeup of his cabinet, his party, and his country, Diori would have surprised
many had he made any friendly gestures toward Biafra. Forty-six percent of

Niger's population and forty percent of the cabinet in 1967 consisted of
Hausa peoples, who spoke the same language and had other historical and
cultural ties to the dominant tribe of Northern Nigeria. As there was a history
of secessionist sentiment on the part of the Hausa,[94] which would only have
increased had Nigeria broken up into three different states,[95] Diori was not
interested in increasing this desire for a separate Hausa state, nor in alienating some of his core supporters. Niger's religious makeup also pointed
toward supporting Nigeria. Between 72 and 85 percent of the population
were Muslims, while the remaining Nigerians were of traditional beliefs.[96]
Furthermore, Niger's political elites were entirely Muslim.[97] Because Islam
"is a force for communality that is said to help override ethnic differences
in Niger," it would be self-destructive for Diori to do anything else but
support predominantly Muslim Northern Nigeria against the Christian
Biafrans.[98]

Because of the cultural ties between large portions of Niger's population
and Northern Nigeria, as well as the dominance of Islam in Niger's leadership and populace, it is hard to conceive of any politician in Niger advocating a pro-Biafran line. Indeed, Diori could take only a pro-Nigerian
position.

Niger's situation was quite similar to that of Cameroon: ethnic ties and
vulnerability correctly predict these two states' behavior while realism cannot. Because Niger faced a potential secessionist movement in the Hausa,
one could argue that vulnerability constrained its foreign policy. However,
realism cannot account for Niger's foreign policy since Niger did not balance
against its greatest threat—Nigeria—by supporting Biafra, but instead supported Nigeria.

Other Allies of Nigeria

Since the Muslim-Christian cleavage defined the civil war between
Northern Nigeria and Biafra, states with large Muslim populations supported
Nigeria. "Arab support was invaluable to the Nigerians, both materially and
diplomatically. . . . Egypt supplied pilots and technicians for the air force
and Sudan and Libya, traditional users of British weaponry, sold Nigeria
some of the equipment Britain refused to provide."[99] It was argued that,
"Egyptian pilots are fighting not so much Biafra as Christianity. . . . "[100] Even
Somalia, with its history of trying to change its own boundaries,[101] supported

Nigeria's territorial integrity.[102] Only Tunisia, due to its French ties, came close to supporting Biafra, but its president, Habib Bourguiba, was constrained by his Muslim constituency.[103] Because of the religious dimension of the civil war, not a single country ruled by politicians relying upon Muslim support recognized or gave material assistance to Biafra.

Neutral and Ambivalent States

While most states took sides in this crisis as they voted for or against OAU resolutions affirming Nigeria's territorial integrity, a few states either took neutral positions or vacillated between Nigeria and Biafra.

Senegal

Senegal's position toward the Biafrans changed over time from weakly supporting some of their demands to denouncing its right to secede. At the outset, Biafran leaders perceived Senegal's President, Leopold Senghor, to be most likely to be receptive to Biafran appeals.[104] Consequently, Biafra aggressively lobbied Senghor.[105] Senghor called for an immediate cease-fire, one of Biafra's demands, as the issues at stake—federalism, confederalism, secession—were not worth the costs of the civil war.[106] Despite Senghor's disgust for the loss of life, Senegal never recognized Biafra. When expectations for Senegalese recognition were high after a series of long meetings with de Gaulle, Senghor distanced himself from France's position and from Biafra, refusing to recognize Biafra and asserting Nigeria's right to maintain its territorial integrity.[107]

Contradictions between Senghor's personal and political interests produced inconsistencies between the perceptions of Senghor, his statements, and Senegal's policies. Senghor's Catholic background and his support of *Negritude* shaped his inclination to support Biafra. As a Catholic, Senghor had great sympathy for his fellow Catholic, Ojukwu, and the mostly Christian Biafrans. Moreover, as the proponent of an ideology stressing the dignity of the African man,[108] the war and its waste of life disgusted Senghor. Therefore, Senghor sought an immediate cease-fire. However, Senghor's political interests constrained him from giving more support to Biafra. The role of religion, particularly Islam, in Senegalese politics cannot be emphasized strongly enough.[109] More than 85 percent of the population are Muslims.[110] In his bid for power in Senegal, despite his Catholic background, Senghor was able to gain and maintain the support of Muslim religious leaders, who "represent the main traditional force in Senegalese politics."[111] Senghor "proved that although he was a Roman Catholic, his more conservative policies had a greater attraction for Muslim leaders," than his opposition's more radical policies.[112] These Muslim elites became even more important for Senghor during the Nigerian Civil War, as crises developed within Senegal. "The dual crises in the countryside and the cities almost swept away the Senghor regime, which owed its salvation . . . [to the] intervention for the second time by the religious chiefs, who broadcast appeals for calm."[113]

Because of his dependence on Muslim elites, Senghor could not support the Biafrans, or else he would have alienated those who helped maintain his position. Senghor was "under considerable domestic pressure from his large Moslem constituency," to support Nigeria, not Biafra.[114] Thus, the religious composition of Senghor's supporters restrained him from following his personal preferences.

The other two arguments fail to explain Senegal's position. Vulnerability cannot predict Senegal's foreign policy since it faced no real separatist threat at the time. Our adjusted realist approach suggests that Senegal would not support Nigeria since Senegal is weaker than Nigeria, and therefore would benefit from Nigeria's disintegration. However, the other components of threat do not suggest that Nigeria threatens Senegal. Thus, at best, realism predicts that Senegal is unlikely to support Nigeria. Instead, Senegal moved from ambivalence to supporting Nigeria.

Sierra Leone

Sierra Leone's policies during this crisis ranged from being somewhat supportive of Nigeria to more neutral stances to weak support for the Biafrans. Sierra Leone supported Nigeria's territorial integrity by taking its side at the Organization of African Unity summit in Algeria in September 1968.[115] However, shortly afterward, along with Gabon, the Ivory Coast, Tanzania, Zambia, Kenya, France, and the Netherlands, Sierra Leone pushed for UN consideration of the Nigerian civil war, which Nigeria wanted to avoid.[116] Sierra Leone also abstained from voting on a resolution in September of 1969 that supported Nigeria's position.[117]

During 1969, serious consideration was given to recognizing Biafra, and the Prime Minister of Sierra Leone, Siaka Stevens, suggested that he might do so. While recognition was never granted, Sierra Leone's stance moved closer to the positions taken by Zambia, Tanzania, the Ivory Coast, and Gabon. Stevens faced serious pressure from his parliament as it passed a resolution calling for Sierra Leone to push for an unconditional cease-fire, a stance favoring Biafra.[118] However, "despite much public sympathy for Biafra there is strong opposition to recognition within the cabinet."[119]

During the Nigerian civil war, Sierra Leone experienced: an election that threatened to put out of office a regime that had been in power since independence; a military coup d'état to keep that regime in place; a counter-coup by junior officers who said they would bring back civilian control but did not; a coup by privates and sergeants to put the winners of the election into office; a national coalition of the losers and winners of the election; and finally, after an additional election and further ethnic violence, a regime that was governed by the winners of the 1967 and 1968 elections.[120]

After this upheaval, the All People's Congress [APC], led by Siaka Stevens, was solidly in office, with the Sierra Leone People's Party [SLPP] in opposition. While Sierra Leone had only a small Christian population, they were influential in the SLPP. Likewise, the APC were affiliated with the Islamic population of the northern region. One would then expect that the SLPP would push for recognition of Biafra and the APC would seek to support Nigeria if religious politics were to influence Sierra Leone's foreign policy. However, neither party was religiously homogenous, as the APC's elites were mainly Christian Creoles, and a prominent faction of the SLPP was Muslim.[121] As neither religion was popular enough to mobilize sufficient political support,[122] and since each party's constituency consisted of different religious groups, politicians had little desire to emphasize religious identity.

Supporting either side strongly would only alienate parts of either party's constituency. Thus, Sierra Leone took a different policy stance than other states. It did not recognize Biafra, but it did not consistently defend Nigeria's territorial integrity. Abstaining and pushing peaceful ways to end the Nigerian civil war were the most that Sierra Leone could do.

Vulnerability suggests that Sierra Leone would support Nigeria because of its vulnerability to separatism, so its ambivalence and neutrality would be surprising. Realism suggests that Sierra Leone would not support Nigeria since it is relatively weaker, but realism is not more determinate since Nigeria, otherwise, posed very little threat.

The leaders of ambivalent states did have some interests in supporting Biafra, but domestic politics generally constrained them. In Senegal, Senghor's own personal background suggested that he might assist Biafra's secession. However, the political importance of his predominantly Muslim constituency outweighed his personal preferences. Similarly, Sierra Leone's leaders were caught between different religious interests within their own constituencies. The best policy, in this case, was to push for an end to the crisis without offending various factions within one's supporting coalition. Likewise, in Uganda,[123] where tribal outbidding was the norm, President Milton Obote sought to play down religion as a political cleavage because his own party, the Uganda People's Congress, consisted of both Protestants and Muslims.[124] Even though Uganda was thought to be a likely supporter of Biafra,[125] Obote's own multireligious constituency inhibited any efforts toward supporting either side in the conflict.

As Biafran leaders created appeals based on religious affiliation, they caused leaders of multireligious constituencies to be handcuffed during this crisis. These politicians could not make significant efforts to support either party in the conflict, because such policies might lead to the loss of critical supporters.

Ethnic Politics and the Nigerian Civil War

The international politics of the Biafran secession is a strong test of the ethnic politics as model as there was much variance in the kinds of ties and enmities existing between the combatants and outside actors. This case is also a good test of the alternative approaches since their critical variables, vulnerability and threat, also varied.

Balance of Threats and the Nigerian Civil War

The adjusted balance of threat approach needs to be applied to the Nigerian Civil War to shed light on both the conflict itself and the value of this approach. It asserts that states will align against states posing the greatest threats. Why then is a particular state perceived to be a threat by some states and not others? To understand the threat Nigeria posed to other states, we need to consider the four components of threat—aggregate power, geographic proximity, offensive capability, and aggressive intentions.

TABLE 4.1 Realism and the Nigerian Civil War

Country	Power Relative to Nigeria*	Nigeria's Threat	Biafra's Threat	Neighbors of Nigeria	Predicted Policy	Actual Policy
Gabon	Weaker	Moderate	Low	Almost	Support Biafra	**Supported Biafra**
Israel	Stronger**	Low	Low	No	No Support for Biafra	*Supported Biafra*
Ivory Coast	Weaker	Moderate	Low	No	Support Biafra	**Supported Biafra**
Portugal	Weaker	Moderate	Low	Almost	Support Biafra	**Supported Biafra**
Rhodesia	Weaker	Moderate	Low	No	Support Biafra	Supported Biafra
South Africa	Stronger	Moderate	Low	No	Indeterminate	Supported Biafra
Tanzania	Weaker	Low	Low	No	No Support for Nigeria	Supported Biafra
Zambia	Weaker	Low	Low	No	No Support for Nigeria	Supported Biafra
Sierra Leone	Weaker	Low	Low	No	No Support for Nigeria	Neutrality and Ambivalence
Uganda	Weaker	Low	Low	No	No Support for Nigeria	Neutrality and Ambivalence
Cameroon	Weaker	High	Low	Yes	Support Biafra	*Supported Nigeria*
Egypt	Stronger	Low	Low	No	No Support for Biafra	Supported Nigeria
Ethiopia	Stronger**	Low	Low	No	No Support for Biafra	Supported Nigeria
Niger	Weaker	High	Low	Yes	Support Biafra	*Supported Nigeria*
Senegal	Weaker	Low	Low	No	No Support for Nigeria	Ambivalence, changed to *support for Nigeria*
Somalia	Weaker	Low	Low	No	No Support for Nigeria	*Supported Nigeria*
Sudan	Weaker	Low	Low	No	No Support for Nigeria	*Supported Nigeria*

* This is coded from a ratio of the country's power relative to Nigeria's, using measures of military and economic capabilities and population measures, as discussed in chapter six.

** Coded stronger, compensating for overly strong influence of Nigeria's population on power measures.

Italics indicates incorrect predictions

Bold indicates correct predictions

Nigeria was (and is) one of the most powerful states in Africa, due to its large population and oil deposits. Because of its near-hegemonic position, Nigeria can be perceived as posing a threat to many African states. However, aggregate power, by itself, is a poor predictor of the behavior of other states, because states of varying capabilities lined up on either side of the conflict. South Africa, Africa's most powerful state, supported the Biafrans, as did Gabon, a considerably weaker state. Similarly, Egypt and Cameroon supported Nigeria despite differing levels of aggregate power. Further, as Nigeria was one of the most powerful states in Africa, this approach would have predicted much more support for Biafra than was actually the case; only a small number of states supported Biafra. As Walt himself argues, aggregate power cannot predict foreign policy behavior by itself.

The second component of threat, geographic proximity, does not seem to clarify the conflict's international politics. Walt argues that the closer a powerful state is, the more threatening it will appear.[126] However, the closest states to Nigeria, Niger and Cameroon, both aligned with Nigeria, and supported its efforts to suppress the Biafrans. In effect, they bandwagoned with Nigeria. Walt allows for bandwagoning when weak states do not have alternative alliance partners, but he generally predicts balancing against threats, rather than aligning with them.[127] This might aid in explaining Niger's and Cameroon's behavior, but fails to account for why states further away from Nigeria did not follow policies similar to each other. Tanzania and Zambia are as close to (or as far away from) Nigeria as Ethiopia, Somalia, and Sudan, but followed completely different policies. The former supported Biafra, and the latter assisted Nigeria. Geographic proximity, thus, is not a very helpful predictor of foreign policy, especially considering the differences between the behavior of Nigeria's neighbors and the Congo's. Nigeria's neighbors did not support Biafra, but the Congo's neighbors tended to support the Katangans.

Nigeria's offensive capability was not very threatening because its military was not then able to intervene directly in other states, except perhaps its immediate neighbors. Even this threat declined greatly during the outset of the crisis, when Biafra's forces invaded Nigeria. This success, at the time, suggested that Nigeria's offensive capability was minimal, and its defensive capability might be suspect. Therefore, the threat Nigeria posed to other states may have declined, just as several states began to support the Biafrans. Expanding the definition of offensive capability to include disrupting other states' territorial integrity does not help things much. Neither Nigeria nor Biafra had a particularly special capability of disrupting other states, compared to the Congo's and Katanga's abilities to threaten other states. Changes in offensive capability, then, do not necessarily predict the perceptions of states nor the policies they follow.

The final component of threat is aggressive intentions. While Nigeria had supported Africa's efforts to sanction Rhodesia and South Africa, Nigeria had not acted directly against the interests of Biafra's other allies. It is difficult to determine what could have caused such diverse states as Gabon, the Ivory Coast, Tanzania, and Zambia to perceive Nigeria as threatening. The latter two are especially puzzling, since they are on the opposite side of the continent: Nigeria can hardly threaten them in any meaningful way. It is even more amazing that Tanzania and Zambia would be on the same side as Rhodesia and South Africa, who are much closer, more powerful, more capable of acting aggressively, and having a history of aggressive behavior. If states act primarily because of the external threats they perceive, one would expect Tanzania and Zambia to support Nigeria as a potential ally against the white minority regimes of South Africa.

While a focus on relative power is helpful to explain whether states are successful in achieving their goals, the realist approach cannot explain the perceptions and preferences of states as they rarely consider the domestic sources of interests and threats. Of the seventeen states studied here, the adjusted realist approach correctly predicts four, is wrong on six, and indeterminate in seven other cases. The white minority regimes balanced against Nigeria, because it was the most powerful state in Africa ruled by blacks. Nigeria was a potential ally of the white minority regimes' internal opposition. Rhodesia and South Africa balanced by supporting Biafra, because their own internal politics determined who their enemies were.

Common Vulnerability and International Cooperation

The history of ethnic instability in Biafra's supporters undermines the vulnerability argument. Of the four African states to recognize Biafra and provide arms, three faced actual or potential secessionist movements. The fourth, Tanzania, the product of a recent union between Tanganyika and Zanzibar, faced the difficult task of integrating a noncontiguous, ethnically distinct territory. While none of the supporters of Biafra outside black-ruled Africa was vulnerable to secession, several of them, specifically Israel, Rhodesia, and South Africa, faced serious opposition along ethnic cleavages. Another outsider, Portugal, was facing opposition along racial lines within Africa to its colonial rule.

Overall, of the seventeen cases, the vulnerability argument correctly accounts for the behavior of four states, wrongly predicts the behavior of nine

TABLE 4.2 Vulnerability and the Nigerian Civil War

Country	Vulnerability to Ethnic Conflict and Separatism	Vulnerability Predictions	Actual Policy
Gabon	High	Support Nigeria	*Supported Biafra*
Israel	High	Support Nigeria	*Supported Biafra*
Ivory Coast	High	Support Nigeria	*Supported Biafra*
Portugal	Low	No Prediction	Supported Biafra
Rhodesia	High	Support Nigeria	*Supported Biafra*
South Africa	High	Support Nigeria	*Supported Biafra*
Tanzania	High	Support Nigeria	*Supported Biafra*
Zambia	High	Support Nigeria	*Supported Biafra*
Sierra Leone	High	Support Nigeria	*Neutrality and Ambivalence*
Uganda	High	Support Nigeria	*Neutrality and Ambivalence*
Cameroon	High	Support Nigeria	**Supported Nigeria**
Egypt	Low	No Prediction	Supported Nigeria
Ethiopia	High	Support Nigeria	**Supported Nigeria**
Niger	High	Support Nigeria	**Supported Nigeria**
Senegal	Low	No Prediction	Ambivalence, changed to Support for Nigeria
Somalia	High	Support Nigeria	**Supported Nigeria**
Sudan	Low	No Prediction	Supported Nigeria

Bold indicates correct predictions
Italics indicates incorrect predictions

states, and is indeterminate in the remaining four. The Nigerian Civil War indicates that vulnerability to secession and ethnic conflict probably is not a very good explanation nor a predictor of the foreign policy toward secessionist conflicts.

The conventional wisdom considers the relatively few supporters of Biafra as evidence of the Organization of African Unity's influence. The OAU's involvement inhibited potential supporters, according Jackson and Rosberg and Herbst. While the OAU's involvement may have influenced non-African states, the OAU could not play that influential a role since some of its most important founders and supporters acted against its resolutions. Although Tanzania's Nyerere was one of the OAU's founders, and supported the 1964 resolution affirming the legitimacy of the existing boundaries, Tanzania supported Biafra. Further, one of the logical underpinnings of Herbst's arguments, reciprocity, is undermined here, as Tanzania supported Nigeria's internal enemy despite Nigeria's assistance to Tanzania in handling its own internal conflicts. Finally, the OAU's independent role is hard to determine because it may merely reflect states' preferences, rather than changing them in some way. The number of states supporting Biafra is a little larger than the number supporting Katanga, but most states supported Nigeria—votes within the Organization of African Unity were on the order of thirty-six or more to four. Those who assert the importance of international cooperation can argue that the Organization of African Unity was as successful in limiting support for secession as the United Nations, but cannot really say why various states defied the two institutions. However, the conflict's religious definition may have produced the appearance of support for Africa's boundary regime, just as the racial definition of the Congo Crisis may have increased support for the Congo.

The Ethnic Politics Model and the Nigerian Civil War

Table 4.3 indicates that the theory of ethnic politics and foreign policy produces much more accurate predictions than the two other approaches. Ethnic ties predicted the policies of fourteen of the seventeen states, with the exceptions of Tanzania, Ethiopia, and Senegal.

Neither ethnic ties alone nor the competing approaches can explain Tanzania's policies. The vulnerability hypothesis does not work: Tanzania was the product of recent merger of two territories separated by water and by cultural differences, and was therefore vulnerable to separatist sentiment.

TABLE 4.3 Ethnic Politics and the Nigerian Civil War

Country	Religious Ties To:	Religious Competition	Ethnic Ties Predictions	Actual Policy
Gabon	Biafra	Low	Support Biafra	**Supported Biafra**
Israel	Biafra*	High	Support Biafra	**Supported Biafra**
Portugal	Biafra	Low	Support Biafra	**Supported Biafra**
Ivory Coast	Biafra	Low	Support Biafra	**Supported Biafra**
Rhodesia	Biafra	High	Support Biafra	**Supported Biafra**
South Africa	Biafra	High	Support Biafra	**Supported Biafra**
Tanzania	Both	Low	Neutrality or Ambivalence	*Supported Biafra*
Zambia	Biafra	Low	Support Biafra	**Supported Biafra**
Sierra Leone	Both	High	Neutrality or Ambivalence	**Neutrality and Ambivalence**
Uganda	Both	High	Neutrality or Ambivalence	**Neutrality and Ambivalence**
Cameroon	Nigeria**	High	Support Nigeria	**Supported Nigeria**
Egypt	Nigeria	Low	Support Nigeria	**Supported Nigeria**
Ethiopia	Biafra	Low	Support Biafra	*Supported Nigeria*
Niger	Nigeria	High	Support Nigeria	**Supported Nigeria**
Senegal	Nigeria	Low	Support Nigeria	*Ambivalence,* changed to **Support for Nigeria**
Somalia	Nigeria	Low	Support Nigeria	**Supported Nigeria**
Sudan	Nigeria	High	Support Nigeria	**Supported Nigeria**

Bold indicates correct predictions
Italics indicates incorrect predictions

* Israel had religious enmities towards Nigeria, which produces the same preferences as ties with Biafra.

** The two different ethnic groups within the politicians' constituencies had different ties and enmities at stake. One shared religious and kinship ties with Nigeria, and the other had enmity against the Ibos, who led the Biafran secessionist movement.

Focusing on international cooperation does not work because Tanzania had a history of cooperation with international institutions and Nigeria before this conflict, but was not interested in continued cooperation. The realist approach cannot account for Tanzania's policies because Nigeria posed no significant threat to Tanzania. Indeed, Tanzania's greatest threats were posed by other states supporting Biafra: Rhodesia and South Africa. Tanzania's policies only make sense once we consider how political competition gave Nyerere more autonomy than other African leaders.

Ethiopia's policies are not predicted by ethnic ties alone, but are not as contrary to the theory's logic as Tanzania's. Since there was no organized competition in Ethiopia, religious outbidding was not prevalent at this time. Because there were no viable exit options for the Emperor's Christian constituency, Selassie could take such a stand in favor of Nigeria. Further, his ethnopolitical strategy aimed at attracting Muslims, so he cared about their preferences, including support for Nigeria. Of course, the Emperor's efforts to define himself as a leader of Africa and of the OAU for his domestic audience increased his willingness to support Nigeria.[128]

Senegal's neutrality and subsequent weak support for Nigeria can be understood once the conflict between the leader's ethnic and political preferences and the ethnic ties of his constituents are considered. Senghor was a Catholic, and cared about the dignity of the African individual. Consequently, he saw the war as a waste, and disliked the repression of the Biafrans. However, he relied on the support of Muslims for his position, and could not act directly against their preferences. His position converged with the expectations of ethnic politics as he eventually supported Nigeria.

Summary

The Nigerian Civil War has several implications for the study of the international politics of secession. First, those approaches focusing on international cooperation are correct in predicting that relatively few states support secessionist movements. However, these arguments are built upon a faulty foundation: vulnerability to secessionism did not inhibit any of the four African states recognizing and assisting Biafra. Vulnerability cannot explain the behavior of these states. Second, the adjusted realist model would have expected that because of Nigeria's predominance in the region, more states would have supported Biafra to balance the threat posed by Nigeria. Yet, relatively few states did so. Instead, many states supported Nigeria because their constituents wanted Biafra to lose and Nigeria to win. The question remains as to whether ethnic politics applies to the present day and outside of Africa.

5   The International Relations of Yugoslavia's Demise, 1991–1995

Yugoslavia's disintegration has frustrated Europe and the rest of the world.[1] Yugoslavia, particularly Bosnia, had stood as a symbol of inter-ethnic cooperation. Sarajevo, where World War I began, served as a stark symbol of the conflict. The site of the 1984 Winter Olympics became a battleground. Olympic venues became gravesites. Once the conflict started, Europeans hoped and expected that they would manage this conflict due to the newly developing Common Foreign Policy of the European Community [EC].[2] These hopes were quickly dashed, as cooperation among EC states failed in two ways: it failed to deter the conflict in Yugoslavia, and dissension with the EC raised doubts about its ability to develop a common foreign policy. Other actors including the United Nations, the Organization for Security and Cooperation in Europe [CSCE], and the North Atlantic Treaty Organization [NATO] stepped in and struggled with the conflict. The world's frustration with this conflict, and ethnic conflict in general, may discourage future interventions, as the Congo Crisis caused the UN to retreat for awhile from intervening in internal conflicts.

Studying the international politics of Yugoslavia's disintegration serves several purposes. First, since Yugoslavia is the first post-Cold War secessionist conflict to involve the international community, academics and policy-makers may use it as an analogy for understanding future conflicts, as the Congo Crisis did for the postcolonization period. "Yugoslavia's fate may well serve as an exemplar for ethnic conflict elsewhere in Europe."[3] Conse-quently, it needs to be studied so that we can draw informed lessons.

Second, studying solely African secessionist conflicts would limit our ability to generalize this book's findings beyond less developed, weakly institutionalized states. We can use this more recent conflict to determine whether vulnerability, ethnic ties, or realist imperatives apply beyond 1960s Africa. Since most of the states reacting to the Yugoslavia conflict fall into two categories—advanced stable, institutionalized democracies, or states undergoing transitions—this case is likely to have stronger and clearer implications for today's international politics, expanding this book's relevance.

Third, this case provides more analytical leverage than the others since there are multiple secessionist movements with differing ethnic identities. While the plethora of separatist conflicts complicates the case study, making it harder to apply some of the hypotheses, it facilitates interesting comparisons, such as why did some states support particular separatist movements and not others. Very few states developed consistent, principled policies toward all actors in the conflict. Given the variety of ethnic identities at stake, such inconsistencies are not surprising, particularly if ethnic politics influences foreign policy.

Before going on, it is important to note the dimensions of the conflict's complexity. First, there were irredentist movements as well as secessionist movements: efforts for a Greater Serbia and a Greater Croatia. The focus of this book is how outside actors react ethnic conflicts, so irredentist states that generated the conflict (such as Serbia and Croatia) are not analyzed here.[4] Second, unlike the other conflicts studied in this book, there were several groups seceding from the host state, Yugoslavia, and groups seeking to secede from the seceding republics. The former category includes Bosnia, Croatia, Macedonia, and Slovenia. The latter category includes Croatian Serbs, Bosnian Serbs, and Bosnian Croats.

Below, the chapter addresses the roots of the conflict briefly, before discussing the role of various international organizations. I analyze the foreign policies of the major actors, which, in turn, largely explain the behavior of the relevant international organizations. The key questions to consider throughout this chapter are: were states inhibited by vulnerability to separatism? Were states motivated by concerns for their security? What role did religious and other ties between important constituencies and combatants play? Can we find some consistency among the complex, contradictory actions taken by states and international organizations?

To preview, vulnerability did not inhibit many states while security motivations played a more prominent role. Most importantly, states tended to support the side with which their constituents had ethnic ties. Rather than following principled positions throughout the conflict, most states varied in supporting secessionists and host states depending on the ethnic composition of the combatants in question.

Roots of the War of Yugoslavia's Dissolution[5]

The original dispute between Serbia and its autonomous republic, Kosovo, increased tension between Serbia and Yugoslavia's other constituent republics. This caused Slovenia to secede after a short battle with the Yugoslav army and catalyzing a war between Croatia and Serbia, which eventually spread to Bosnia. While the combatants can trace their disputes back to World War II and before, the pivotal period was the mid-1980s. The circumstances were ripe for ethnic conflict. Economically, two factors essentially invited politicians to engage in ethnic politics: the extreme decline of Yugoslavia's economy in the 1980s and the uneven development of the republics.[6] Politically, incentives existed for elites to take advantage of ethnic identity. Because power was regionally focused, each republic having its own party system, resources, and political institutions, it made sense to play to a limited audience: only the key supporters within the existing republic boundaries.[7] This particular federal structure meant that politicians could gain and maintain their positions if they attracted support from only one ethnic group: Serbs in Serbia, Croats in Croatia, and Slovenes in Slovenia.

Specifically, the stage was set for the rise of Serbian nationalism, which resulted from Slobodan Milosevic's efforts to gain power in Serbia. In 1987, the League of Communists of Serbia was divided, facing the difficult problem of maintaining legitimacy in the face of economic disaster. Milosevic found a successful formula for providing the party with a mission and for his leadership of the party: defending Kosovo's Serbs against the Albanian majority. The approaching 600th anniversary of the Battle of Kosovo gave Milosevic the opportunity to take stands on the Kosovo issue, creating a supporting coalition of nationalists and conservatives. Because Kosovo has a critical role in Serbian history and nationalism, Milosevic was able to purge the party of those who opposed his nationalist strategy.[8]

Milosevic's successful use of the Kosovo issue created increased insecurity for other ethnic groups within Yugoslavia, particularly as Milosevic's statements and actions threatened to alter existing institutions that gave other ethnic groups some control over Yugoslav decisionmaking. Reasserting Serb control over Kosovo threatened to alter the balance of power within federal institutions, as Serbia could add Kosovo's vote to Montenegro's and its own (and later, Vojvodina's), giving Serbia the ability to block decisions at the federal level. The policies taken toward Kosovo were perceived to be part of a larger effort to recentralize the Yugoslav political system, which would lessen the ability of the various ethnic groups to control their destinies.

Ethnic conflict spread swiftly within Yugoslavia because changes in the federal structure threatened all ethnic groups. Slovenia and Croatia were threatened by any increase of Serbia's influence at the federal level. Bosnia and Herzegovina and Macedonia felt insecure in a Yugoslavia without Croatia and Slovenia, compelling them to secede as well despite their initial reluctance. War broke out when Slovenia and Croatia seceded in June 1991. Slovenia was able to defeat a half-hearted attempt by the Yugoslav army to maintain the country's territorial integrity. Croatia's secession was much more bloody, producing a UN-enforced stalemate that lasted until August 1995, when Croatia reconquered the territory that the Serbs had taken in 1991. The exit of these two republics left Bosnia and Macedonia with a difficult choice: remain in a Serb-dominated Yugoslavia or try to become independent despite the probable costs. Both chose the latter, though only Bosnia has had to pay the price thus far. The Bosnian conflict defied the ambivalent efforts of the West and of the world at large to settle the conflict. Only in 1995, after the Bosnian Muslims and Bosnia Croats settled their differences, after a series of successful offensives by the Croatian army and the Bosnian Muslims, and after NATO's bombing campaign, did the three sides agree to peace and *de facto* partition.

Intervention by International Organizations: the EC, UN, and NATO

Interventions by the international community during Yugoslavia's dissolution were similar to the Congo Crisis, rather than the Nigerian Civil War. That is, the UN's mandate was unclear at first, and only as the crisis progressed did international organizations, particularly NATO, escalate to the use of force to end the conflict. International organizations facilitated and supported negotiations, cease-fires, sanctions, and the use of force, but these efforts did not provide consistent assistance to one side or the other. Cease-fires and the introduction of peacekeepers assisted Serb separatists in Croatia, but may have allowed the Bosnian government to survive despite the best efforts of Bosnia's Serbs. Like the Congo Crisis, international involvement eventually assisted a weak state to defeat a separatist movement. In the Congo, the UN forces defeated the Katangan secessionists. In Bosnia, the United Nations and NATO gave critical assistance, making Bosnia's survival possible, though at grave cost. Below, I briefly detail the various efforts of several international organizations.[9]

"There was a strange initial reluctance within the Community to involve the United Nations. . . . This was going to be the time when Europe emerged with a single foreign policy and therefore it unwisely shut out an America only too happy to be shut out."[10] The Yugoslav crisis was the first real opportunity for the European Community to apply its efforts toward a common foreign policy. At the outset, the EC was united, but ultimately this conflict caused Europe and the world to lose confidence—a common European foreign policy was not to be.

At first, the European Community and other actors encouraged the Yugoslav republics to remain united. Once Slovenia declared its secession and violence broke out between Slovenia and the Serb-dominated Yugoslav armed forces, the European Community took the lead, trying to broker a cease-fire. On July 8, 1991, EC representatives successfully brokered a cease-fire in Slovenia, the Brioni Accords. The Accords required Slovenia to delay any moves toward independence for three months in exchange for the removal of the Yugoslavia army from Slovenia. The deal essentially gave Slovenia *de facto* independence, but delayed *de jure* recognition. After July 8, the fighting shifted to Croatia.

EC representatives brokered a series of cease-fires between Croatia, the Yugoslav Army, and Serb paramilitary groups. These cease-fires did not hold up until Croatia and Serbia agreed in November 1991 to United Nations peacekeepers. These peacekeepers, UNPROFOR I, separated Serb-held Croatian territories from the rest of Croatia, allowing the Serbs to keep and consolidate the gains made through ethnic cleansing. Croatia defied the United Nations by reconquering these territories in 1995.

At the same time that the peacekeepers were considered for Croatia, EC members debated whether to recognize Slovenia and Croatia, with Germany pushing for immediate recognition. Resolving this debate, the EC agreed to a set of rules on December 17, 1991, clarifying the conditions for recognizing those seceding from Yugoslavia and Soviet Union. Among these conditions were respect for human rights, guarantees for ethnic groups in accordance with the Conference on Security and Cooperation in Europe, and respect for all boundaries. To decide which Yugoslav republics met these criteria, the EC appointed the Badinter Commission, which eventually determined that Slovenia and Macedonia qualified. However, before the commission's decision, Germany recognized Slovenia and Croatia, with the rest of the European Community following suit in January 1992. The EC withheld recognition of Macedonia due to Greek opposition.

After this debate, attention focused on Bosnia. War broke out in March 1992, and only stopped with the Dayton Accords in late 1995. Once the conflict spread to Bosnia, the EC played a lesser role and the United Nations played the leading role along with increased NATO involvement as the conflict continued. On April 7, 1992 EC and US recognized Bosnia in hopes that it would help stabilize the situation, but it did not. In May 1992, the UN General assembly admitted Slovenia, Croatia, and Bosnia, but not the new Yugoslavia consisting of Serbia and Montenegro. Then, the UN voted to levy economic sanctions against the new Yugoslavia (only China and Zimbabwe abstained). Eventually, the West European Union and the North Atlantic Treaty Organization sent ships to the area to monitor compliance. An arms embargo was placed upon the entire former Yugoslavia, which, in effect, assisted Serbia, since it had largely inherited the armed forces of Yugoslavia. The embargo hurt Bosnia, which was poorly prepared for war.

After the international media revealed the most significant atrocities in Europe since World War II, the United Nations Security Council passed a resolution calling for humanitarian aid to Bosnia—these efforts became UN-PROFOR II.[11] The efforts to feed the Bosnians, particularly the Bosnian Muslims, essentially undermined the Serb separatists and helped Bosnia since starvation was part of the strategy of ethnic cleansing. This humanitarian endeavor required access to the countryside, so the peacekeepers often had to pay off the Bosnian Serbs guarding the roads. Thus, even attempts to feed the Bosnian Muslims had some positive payoffs for the Serbs. In the process of getting through the various blockades and getting food and medicine to the Bosnian Muslims, the UN eventually promised to defend particular areas where displaced Bosnians gathered—so-called safe areas, including Sarajevo, Bihac, Gorazde, Zepa, and Srebrenica.[12] The UN made some threats and used force in response to the shelling of the Sarajevo marketplace, resulting in the monitoring of larger artillery near the city. The safe areas were hardly safe, as the Bosnian Serbs attacked each in turn, resulting in the massacres at Srebrenica.[13]

After the Bosnian Serbs took UN peacekeepers hostage in spring 1995, the European contributors to the UN mission became more assertive. France and Britain sent reinforcements, and then redeployed their troops to be less vulnerable. Once this occurred, NATO was much freer to use force, which it did in August and September 1995. Along with the Croatian reconquest of Serb-held territory, the Bosnian Muslims enhanced ability to wage war, and Milosevics decreased enthusiasm for the irredentist project,[14] the NATO bombing campaign brought the adversaries to Dayton and to a lasting cease-fire.

The policies of the various international organizations were not consistent. These efforts often had unintended consequences benefiting one side or the other, and they were rarely without controversy. To understand the behavior of these actors, we need to understand states' preferences. Hard bargaining between states shaped each international organization's actions, so we need to know why states chose their particular courses of action. An important factor shaping states' behavior was how they viewed the combatants, which, in turn, was shaped by the secessionists' efforts to define themselves.

Identifying the Separatists

In the case studies of Katanga's and Biafra's attempted secession, the ethnic definition of each conflict influenced how outsiders reacted. The same held true for the wars of Yugoslavia's dissolution. Many different identities overlapped during this conflict: democratic, multiethnic, Slavic, Catholic, Orthodox, Muslim, Slovene, Serb, Croat, Bosnian, and Macedonian. Slovenia and Croatia positioned themselves as pro-Western and democratic, facing authoritarian Serbia. Bosnia appealed for support by arguing that it stood for the possibility of multiethnic society, but also sought support from Islamic states. Serbia appealed to its Slavic brethren, particularly Russia. While the conflict was not directly focused on religious differences, such identities mattered both within Yugoslavia (much of the violence targeted mosques and churches) and beyond as outsider actors supported those with whom they shared religious ties. Finally, each group's nationality was very important for the conflict's domestic politics: improving the economic opportunities of Slovenes; protecting Serbs outside of Serbia; empowering Croats in a Croatian state; defending the idea of multiethnic Bosnia; and maintaining Macedonia in the face of Greek opposition. Below, I briefly discuss each ethnic group in turn to determine how these various identities came into play.[15]

Serbian Identity and Nationalism

While the various combatants and many outsiders trace the conflict's roots to events centuries ago, the violent decade began with the reassertion of Serb nationalism, which shaped the reactions and strategies of the other groups. Milosevic apparently emphasized every aspect of Serb identity to gain support. The Kosovo issue resonated deeply because of its place in Serb mythology.[16] Milosevic sought greater use of Cyrillic to make the language of Serbs more distinct from Serbo-Croatian.[17]

Most importantly, he allied himself with the Serbian Orthodox Church. Despite his communist past, Milosevic began to favor the Church in policy and in the media. Milosevic began a construction program to rebuild Orthodox Churches, gave the Church permission to distribute its publications, and replaced the teaching of Marxism in the schools with religious teachings.[18] The government-controlled media even declared that Orthodoxy was the spiritual basis for and the most essential component of the national identity [of Serbs].[19] Milosevic's embrace of the Serbian Orthodox Church was reciprocated, as the Church provided legitimacy to Milosevic's claims. As the Kosovo Crisis developed in the late 1980s, the Church defined any conflict with the Albanians as part of a deliberate anti-Serb Albanian master plan of genocide.[20] Historically and more recently, the Serbian Orthodox Church has been all but synonymous with Serbian nationalism.[21] While it is doubtful that Milosevic is a true believer,[22] it is clear that he has relied upon any and every Serb nationalist symbol to build support for his regime and to undermine his opponents.

The Serbs also tried to portray the conflict as one between Christianity and Islam, with the Serbs playing the role of defenders of Western Civilization. Serbian media sought to define those who supported the Bosnian government as Islamic fundamentalists, " 'Khomeinis.' "[23] This definition of the conflict aimed to attract support from Christian countries, particularly Orthodox ones, or at least deter support for the Bosnian government.

One of the most puzzling dynamics of this conflict was the identification of Serbs with Slavs, and other groups as non-Slavs, particularly the Bosnian Muslims. While the Albanians are not Slavs, Croats, Serbs, and Bosnian

Muslims are. The Serbs defined themselves as Slavs and the Bosnian Muslims as non-Slavs, as Turks. While this runs contrary to history and to the demographic realities, the Serbs, for the past hundred years or so, have considered anyone who converts from Christianity to Islam to have not only changed their religion, but their race as well.[24] This matters, of course, because outsiders, particularly Russia, viewed the Serbs as Slavs and their enemy in Bosnia as non-Slavs.

Slovene Identification with Democracy

The two key ethnic divisions between Slovenia and Serbia are linguistic and religious, but the most important differences, the Slovenes would argue, is political—that they are genuinely democratic. Slovenian is distinct from Serbo-Croatian, and this mattered politically.

One of the key events driving Slovenia's secession was the trial of four Slovenians in 1988 for publishing military documents suggesting that the Yugoslav military was likely to crush the growing democracy in Slovenia. While the trial itself was seen as being anti-democratic, the fact that it was held in Serbo-Croatian despite being tried in Slovenia angered Slovenes. This trial led to large demonstrations, and spurred moves to democratization. A second identity also mattered. Slovenes are predominantly Roman Catholic. While the Catholic Church did not play as an important role in Slovenia as it did in Croatia as the Orthodox Church in Serbia, it still influenced politics, primarily through the Christian Democrats.[25]

However, the Slovene secessionist efforts focused on its political distinctiveness. The argument was that Slovenia was democratic while Serbia and Yugoslavia were obstacles to realizing true freedom. Slovenia was the first of the Yugoslav republics to allow multiple parties to compete. Its press seemed to be the freest. Slovene politicians and their supporters focused on liberalization, decentralization, and opposition to the draft, rather than strictly to nationalist identities. Indeed, Susan Woodward argues that this was a strategy to get international support: "for it [Slovenia] did not portray Slovenes' desire for self-determination in nationalist terms, but as a fight for 'liberty' and 'democracy.' "[26] The reality of Slovenian democracy and its efforts to define the conflict as one of democracy versus authoritarianism succeeded in shaping the views of outsiders, including the American Ambassador to Yugoslavia.[27]

Contradictions of Croatian Nationalism and Democracy

The Croats also sought to define the conflict as one between democracy and authoritarianism, and between "civilization and barbarism,"[28] but President Franjo Tudjman and his supporters clearly relied much more heavily upon Croatian nationalism to rally support. Unlike Milosevic, Tudjman did not come to nationalist beliefs recently as he had been arrested for advocating Croatian nationalism in the past and was considered obsessed with Croatian nationalism.[29] Tudjman's party, the Croatian Democratic Union [HDZ], has focused almost entirely on Croatian-ness, and promised in its campaigns to reduce the power of Croatia's Serbs.[30]

History and religion play key roles in Croatian identity, and the leaders of Croatian separatism focused on both. The Ustashe regime that ruled in Croatia during World War II served as an important focal point for Serbs and Croats alike. Serbs remembered the atrocities committed by the fascist regime, particularly those crimes committed against Serbs, arguing that they had good reason to fear an independent Croatia. Tudjman and his allies harkened back to the glory of the last independent Croatian state, and appropriated the Ustashe's flag and other symbols as their own. The HDZ also tried to tie itself to the Catholic Church. Just as Milosevic sought comfort and cover from the Serbian Orthodox Church, Tudjman argued on television that the Catholic Church had nurtured Croatian national consciousness.[31] These claims are not idle ones, as the Church has played an important role, trying to defend the Croatian nation.[32] Further, the Croats became more interested in the Catholic Church, which may have been more about feeling their Croatian identity than about faith.[33]

Like Milosevic, Tudjman and his government-controlled media tried to define the Bosnians as Islamic fundamentalists. American Ambassador Warren Zimmermann noted that the government-controlled presses of Croatia and Serbia "became nearly identical—the Muslims were trying to establish an Islamic state in the heart of Europe."[34]

Politics played an important role,[35] as Tudjman relied heavily on the "Hercegovina" lobby, who were largely wealthy émigrés living in the United States and Canada. They were significant contributors to Tudjman's Presidential campaign in 1990. This lobby's nationalist stance included a strong desire to annex parts of Bosnia to Croatia.[36] Tudjman's subsequent anti-Muslim statements and policies alienated outside actors and risked the loss of American support.[37]

Tudjman and Croatia's harsh policies toward Serbs in Croatia and Muslims in Bosnia weakened claims that Croatia deserved international support due to its democratic nature. Once in power, Tudjman and the HDZ acted in an authoritarian manner.[38] Government control of the media meant that the HDZ received favorable coverage, improving its electoral chances. Of course, rewriting electoral laws also benefited the HDZ.[39] Documenting repression of the media and severe policies toward Serbs, the Organization for Security and Cooperation in Europe criticized Croatia. " 'There has been no progress in improving respect for human rights, the rights of minorities and the rule of law.' "[40]

The contradictions between Croatian nationalism and genuine democracy have perhaps become clearer since the end of the fighting. During the conflict, Croatia was able to justify its harsh measures due to wartime necessities, so countries predisposed to supporting Croatia focused more on its religious identity and its pro-Western orientation.

Complexities of Bosnia's Multiethnic Composition

Elections in Bosnia produced a multiethnic coalition, formed by three parties, each representing an ethnic group.[41] Quickly, the Serbs disagreed with the other two groups, and as Bosnia approached secession, the Serbs sought their own self-determination—independence from Bosnia. Consequently, Bosnia's claim to being a multiethnic state literally came under fire. Bosnian leaders faced an important dilemma: emphasizing the Islamic identities of many of their supporters might cause Islamic countries to give it support, but would weaken the multiethnic basis of the regime at home and potentially alienate Western countries.

Even after Bosnian Serbs announced their own independence, the Bosnian government was genuinely multiethnic, and saw this pluralism as crucial for Bosnia's survival.[42] As late as April 1994, the Bosnian cabinet had members from all three ethnic groups, although Muslims possessed the most important positions. The defense of Sarajevo was in the hands of a military that included many Serbs.[43] Sarajevo's population remained multiethnic, and non-Muslim groups gave significant support. Further, Bosnian leaders sought to use its multiethnic identity to get help from the West. By defining itself as the victim of ethnic cleansing and the sole multiethnic combatant, Bosnia hoped to gain international assistance. However, as the war endured, domestic and international dynamics pushed Islam to the forefront. The war itself radicalized Bosnia's population, increasing interest in Islam.[44] As war broke out between the Bosnian government and the Croats, the ideal of a multiethnic Bosnia frayed further. "This shift to a more well defined Islamic identity paralleled the decision to rely more on military means, reflected disillusionment with Western protectors, and positioned the Bosnian government to seek money and arms from traditional Islamic states in the Middle East in the event that the strategy of mobilizing a higher level of NATO military engagement failed."[45] Iran, Saudi Arabia, Turkey, and other predominantly Muslim countries, as I discuss below, were much more willing to give arms and sponsor volunteers to fight on behalf of the Bosnian Muslims.

Other actors defined Bosnia as a Muslim ethnic group, rather than a multiethnic state. Politicians in both Croatia and Serbia used fears of an Islamic government to rally support. "Militant Serbian nationalists spread the fear of an Islamic-Catholic ('Khomeini-Ustashe') conspiracy by the Moslems and Croats.' "[46] Tudjman argued that Islamic fundamentalists were to blame for the conflicts between Croats and Bosnia.[47] Whether these fears were real or created by politicians, Bosnian Serbs were concerned that Bosnia would become an Islamic Republic akin to Iran.[48] Further, support from Islamic countries also served to emphasize the religious identity of many, but not all, constituents of the Bosnian government.

Macedonia—What Is in a Name?

While the Bosnian government was ambivalent about the religious identity thrust upon itself, all of Macedonia's neighbors sought to deny Macedonia its identity. Bulgaria, Greece, and Serbia all deny that Macedonians exist as a separate nation. Bulgaria considers Macedonians to be Bulgarians, but have generally been much friendlier to Macedonia than the others. Serbs consider Macedonians to be South Serbs, which suggests that the territory called Macedonia should belong to Serbia (or the rump Yugoslavia). Greece, of course, has been the most hostile to Macedonia's existence, using nearly every possible foreign policy instrument to deny Macedonia its own identity, including embargoes, boycotts, and hard bargaining within the European Union.

Given all of this conflict, what does it mean to be a Macedonian? Macedonian is a distinct language (although Bulgaria considers it to be a dialect), spoken by seventy percent of the population, with most of the remaining population speaking Albanian. The Macedonia Orthodox Church became autocephalous in 1967 from the Serbian Orthodox Church, though the Serbian Orthodox Church opposed this.[49] The population is mostly Slav. Because of the large Albanian minority, Macedonia has been quite careful on nationality issues. President Kiro Gligorov had to balance the demands of Albanian parties with some of the extreme Macedonian parties.[50] Thus, he and other leaders could not focus solely on language or religion as a basis for Macedonia's identity. Instead, the focus has been on the history of Macedonia's territory, relying upon symbols from ancient Macedonia.[51]

President Gligorov asserted in an interview in 1992:

We are Slavs who came to this area in the sixth century. . . . we are not descendants of the ancient Macedonians. We have borne this name [Macedonians] for centuries; it originates from the name of this geographic region, and we are inhabitants of part of this region. This is the way people can differentiate us from neighboring Slav peoples, the Serbs and the Bulgarians. Our country is called the Republic of Macedonia.[52]

Other countries proposed a variety of names, but either Macedonia or Greece found the various substitutes to be unacceptable. Macedonia was allowed into the United Nations as the Former Yugoslav Republic of Macedonia [FYROM]. For Macedonia, the problem is if they are not Macedonians, then what right do they have to exist? If the territorial identity ceases to exist, then focusing on language or religion would probably result in the loss of the Albanian-majority regions to Albania.[53]

Summary

If the groups struggling during Yugoslavia's demise differed only because of nationality or language, it might still have been as violent, but outsiders would probably not have cared as much. However, multiple identities coexist, so both insiders and outsiders can consider certain identities as being important at the expense of others.

Analysts persuasively argue that "Religion here serves merely as a national identifier. Thus one can have a 'Christian' or 'Muslim' atheist."[54] In other words, Bosnia's conflicts were not really about religious dogma. Still, because the Bosnian government and its constituents were and are predominantly Muslim, the Croats are largely Catholic, and the Serbs are Eastern Orthodox, the conflict was widely viewed as a religious one. Clearly, without the religious dimension, no one could consider the conflict to be a "clash of civilizations."[55] Consequently, the wars resonated more deeply in some countries than others, resulting in countries taking certain sides.

The nature of the groups, the strategies of their leaders, the stances of their opponents, and the predilections of the outside actors determined which actors perceived which identities to be at stake. Because Croatia and Serbia were defined by their exclusive nationalisms, they had incentives to define the identities at stake in Bosnia to be ethnic ones and deny the existence of a multiethnic Bosnia. Further, outsiders assumed that Bosnia was essentially a construct of the Muslims, rather than an independent entity, of which the Muslims were merely a part. Debates between Macedonia, Greece, and other actors have shaped the very the meaning of what it is to be Macedonian. The relevance of these different identities become clear once we examine how states reacted to the conflict.

Understanding the Puzzling Behavior of Key Actors

To assess the competing arguments, and particularly the value of the ethnic ties approach, we need to examine the behavior of the most significant players. Since this conflict had three sides, this section is not organized as the previous chapters. Instead of focusing on the supporters of one side or another, I first examine the states that acted most unexpectedly, and then I discuss more briefly the remaining major actors. First, I consider France and Romania because they do less than what the ethnic politics argument expects. Then, I address Germany's policies since its role is clearly the most controversial. Third, Hungary's foreign policy is worthy of examination since we could have expected that Hungary would have been more assertive. By examining these "hard" cases, we can develop a better assessment of the roles played by ethnic ties, vulnerability and international organizations, and power. Later, I briefly analyze the behavior of Russia, Greece, Turkey, Iran, the United States, and the neighboring countries as well as some more distant actors. Including these observations facilitates comparison of this chapter with the other two case studies since each case study examines the most active supporters of each side and considers the behavior of neighbors.

France

French policy toward the Yugoslav conflict poses a challenge to the theory of ethnic politics and foreign policy because of the religious ties between the French populace and the Croatian people and due to the apparently good fit with the vulnerability hypothesis's predictions. Since France is largely Catholic, one would have expected greater support for Slovenia and Croatia. Moreover, the case seems to provide evidence for the vulnerability argument since France's vulnerability to Corsican separatism may have deterred it. By considering the changes in French foreign policy, we can assess the competing arguments in a difficult case. Ultimately, because reigning French politicians faced little threat from the potential exit of Catholic voters, France could pursue its usual course of setting a foreign policy independent from the United States and others.

France's policy was inconsistent over the course of the conflict. Before and after Yugoslavia fell apart in the spring of 1991, France supported Yugoslavia's territorial integrity. At this point, France, along with Britain, led efforts within the European Community to provide incentives to Yugoslavia if it remained intact. Once war broke out and Germany began to push for recognition of Slovenia and Croatia in fall 1991, France resisted these efforts.[56] France only relented in December after gaining concessions on the Maastricht Accords, which were negotiated at the time.[57] France provided the most troops to UN peacekeeping missions in Croatia and Bosnia. Throughout the Bosnian conflict, France was more willing to support partition and more reluctant to bomb the Bosnian Serbs due to the threats posed to the French troops in the area.

At first glance, vulnerability to separatism may have deterred France from supporting the Croats and Slovenes. "Acceptance of the dissolution of Yugoslavia was felt to have implications for France over Corsica."[58] Separatist violence in Corsica continued during the Yugoslav war, so it makes sense that France would want to avoid setting a precedent that might encourage separatism within its territory. There are two problems with this argument. First, Corsican separatism did not deter France from supporting separatist movements elsewhere, such as Katanga and Biafra. While these more distant movements may not present such a clear precedent as a European conflict, the vulnerability argument does not make such distinctions. Second, France was among the first to support the partition of Bosnia, which would seem to contradict the vulnerability argument.

Analysts also argue that France did not want an unfortunate precedent set that might encourage the breakup of the Soviet Union.[59] France had supported Mikhail Gorbachev's efforts to reform the Soviet Union, and feared that increased separatism might threaten his efforts. This worry had substance, as the Union Treaty allowing the Baltic Republics to secede spurred a coup to depose Gorbachev. While this helps to explain French reticence during the summer of 1991, this concern cannot account for French foreign policy after August 1991, when the Soviet Union's disintegration was a foregone conclusion.

Further, historical ties to Serbia, going back to World War I, might have caused France to give more support to Serbia than otherwise would have been expected. While some decisionmakers may have had ties to Serbia, how such ties could risk conflict with Germany and others is hard to understand. While the historical parallel of Germany opposing Serbia and France supporting Serbia to 1914 Europe is interesting, there must be something else at work, as France, like many others, has gathered and discarded alliance partners over the years.

A fourth and more likely approach is that the French wanted to develop a foreign policy independent from Germany's and from that of the United States. "Among the various principles guiding French policy, the most significant was probably 'difference.' A priority continued to be asserting itself on the international stage."[60] This is a historical tendency in French foreign policy that had implications for the other secessionist crises discussed in earlier chapters.[61] The desire to play a leading role in European institutions and international politics runs deep within French politics, so it should not be surprising that France attempted to take the lead in this conflict. In his attempts to control foreign policy and have foreign policies independent from other countries, President François Mitterand has been called " 'more Gaullist than de Gaulle.' "[62] Indeed, Mitterand's surprise flight to Sarajevo on June 18, 1992 opening the airport for humanitarian aid defied the United Nations and gave France a prominent role in the conflict.

Because French foreign policy greatly depends on the President's interests, it is important to note that Mitterand was President during almost the entire conflict. François Mitterand was President until 1995, and as leader of the Socialist party, was less dependent upon devout Catholics for political support. He was also less constrained by political competition since his second term as president, 1988–1995, would be his last. While he might have had some concern for his party regardless of whether he was to run for reelection, tensions between Mitterand and the party before the 1993 elections may have lessened such concerns.[63] Further, the focus of domestic political debates over French foreign policy centered on the Maastricht agreement and deepening European integration.

Admittedly, ethnic ties did not play a great role in French foreign policymaking. This is in part because the pull of Catholic ties between the French and Croatia was lessened by the disdain the French had for Croatia's Ustashe past.[64] However, rising enmities within France toward its Muslim population might help to explain why France weakly opposed Serb aggression toward Bosnia.[65]

Regardless of the reasons why France placed troops in the region, their presence became the most important influence upon French foreign policy. Fears that French soldiers would either become targets or hostages inhibited the French government from supporting an end to the arms embargo or more decisive NATO action. NATO's bombing campaign in the summer of 1995 became possible only after France reinforced its troops and moved them out of harm's way.

The French case, therefore, does not lend support to the ethnic ties argument, but neither of the competing arguments accounts well for France's policies either. Vulnerability might have encouraged France to support Yugoslavia's territorial integrity, but cannot account for why France supported Bosnia's partition. None of the actors in the conflict could reasonably pose a threat to France nor serve as a valuable ally so it is hard to argue that security interests motivated France's policies. The traditional French desire to have an independent foreign policy is a key part of French identity, so French nationalism may have played a role in this conflict.

Romania

Romanian foreign policy is also a puzzle for those focusing on ethnic ties. Given the historical and ethnic ties between Romania and Serbia, we could expect that Romania would support Serbia, but instead, Romania played more of a neutral role during the conflict. We can explain Romania's anomalous foreign policy by focusing on two different dynamics. First, Western pressure on Romania caused it to conform. Second, perhaps ethnic politics within Romania was so focused on other ethnically defined adversaries that politicians did not need to use foreign policy toward Yugoslavia to build domestic political support.

Before explaining Romanian foreign policy, we must specify what Romania did and did not do as Yugoslavia broke apart. As the conflict began to develop, Romania supported efforts to maintain Yugoslavia's territorial integrity.[66] At the same time, Romania allowed the smuggling of oil and other supplies to Serbia.[67] Romania clamped down on the smuggling after the West pressured Romania to comply. Romania was one of the few countries in the region to have diplomatic ties to the rump Yugoslavia while enforcing the sanctions. In a similar vein, Romania publicly took a stand for neutrality. "Foreign Minister Melescanu reaffirmed the intention to create 'very good relations with all of the republics that appeared as a result of the disintegration of the old Yugoslav federation,' explicitly noting that 'there exists no intention on Romania's part to be an ally of any one of the [post Yugoslav] republics against any other one.'"[68]

What caused Romania to change its policy and enforce the sanctions? How was this permissible in Romania's domestic politics? International pressures combined with domestic politics making it possible for Romanian leaders to stop the smuggling of goods via the Danube to Serbia. The 1992 G-7 summit meeting singled out Romania as a violator of the embargo against Serbia, and shortly after this meeting Romania more seriously enforced the embargo.[69] This pressure mattered because Romania greatly desired to a part of the European Union's integration plans.

Supporting the sanctions was possible, despite the severe cost of approximately $7–8 billion,[70] because Romania's nationalist politics focused on internal enemies and other neighboring states, and largely ignored Yugoslavia. The inheritors of post-Ceauçescu Romania, particularly the ruling National Salvation Front [NSF], showed few inhibitions toward using nationalism to gain votes and avoid the loss of supporters. All parties contained at least some extreme nationalists, and several parties relied on nationalism as their only major issue. While not as avowedly nationalist as the Romanian National Unity Party or the Greater Romania Party, the NSF also used ethnic appeals to gain support. "Whenever threatened in its control of political power, the government has resorted to populist, often chauvinist demagogy."[71] Often, the NSF found it necessary to rely on these nationalist parties to form winning coalitions.[72]

Given the prevalence of Romanian nationalism and ethnic outbidding, how could Romania not support Serbia, its closest ethnic kin in the region? The answer is that Romanian nationalists had plenty of issues and targeted ethnic groups that mattered more to the average Romanian. Specifically, nationalists cared about and fought over two issues: the Romanian majority in Moldova and the Hungarian minority in Transylvania. Moldova, or Bessarabia as it once was known, was one of the Soviet Union's fifteen republics, a slice of Romanian territory gained during World War II as the result of the Ribbentrop-Molotov pact. Roughly two-thirds of the population is Romanian. After gaining independence from the Soviet Union, the issue of whether Moldova would be reunited with Romania arose on both Moldova's and Romania's political agendas. A majority of Romanians in Romania wanted to annex the lost territory.[73] If politicians wanted to prove to their supporters that they were good Romanian nationalists, they could (and did) take strong stands on reunification with Moldova.

Similarly, rather than focusing on some relatively distant target, Romanian elites emphasized an apparently greater threat: Hungarians in Transylvania. Indeed, "The NSF began to frequently use the 'Hungarian threat' in order to divert attention from pressing issues of democratization."[74] Politicians used fears of Hungarian separatism and of Hungary's intervention to mobilize support. "With Romania politically calm in 1994 despite declining living standards, and the Yugoslav war an issue of relative unimportance, it was ties with Hungary and Moldova which focused attention on Romania's position in a region shaken by numerous internal and inter-state disputes."[75]

Romanian foreign policy provides strong support for none of the arguments that this book addresses. The presence of Hungarian separatism might have compelled Romania to support Yugoslavia's territorial integrity, but cannot account for its subsequent support of Serbia as Serbia was a force for disintegration. Realist accounts can make some sense of Romania's foreign policy, as Serbia (and Slovakia) could be seen as allies against the common Hungarian threat, but Hungary was threatening due to ethnic politics, not due to traditional realist concerns. An initial glance at Romania's ethnic composition would suggest support for Serbia, and this was Romania's policy at the outset. A somewhat deeper analysis suggests that the Romanian government did not have to take strong stands on Yugoslavia as long as it took strong stands on issues of greater relevance to Romanian nationalism.[76] Thus,

ethnic politics greatly influenced Romanian foreign policy, just not in the
ways specified by ethnic ties alone.

Germany

Many have blamed Germany for the war in Bosnia, so it deserves special
attention. The accusation is that Germany's early support for Slovenia and
Croatia undermined efforts to keep Yugoslavia together, and encouraged the
politicians in those two republics to push for independence. In the fall of
1991, after Slovenia was *de facto* independent and Croatia was in the process
of being divided, Germany aggressively pushed for recognition of the two
republics. Critics then argue that this pressure caused Bosnia to declare
independence, which then produced war. Regardless of the accuracy of
these accusations,[77] Germany's assertive push for recognition, even at the
risk of aliening its most important partners, is something that needs to be
explained. Below, I consider what Germany did, the various explanations
analysts have posed, and I apply the theory of ethnic politics and foreign
policy after considering the competing arguments. The key to understanding German foreign policy toward Yugoslavia is its discrimination—strong
support for Slovenia and Croatia, and much less support for Bosnia and
Macedonia.

Policy Toward Yugoslavia   Most accounts agree that Germany did not actively support Slovenia and Croatia until violence broke out at the end of
June 1991. German Foreign Minister Hans Dietrich Genscher met with
Slovenian and Croatian officials earlier in that year, but did not encourage
them to secede unilaterally.[78] Still, meeting with such officials may be considered implicit support and perhaps *de facto* recognition. Importantly, German officials did not meet with representatives from other Yugoslav republics
at this time. Until the conflict broke out in Slovenia, Germany's official
position supported the EC's efforts to maintain Yugoslavia. This quickly
changed once violence broke out. Arguing that Serbia's aggression caused
the conflict, German decisionmakers quickly seized upon recognition as a
means to coerce the Serbs. As the Yugoslav Army began to use force in
Slovenia, German reaction was strong. Once the conflict in Slovenia was
settled, violence broke out in Croatia with the YPA strongly taking the side

of the Serbs, causing Germany to make clearer its threat to recognize the secessionist republics.

Throughout fall 1991, Germany tried to get the rest of the EC to act jointly in opposition to Serbia and in support of the secessionist republics. Chancellor Kohl promised to recognize Slovenia and Croatia before Christmas, resulting in a final push by German diplomats in December 1991. Shortly after the Maastricht meeting of the EC,[79] on December 16, 1991, the European Community agreed to follow the decisions of the Badinter Arbitration Commission, who would determine which Yugoslav republics were worthy of recognition. Instead of waiting, German decisionmakers agreed on December 19 and announced on December 23, 1991, that Germany recognized the independence of Slovenia and Croatia. It would open embassies in these two states on January 15, 1992, when the rest of the EC would be implementing whatever decision the Badinter Commission made. The Commission agreed that Slovenia and Macedonia met the various requirements, including guarantees to minorities, while Croatia fell short. German diplomats argued that Croatia was in the midst of implementing new policies that would guarantee the rights of Serbs, and therefore deserving of recognition.[80] It is quite striking that Germany was quite willing to go along with Greece in denying Macedonia recognition despite pronouncements of support for self-determination and democracy. "With respect to the recognition of Macedonia, the German government kept its promise to protect Greece's interests," Foreign Minister Genscher admits in his memoir.[81]

After recognition, Germany took a backseat to the U.S., Russia, Britain, and France. German diplomats argue that since the United Nations handled Bosnia, and not as much by the European Community, the responsibility shifted toward the permanent members of the Security Council. Once the question became one of military intervention, Germany could not take a strong position because their troops would not be at risk. "The fate of Bosnia was now exclusively in the hands of those powers willing to put their own troops on the ground, and they certainly would not have been enthusiastic about any German advice on how to make the best use of these troops."[82] Despite constitutional battles over the use of force outside of NATO's territory, Germany gave military support to the no-fly zone over Bosnia and later to the NATO forces enforcing the Dayton accords.

Dominance of the Region—Realpolitik or History   Critics of Germany's policies have argued that a desire to dominate the Balkans motivated Germany. These analysts tend to argue that both power politics and traditional German nationalistic attitudes cause this desire to be manifested in German support for Slovenia and Croatia. British officials apparently believed that Germany's efforts were "an attempt to reconstitute a special German sphere of geopolitical influence in the Balkans in collusion with Croatian heirs of the old Ustashi . . . with the Bavarian, Austrian, and German Roman Catholic hierarchies, and with suspect German nationalists at the *Frankfurter Allgemeine Zeitung*."[83] Aleksa Djilas argues that "Germany will find it much easier politically to dominate Slovenia and Croatia than all of Yugoslavia. . . . Under the guise of Western democratic values and human rights during the disintegration of Yugoslavia, traditional German nationalistic prejudices reappeared."[84]

To address these arguments, I first consider the role of power politics and then deal with the focus on traditional nationalist tendencies. Does a desire for security or power explain Germany's foreign policy? This question ultimately depends on what is meant by security. The Balkans present an insignificant military threat, particularly since Germany is a member of NATO, and Serbia, Germany's supposed threat, is not. Germany is one of the most militarily capable countries in the world, and is backed by the world's most powerful alliance. While the Yugoslav military was sizable and well armed compared to some of its neighbors,[85] its disintegration and its geographic distance from Germany produce a very weak threat to Germany's security. If one means refugee flows, which most critics ignore, then security concerns might have driven German foreign policy. Germany has received more refugees from Yugoslavia than any other Western European country (at least 400,000). However, these refugees became quite numerous after Germany decided to support Slovenia and Croatia and after German public opinion shifted toward greater support.

Of course, if power motivated Germany, rather than security, then domination of the Balkans might make some sense. There are two problems with this assertion: a) that dominating the Balkans would really increase German power much; and b) Germany's policies toward Yugoslavia were not cost-free as they expended resources (power) to achieve their goals. What would domination of the region add to German power? It is not clear how this would advance German interests in the world. Given that Germany's economic interests are elsewhere, and there is no perceived need for conquering "living space," as was argued before World War II, asserting that Germany sought domination strains one's credulity. Further, Germany's assertive support for Slovenia and Croatia damaged their relationships with other, much more important states: the United States, Russia, France, and Great Britain. Germany was apparently willing to compromise on the Maastricht Treaty to get support for recognition, but clearly the Maastricht Treaty is more likely to have an impact on German sovereignty and on its relative power than the status of Slovenia, Croatia, or Serbia. Moreover, if the European Union is a tool for maximizing German influence in the world (as some of Germany's critics would argue), then damaging the institution by acting unilaterally would be counter to Germany's long-term interests. Moreover, Germany's willingness to let the United States and others take the lead after December 1991 suggests that Germany is not so power hungry.

While arguing that ethnic politics shapes foreign policy, I do not aver that history simply repeats itself, as many seem to assert when explaining German foreign policy. Scholars arguing that traditional German nationalism motivated the country's foreign policy in the 1990s make two mistakes. First, they oversimplify by suggesting that German foreign policy was very similar to what it was before and after World War I. Second, they ignore the possibility that German nationalism then and now may be shaped by some other forces. During the Yugoslav conflict, Germany gave diplomatic recognition to Slovenia and Croatia, Germany perhaps looked the other way as private actors facilitated the transfer of arms, and it gave some direct military support to UN and NATO forces in the region. That is very different from what Germany did in the early twentieth century. Germany has not invaded Yugoslavia; it has not created puppet fascist regimes in Croatia; and its economic policies are not as domineering, intentionally or otherwise, as they were before World War II.[86]

Further, Germany supported Yugoslavia's territorial integrity before the outbreak of violence, and Germany had a very strong, very positive economic relationship with Yugoslavia before the conflict. "German traditional tendencies" cannot account for either of these predisintegration policies. Thus, while some notion of German traditional feelings toward the region might help explain some German perceptions of the conflict or some influence on public opinion, such arguments cannot account for German behavior. Second, these arguments fail to explain why Yugoslavia is a target for German traditional nationalism. They assert that this is a traditional tendency, but fail to explain why. Ethnic politics might provide some of the microfoundations for these broader generalizations, by showing how particular political forces matter in German domestic politics then (which this book does not address) and now.

Support for Self-Determination   Both German diplomats and American analysts argue that Germany was motivated by a sincere belief in self-determination. "The crucial motives for German behavior during the first two years of the crisis were rooted in a pervasive pattern of moral and political values. Outstanding among these was a particular affinity, enhanced by German unification, for the ideal of self-determination. . . . Equally important was the rejection of violence as a means of politics."[87] The timing of this crisis as the first European crisis after Germany's reunification made the principle of self-determination particularly salient. If Germany demanded self-determination for its own people, then it would have been hypocritical to deny the Croats and Slovenes. German decisionmakers viewed self-determination as applying to those decisions made democratically, which should not be altered forcefully. Thus, Slovenia, Croatia, and Bosnia deserved international support since they made decisions through elections and elected bodies, whereas the democratic credentials of Milosevic, the Croatian Serbs, and the Bosnian Serbs were suspect. By using force, the old Yugoslavia government and the new Serbian leadership delegitimated their efforts to protect Serbs and to assert the rights of the Serbs in the seceding republics. Beverly Crawford asserts that "the self-determination principle was an important component of Germany's foreign policy culture; it was a central foreign policy norm."[88]

The problem with such arguments is that Germany did not support the efforts of every group desiring self-determination. While they did not oppose Bosnian efforts to get assistance, Germany certainly did not lead the way as it had with the Slovenes and Croats. Further, Germany assisted Greece in denying Macedonia recognition, and Germany did not significantly help the Albanians in Kosovo until its involvement in NATO efforts in 1999. Finally, Germany was not terribly sympathetic to the claims of Serbs in Croatia and Bosnia for self-determination. Crawford addresses only the latter. She argues that Germany had not traditionally considered a unitary Yugoslavia as a solution to Serbia's self-determination problems since Germany did not help with the creation of Yugoslavia. In addition, the Christian Democrats did not view the Serbs as worthy of self-determination since they were associated more strongly with the communist authoritarian regime.[89] Libal argues that self-determination applied to the constituent republics of Yugoslavia, but that ethnic groups within each republic, such as the Albanians of Kosovo, the Muslims of Sanjak, and the Hungarians of Vojvodina would not receive international support.[90]

These claims still do not explain why Germany did not recognize Macedonia, especially since it, like Slovenia, met the Badinter Commission's standards for recognition. "At the governmental level, it [the pro-Croat bias] manifested itself in the contrasting attitudes of Bonn toward recognition of Croatia and Slovenia on the one hand, and FYROM [Macedonia] on the other."[91] Obviously, when it came to Macedonia, there were conflicts between principles and other interests, such as winning Greek support for Germany's policies. What is quite striking here is that Germany was quite willing to bear significant international costs (in the form of alienated allies and increased insecurity by potential foes) when it pushed others to recognize Slovenia and Croatia, and when Germany did so by itself, but was unwilling to bear such costs for Macedonia. Although conflict in Macedonia certainly poses a greater danger to international stability, Germany chose not to support self-determination in this case. What is also quite interesting is that there is no mentioning of German public opinion concerning Macedonia's plight.

Domestic Politics   Analysts of Germany's policies have also stressed the importance of domestic politics in shaping German policy. These analysts focus on Croats in Germany; the German media; public opinion; and party politics. Each variant suggests that domestic politics influenced German foreign policy, and each suggests that ethnic ties matter in some way. The first claim is that Croats living in Germany were able to mobilize support for their ethnic kin.[92] The 500,000 or so Croats in Germany, it is argued, had strong ties to the Christian Social Union [CSU]—the Bavarian wing of the Christian Democrats, and influenced the party to support Croatia. There are three problems with this argument. First, the Croatian minority is not very large, so it is hard to understand how their preferences would override the desires of other groups. Second, the CSU did not push for recognition and greater support of Croatia until violence broke out.[93] Third, the CSU's support for Croatia is overdetermined. The CSU is more closely tied to the Catholic Church than other German parties, and while the Croats in Germany may have helped shape perceptions of the Yugoslav conflict, the CSU would have been likely to support the Catholic, anticommunist side regardless of Croat lobbying.[94]

The second line of argument is that the German media, particularly the *Frankfurter Allgemeine Zeitung* [FAZ], shaped public perceptions and pressured politicians to support Slovenia and Croatia. Timothy Garton Ash goes so far as to argue that, the publisher of that particular newspaper "single-handedly did more than any politician to change Bonn's policy toward the former Yugoslavia."[95] Many analysts shared this view,[96] as did the British foreign office.[97] The FAZ and other media outlets portrayed the conflict in very stark terms—democratic Croats versus authoritarian Serbs. Interestingly, all accounts of the FAZ's influence focus on the conflict between Croatia and Serbia. Few, if any, analysts discuss the German media's coverage of Bosnia, Macedonia, or Kosovo. While one could focus on the personality of one publisher,[98] that would fail to address why other media outlets covered the Balkans as they did. This account also seems to exaggerate the role of the media—why were Germans receptive to the FAZ's coverage?

Policymakers and analysts agree that German public opinion influenced Germany's foreign policy. Libal argues that "the outpouring of German public sympathy" influenced the foreign minister's reactions toward the growing conflict.[99] Maull argues that the German public placed significant pressure on the government to give Croatia more diplomatic support.[100] Clearly, the German public supported Slovenia and Croatia. The question, then, is why? Germans' past experiences in the region and their reaction to the use of force shaped public opinion. The lasting effects of tourism are often cited when accounting for German public opinion.[101] Before the war, many Germans spent the vacations along the Dalmatian coast of Croatia. Consequently, Germans responded more passionately when the Yugoslav People's Army shelled Croatian historic sites they had visited, including Dubrovnik. The second major factor shaping German public opinion was the abhorrence of violence. Because of Germany's role in World War II, many Germans are opposed to violence, and to see artillery used against European civilians caused tremendous outrage. "The prevailing public sentiment was the desire to see the carnage stop."[102]

However, assessing public opinion's influence is difficult because, as Crawford points out, opinion polls tended to follow policy changes, not precede them.[103] This particular order of events may be interpreted in two ways. Either politicians shaped public opinion through their speeches and policies, or that politicians anticipated what the public wanted and gave it to them as the public began to realize what they wanted to government to do. To get at this question, we need to consider how German party politics played out during this conflict.

Crawford and many others make convincing arguments that competition among Germany's leading parties was important in shaping policy toward Yugoslavia.[104] The basic argument is that a few parties genuinely preferred particular outcomes in Yugoslavia, and the others "bandwagoned," as they did not want be the only ones opposing self-determination for Slovenia and Croatia. Two parties at the opposite ends of Germany's political spectrum, the Greens/Alliance '90 and the Christian Socialist Union, most clearly reacted to the growing conflict due to their ideologies, principles, and perceptions of the world. Because the Green Party has historically been opposed to violence, and because Germany's reunification produced the Greens/Alliance '90, when viewing Yugoslavia's spiral into conflict, this coalition supported the peaceful self-determination of Slovenes and Croats before any other German party. They called for recognition as early as February 1991.[105] The CSU is the second party that had very strong preferences, as its religious ties to the Croats, as well as historical ones, were quite deep.[106] With the Catholic Church already pushing for international support for Slovenia and Croatia, the CSU, with its strong ties to the Catholic Church, had a side in this conflict that it clearly favored, and pushed for recognition.

The other parties had a less direct stake in the conflict, but each eventually gave strong support for recognition as they felt themselves being outflanked by the other parties.[107] The Free Democrats, the Christian Democrats, and the Social Democrats all feared losing support to other parties, as the most recent election suggested that the party system was beginning to fragment.[108] The SPD had begun to lose votes to both the Greens/Alliance '90 and to the Republikaner Party, while the CDU/CSU was losing supporters to the Republikaners as well. Therefore, each party cared greatly about what the other parties were doing. With the Greens/Alliance '90 pushing for recognition, the SPD had to follow or else lose even more support. With the CSU pushing for greater support, and with the SPD then also supporting recognition of Slovenia and Croatia, the CDU began to support greater efforts on behalf of the northwestern Yugoslav Republics. The Free Democrats, with Foreign Minister Genscher, were the last to cave in to these pressures, but as pressure increased, the FDP also began to call for recognition. Genscher later wrote that "we [German policymakers] were even considered too cautious—an attitude that became evidence especially in response to the request for the recognition of Croatia and Slovenia."[109] The FDP could not stand alone against all of the other parties, despite whatever misgivings Genscher might have had. Having beaten the EC into submission on this issue in December 1991, Germany went ahead and recognized

Slovenia and Croatia before the EC timetable allowed as "a gesture for the domestic audience."[110]

Explaining Inconsistency: Ethnic Ties   While domestic politics clearly drove Germany to alienate friends and potential foes by granting early recognition to Slovenia and Croatia, these accounts omit the discriminatory nature of its foreign policy. Libal and others admit that Germany's hands were tied over Bosnia, since Germany could not use its own military to assist international intervention (though it eventually did so in the face of constitutional challenges). Still, this fails to account for why Germany did not care about Macedonia or Kosovo. If Germany's foreign policy culture or its people at large were devoted to self-determination and nonviolence, then Germany should have given much greater support to Macedonia. What was different about the republics that gained German support and Macedonia? The Badinter Commission, as well as others, considered Slovenia and Macedonia to be deserving of recognition because of their superior treatment of minorities, so that fails to account for German policy. Serbia did not turn its armed forces on Macedonia as it did toward Croatia and Slovenia, so Germans did not see Macedonia on television as much as Croatia or Slovenia. However, the Greeks kept Macedonia on the European agenda by opposing recognition and levying economic sanctions. Thus, Macedonia was on the German political agenda, and deserved recognition according to the principles justifying recognition of Slovenia and Croatia. In the debates explaining German foreign policy toward Yugoslavia, little mention is made of Macedonia. Did the German people not care about Macedonia? Why did German politicians focus so much on Croatia but ignore Macedonia? Given that conflict in Macedonia presented then and continues to do so today a greater threat to international peace and stability, how could Germany give in to Greece? How could German leaders allow Greece to determine policy, given both Germany's relative power advantage and Germany's support for self-determination?

The most obvious distinction between Macedonia and the northwest republics is that Germans saw the Croats and Slovenes as being similar to themselves. Certainly, the CSU would consider the plight of the Catholics of Slovenia and Croatia as more important than the situation of the predominantly Orthodox Macedonians. While we have no direct evidence of religious and other ties having a direct role, it is hard, otherwise, to explain the discrimination in German foreign policy.

Germany played quite a controversial role in the Yugoslav conflict. It was more assertive in this conflict than in any other since World War II. Germany pushed allies into supporting particular groups, while allowing themselves to be pushed into denying Macedonia recognition despite its *de facto* independence. Arguments about history and desires for regional dominance have little credibility as Germany moved faster than the other European states, but slower than it could have in its efforts to support Slovenia and Croatia. The domestic debate clearly mattered, as German parties competed with each other, outbidding each other to be the best supporters of Croatian and Slovenian self-determination.

Hungary

Hungary's foreign policy evolved throughout the crisis. It began as one of the strongest supporters of Croatian and Slovene independence, but became more ambivalent over time. The foreign policy change did not coincide with changes in the composition of relevant constituencies, so the Hungarian case challenges the theory of ethnic politics and foreign policy. While ethnic ties to Croatia and Slovenia and enmities toward Serbia motivated Hungary's early support for the two secessionist republics, ultimately concern for the Hungarian minority in Serbia's Vojvodina region constrained Hungarian foreign policy.

Hungary became embroiled in controversy even before Yugoslavia broke apart. In 1990, Hungary sold more than thirty thousand Kalashnikov rifles to Croatia. When the deal was revealed in 1991, Hungary claimed that the arms deal had been a mistake, but the situation implicated more than a few Hungary officials. Hungary was one of the states pushing for early recognition of Croatia and Slovenia.[111] Hungary also enforced sanctions on Serbia once the international community imposed them, despite their tremendous cost.[112] Hungary even allowed NATO to base its planes on Hungarian territory.

However, as the conflict continued, Hungary supported Croatia and Slovenia much less, as its foreign policy became more ambivalent. The first arms shipment to Croatia was apparently the only one during the war. Furthermore, after Hungarian Foreign Minister Gáza Jeszenszky met with Serbia's President Milosevic in March 1994, Hungary indicated to NATO that it did not want the planes based in Hungary to be used in airstrikes against Bosnian Serbs.[113]

Why did Hungary support Croatia early on and then lessen its support? Why did Hungary give less support to international efforts to punish the Serbs in Bosnia? Ethnic politics can explain both why Hungary initially supported Croatia and Slovenia, and then why it became less supportive than one might have expected. Hungarians tended to support Croatia's and Slovenia's right to self-determination,[114] as Hungary shares religious and historical ties to Croatia and Slovenia. While religion [Catholicism] is not a particularly strong component of Hungarian national identity,[115] it is still something that binds Hungarians to Croats and Slovenes, and serves as a cleavage between Hungarians and Serbs. Religious ties may also explain the discrimination in Hungary's foreign policy: Hungary gave support to Slovenia and Croatia early on, but was less inclined to support airstrikes aiding the Bosnian Muslims. Their plight might be less compelling to Hungarian politicians, so that the risk involved in supporting them probably outweighed any desire to help them.

The potential cost of supporting any secessionist republic for Hungary was the threat Serbia posed to the Hungarian minority in Vojvodina. The salience of Hungarians abroad within Hungary's domestic politics would be high, given their numbers and the risks they face. This would be true even if Hungary had not been governed by a center-right coalition, relying on nationalist parties and strategies to gain and maintain its position.[116] Prime Minister Jozsef Antall "tried to enhance its [the coalition's] domestic political support by placing ethnic concerns into the focal point of its foreign policy agenda."[117] These concerns have focused on Hungarians in Romania, Slovakia, and Serbia.

The main Hungarian strategy for dealing with this problem has been to negotiate bilateral treaties with states inhabited by Hungarian minorities. Serbia's Hungarians have been less salient than Romania's because those in Serbia have "enjoyed rights, privileges, and a sense of security no other Hungarian minority enjoyed in Eastern Europe."[118] Indeed, analysts argue that the Hungarian minority has not tried to secede because their treatment has been relatively good.[119] Not only have the Vojvodina Hungarians avoided separatism, but they have also pressured the Hungarian government to take a neutral stance toward Yugoslavia's wars of dissolution.[120] This effort is probably the result of fear. Indeed, they seem to play the role of hostage in the Serbia-Hungary relationship—that the welfare of the Hungarians in Vojvodina is contingent on Hungary's behavior toward the former Yugoslavia.[121] It is quite suggestive that Hungarian opposition to NATO airstrikes occurred after Hungary's foreign minister met with Milosevic about the treatment of Hungarian minorities in Serbia.[122] It seems that Serbian leaders threatened to harm the Hungarians in Vojvodina if Hungary continued to support NATO's air attacks, and, apparently, this blackmail worked at least in the short term.

The crisis occurred at a time when most parties were using nationalism as one of their appeals for popular support. The reigning government was particularly dependent on nationalist parties to hold onto their position. Hungarians generally preferred supporting Croatia and Slovenia due to their shared ethnic ties, but cared somewhat less about the plight of the Bosnian Muslims due to the absence of ethnic ties. As Serbia made the Vojvodina Hungarians appear to be hostages, Hungary became a less enthusiastic supporter of Serbia's adversaries.

Perhaps Hungary was better equipped to take the side of separatists since it is relatively invulnerable to separatism, but this invulnerability says very little about what Hungary might do. The imperatives of national security predict more support for Slovenia, Croatia, and Bosnia than actually occurred. Yugoslavia and then Serbia presented the most severe military threat, so we ought to expect strong support for efforts to weaken Yugoslavia and later Serbia. Further, Hungary was also strongly motivated at this time by the desire to join the European Community and the North Atlantic Treaty Organization. This desire does not explain Hungary's early support for Slovenia and Croatia, but it may account for the willingness to enforce sanctions later on, despite the risk posed to Hungarians in Vojvodina. Ultimately, Hungary was cross-pressured by its desire to maintain its security and its efforts to secure their ethnic kin in Serbia.

Brief Analyses of Other Major Players

While France, Germany, Hungary, and Romania appeared to be anomalous, during this conflict most countries acted according to the imperatives of ethnic politics. Most of the major actors in the conflict generally acted as if motivated by ethnic ties, and they less consistently met the expectations of the other approaches.

The Soviet Union/Russia

Soviet behavior toward Yugoslavia neatly reflected vulnerability's implications while Russian foreign policy more closely followed the logic of ethnic politics. Before he lost power and before it was a lost cause, Mikhail Gorbachev supported Yugoslavia's territorial integrity. The parallels between the federations were clear, as republics within both countries were seceding. Gorbachev was concerned about what precedents a violent secessionist conflict in Yugoslavia might set for the Soviet Union. Hence, he worked with the United States, even affirming Yugoslavia's territorial integrity in a joint statement in July 1991, when, arguably, the end of Yugoslavia was a *fait accompli*.[123] Both Gorbachev and Boris Yeltsin lost their enthusiasm for Serbia and for Yugoslavia's unity when it became clear that Milosevic and his allies supported those who launched a coup against the both of them.[124]

Although the Soviet Union ceased to exist, Russia continued to play an important role in the Balkans, but was motivated differently. Ethnic ties and political competition shaped Russian foreign policy toward Yugoslavia instead of vulnerability influencing foreign policy. Domestic political competition between President Boris Yeltsin and nationalists within Russian legislature and elsewhere clearly shaped the patterns of support for Serbia. The more competitive pressure Yeltsin faced, the more Russia tended to support Serbia and the Bosnian Serbs. Russian support for sanctions against Serbia declined, and foreign policy became more conflictual with West. Most accounts of Russian foreign policy at this time agree that there were at least three distinct phases in policy toward Yugoslavia. At each stage, Russian foreign policy became increasingly assertive toward the West and protective of Serbia, and that these stages coincided with changes in the domestic political scene.[125]

The preemption of NATO airstrikes by the imposition of Russian peacekeeping troops to Sarajevo in the winter of 1994 illustrates the dilemmas and opportunities the Yugoslav conflict posed for Yeltsin and his competitors. This move allowed Yeltsin to appear to be defending the Serbs while acting in the service of peace. It not only preempted NATO, but also denied the nationalist opposition a key issue. While the reformers wanted a smooth relationship with the West, Yeltsin had to risk conflict with the United States and others to accommodate or anticipate the nationalist backlash. Russia took a strong stand against the Bosnian Serbs only after Serbia itself did, which then gave Yeltsin cover.

"The opposition objected to the Foreign Ministry's lecturing 'Slav broth-ers'; favoured unconditional support for fellow Slavs against Islam and the Vatican; was for lifting sanctions against Serbia and imposing them on Cro-atia; was against the Vance-Owen plan, which compromised Bosnian Serb interests."[126] The Slavic and Orthodox ties between Russians and Serbs may not be as deeply felt as the nationalists in both countries often assert. Still, it is clear that even if these ties served as merely a pretext for attacking the Russian government, they significantly influenced Russia's foreign policy during this crisis. Once Yugoslavia ceased to exist and once Russia was cre-ating its own foreign policy, vulnerability did not influence policy as much as it influenced Gorbachev. As Russia combated Chechen separatists and had to deal with other groups seeking autonomy or independence, Russia gave significant political support to the Bosnian Serbs, who were seeking to secede from a former republic of a federal state. This is not something the vulnerability argument would expect.

Regarding realist accounts, Russia, even in its current state, is consider-ably stronger than Yugoslavia was or any successor, so one cannot argue that Russia supported Serbia because of Bosnia's, Slovenia's, or Croatia's threat. However, one realist argument would be that Russia needs as many allies as possible now, and that Serbia was a likely ally due to shared concerns about the West. Within domestic debates, members of parliament argued along these lines. However, it is hard to see how Serbia adds anything to Russian security, except as a diversion of NATO troops and material to the Balkans.

In sum, we can explain Russian support for Serbia, including its initial ambivalence, by focusing on Russia's domestic politics as nationalists pres-sured the Yeltsin regime to take stronger and stronger stands on behalf of their "brothers" in the Balkans.

Greece

Perhaps Greece's behavior exemplifies the dynamics of ethnic politics more clearly than any other state during Yugoslavia's disintegration. Greece has argued that Macedonia presents a threat to Greece's security, but Greek demands suggest that the real threat is one of domestic politics. Politicians who do not take strong stands against Macedonia lose power. Regardless of the sources of Greece's antipathy toward Macedonia, Greece's obsession

with it led to aggressive efforts toward Macedonia, threatening to destabilize
the region.

Greece used its position within the European Union to deny recognition
of Macedonia. After European states finally recognized Macedonia, Greece
embargoed its goods. Since international sanctions limited Macedonia's
trade with Serbia (rump Yugoslavia), Greece's embargo greatly damaged
Macedonia's landlocked economy. In addition, Greece tended to support
Serbia during the conflict, as it was seen as an ally against the common
Turkish and Macedonian threats, including violating the trade embargo
against Serbia.[127]

Greece's fears are not entirely imaginary as some important political
movements within Macedonia, particularly the Internal Macedonian Rev-
olutionary Organization—Democratic Party for Macedonian National
Unity, espouse irredentist claims toward Greece. However, if Greece truly
worried about either a conventional invasion or subversive movements,[128]
its policies would have been much different. Greece would have tried to
negotiate security guarantees with Macedonia, and with outside actors to
enforce the agreement. UN peacekeepers might have patrolled the border
between Macedonia and Greece, rather than or in addition to guarding the
boundary between Macedonia and Serbia. Greece might have engaged in
positive economic policies to build support in northern Greece to reduce
Macedonian nationalism's appeal. Instead, Greece's demands focused on
Macedonia's name, its flag, and other symbolic issues.

Macedonia's name was objectionable since it laid claim to some of
Greece's past and its identity.[129] "By proposing names for the republic that
did not include the word 'Macedonia,' the Greek government was attempting to sever completely the symbolic ties between the republic and its people
with anything Macedonian."[130] The use of the star of Vergina as part of the
Macedonian flag upset Greeks since it was an emblem of the ancient Macedonian royal family, to which Greece laid claim. Macedonia, at the most,
posed a threat to the identities of Greeks by "usurping" its history. As a result,
ethnic ties do not explain Greece's policies, but ethnic enmities do.

"Greek politicians and diplomats have generally done their utmost to
make life difficult for Macedonia, and have generally succeeded. Athens'
fierce opposition to Macedonian statehood is based on disputed ethnic territory but essentially reflects domestic political needs . . . ."[131] Intense competition, due to a one-seat majority in the parliament,[132] caused politicians
to outbid each other in proposing anti-Macedonia policies. The elections of

October 1993 brought socialist Andreas Papandreou to power, and he immediately asserted that Greece would close its border to Macedonia if a name change did not occur.[133] One key to Papandreou's recent success was his newfound popularity with the Greek Orthodox Church, which supported a hard-line policy toward Macedonia.[134] Macedonia was only allowed to enter the United Nations under the name of the Former Yugoslav Republic of Macedonia. Greece only relented and removed its embargo in 1995 once Macedonia changed its flag.[135]

The other approaches cannot provide as good an explanation than one focusing on Greek nationalism and ethnic enmities. Given Greece's alleged vulnerability to Macedonian irredentism, it should have opposed Serbian irredentism toward Bosnia, but it did not.[136] Likewise, Macedonia did not threaten Greece militarily, but Serbia might have since it inherited most of Yugoslavia's armed forces. The other components of threat—proximity, offensive capability (supporting opposition movements within Greece), and perceived intentions—suggest that Macedonia was a threat to Greece. However, domestic politics significantly influence the latter two indicators, and as discussed above, if Greece genuinely felt that its security was threatened, Greek demands would have been different.

Turkey

Given Turkey's antipathy toward Greece, it is not surprising that Turkey chose to support Greece's enemies. However, domestic politics may have driven Turkey's assistance to Bosnia and Macedonia as much or more than its rivalry with Greece.

Turkey pushed both NATO and the UN to give more support to Bosnia. Turkey designed and introduced a resolution calling for air strikes against the Bosnian Serbs, lifting the arms embargo against the Bosnian government, and confiscating Serbian heavy weapons.[137] Turkey donated more than 1,400 troops to UNPROFOR,[138] sent planes to help enforce the no-fly zone over Bosnia, and sent ships to enforce the embargo. Turkey hosted the foreign ministers' meeting of the Organization of the Islamic Conference in 1992, where it put Bosnia at the top of the agenda. Turkey was also among the first to recognize Macedonia, and began giving assistance in 1993.[139]

Why such active support for these two states? There are two competing explanations: enmity with Greece and the ethnic ties between Turkey and

Bosnia's Muslims. Rivalry with Greece helps to explain Turkish policy toward Macedonia. Given their history and the ongoing conflict over Cyprus, Turkey probably does seek out opportunities to frustrate the Greeks, and vice versa. Because the Greeks were obsessed with Macedonia, it is not surprising that Turkey assisted the Macedonians.

The better explanation for Turkish support for Bosnia is domestic politics. First, the Turkish people more intensely feel ties to minorities in Orthodox states and in areas once part of the Ottoman Empire.[140] The Bosnians fit both categories. Second, Bosnians and Turkish citizens have similar, relaxed attitudes toward Islam.[141] Because Turkey's citizens felt these bonds with the Bosnians, they pressured the government to support Bosnia.[142] Turkey has faced the difficult problem of maintaining a secular polity in the face of increasingly popular Islamic parties. During much of the Yugoslav conflict, a coalition government, including parties representing moderate Muslims, controlled the government. Even the Social Democrats who were more concerned with secular governance realized "that a lack of concern about Bosnia would hasten their political decline."[143]

Realism does provide similar predictions as ethnic ties in this case. The greatest threat to Turkey in this region is Greece, and Turkish foreign policy in this case aimed to thwart Greece's objectives and to assist Greece's enemies. Vulnerability is unclear here because supporting Bosnia and Macedonia before they were recognized as states is puzzling from this perspective as Turkey is vulnerable to separatism. However, once these two entities can be considered states, Turkey's support of their territorial integrity supports the vulnerability claims.

The United States

The United States moved from playing almost no role in the conflict to becoming the dominant actor, forcing the Bosnians and Croats to get along, leading airstrikes, and, finally, mediating the Dayton Accords.[144] The Bush Administration considered the conflict to a European affair, and gave primary responsibility for managing the conflict to the European Community. Bill Clinton promised to do more to help when he ran for President in 1992. Although his initial policies fell short of his promises, his administration eventually escalated American involvement from encouraging sanctions and enforcing a no-fly zone to bombing Serb positions and negotiating the Dayton Accords. Analysts explain American foreign policy by focusing on the lack of compelling strategic interests, conflicts with and deferring to allies, and the desire to avoid casualties. Ethnic politics did not strongly shape American behavior toward Yugoslavia, with one notable exception—the Greek-American lobby significantly influenced policy toward Macedonia.

Former Secretary of State James Baker's memoir makes clear that three factors drove American policy: "There was never any thought at that time of using U.S. ground troops in Yugoslavia—the American people would never have supported it. . . . The Bush administration felt comfortable with the EC's taking responsibility for handling the crisis in the Balkans. The conflict seemed to be one the EC could manage. . . . Our vital interests were not at stake."[145] Neither Bush nor Clinton wanted to commit ground troops and thereby risk American casualties. For Bush, the Yugoslavia conflict broke out very shortly after the Gulf War. For Clinton, much of the Yugoslavia conflict occurred after the debacle in Somalia, where the loss of less than twenty Rangers caused the United States to bail out. Further, the American military strongly opposed involvement in Yugoslavia.[146] A second important constraint was the desire to defer to the Europeans. During the Bush administration, it was felt that this was a European problem and that they should and could handle it. Once British and French troops were placed in harm's way as UN peacekeepers, Clinton frequently had to backtrack from promises to use force due to British and French resistance. Because their soldiers' lives were at stake, and American lives were not, it was quite difficult for the United States to overcome the opposition of its allies.[147] Finally, it was not clear what American interests were in the conflict. Baker, as cited above, flatly denied the existence of strategic interests in Yugoslavia. Now that Yugoslavia was not an ally against the Soviet bloc, it was less important to the United States.

The turning point in American foreign policy was the spring and summer of 1995. Clinton promised its NATO allies that the U.S. would commit 25,000 troops to facilitate the withdrawal of UN peacekeepers if the decision was made to pull these troops, primarily French and British, out of Bosnia.[148] Once this commitment was made and once the Bosnian Serbs briefly held UN troops hostage, the United States faced a choice. Either the U.S. could commit these troops to help withdraw the UN forces under fire, or it could more actively negotiate an agreement, which would then be enforced by 25,000 troops. Because this commitment was to help NATO allies, Clinton could then defend more aggressive action in Bosnia as part of America's commitment to NATO, and, therefore, such actions would be in America's strategic interests.[149] It is important to note that the fall of several safe areas, most importantly Srebrenica, increased American interest and support for more assertive action.

Where does ethnic politics fit into all of this? Ethnic ties did not play much of a role in American foreign policy toward Bosnia, but shaped policy toward Macedonia. Croatian-Americans pushed President Bush to recognize Croatia, threatening not to vote for him if he did not grant recognition.[150] Serbian-Americans protested American support for Bosnia. Muslim groups protested the weak and erratic support that characterized American policy until late summer 1995. "Individual members [of Congress] were driven by ethnic constituents,"[151] but because each group had ties to more than a few Representatives, the overall effect was to cancel each other out. Since none of these groups, by themselves, was large or well organized, they could not influence politicians much.[152]

The influence of the Greek-American lobby indicates that ethnic ties can shape foreign policy if the ethnic group is well organized, has access to decisionmakers, and is focused on a particular objective. Greek-Americans supported Greece's opposition to Macedonia, including denying it recognition. When the U.S. was deciding whether to recognize Slovenia, Croatia, Bosnia, and Macedonia, President Bush "was put on notice by the powerful Greek-American lobby that it would work against the president's reelection if the United States recognized Macedonia."[153] The U.S. recognized Bosnia, Croatia, and Slovenia in spring 1992, but refused to recognize Macedonia, even though it met the Badinter Commission's standards. Clinton, too, delayed recognition, finally announcing on February 9, 1994 that the U.S. would recognize Macedonia. However, Clinton changed his mind within a month due to pressure from the Greek-American lobby. Senator Paul Sarbanes, Representative Michael Bilirakis, and powerful Greek-Americans all pushed Clinton not to recognize Macedonia. Indeed, Bilirakis wrote a bill that would forever prevent the U.S. from having diplomatic relations with Macedonia.[154]

The concern for NATO suggests that some strategic concerns shaped American policy. However, the adjusted realist model cannot explain American policy since it is indeterminate. None of the actors seriously threatened the United States. Still, the spread of conflict to Greece and Turkey could pose a threat to the United States, but Bosnia never really threatened to spill over to other states. Kosovo was always thought to present that possibility, which explains American threats to Serbia in 1992[155] and actions in 1999.

Vulnerability cannot account for American policy since the U.S. did not face a serious separatist threat. This is ironic since the U.S. was the most devout defender of the principle of territorial integrity throughout the conflict.

Others

Other countries listed in the tables below tended to follow the patterns of countries discussed above. Countries with largely Islamic populations acted like Turkey and gave considerable support to Bosnia. Austria and Italy acted much like Germany. Albania and Bulgaria perceived their kin to be at risk and acted accordingly.

Aside from Turkey, Iran lent perhaps the most energetic support to Bosnia. Iran sent weapons and ammunition, facilitated the recruitment of volunteers (veterans of Lebanon's and Afghanistan's wars),[156] and led the Islamic community in criticizing the United Nations. Egypt, Malaysia, Saudi Arabia, and others gave assistance as well. For Iran, this conflict served to emphasize the divisions between the Islamic world and the West. For more secular countries with largely Islamic populations, public opinion compelled leaders to take strong stands against Serbia and for Bosnia.[157] Ignoring the public's support of Bosnia would have strengthened the Islamic fundamentalists that several of these states faced.

Austria and Italy focused their efforts in support of Slovenia and Croatia, and played a much lesser role during the Bosnian conflict. Austria and Italy, like Germany, were among the first to push for recognition of Croatia and Slovenia. Austria introduced resolutions and pushed for action both within the Conference for Security and Cooperation in Europe and the United Nations Security Council. While Austria did not face any serious conflict of its own, separatism was rising in Italy, so support for Croatia and Slovenia conflicts with the vulnerability argument. Realists could claim that Serbia/Yugoslavia was a threat to both, and the independence of Slovenia and Croatia would create a buffer between the most threatening state to the East, Serbia, and themselves. Of course, supporting Bosnia and Macedonia as aggressively as they supported the other two secessionist republics would have also weakened their adversary. Yet neither Austria nor Italy were as energetic in their support of Bosnia and Macedonia as they were of Croatia and Slovenia. Given the largely Catholic populations of these two states, it should not be surprising that they tended to take the same side as the Vatican throughout the conflict.

Albania has focused on the plight of ethnic Albanians next door, and Bulgaria has concentrated on Macedonia, a group it considers ethnically Bulgarian. Albania has supported ethnic Albanians in Kosovo and Macedonia. Given the weakness of Albania's political system, the government has had few resources to give to its kin. However, the government's breakdown in 1997 and the seizing of guns from its armories resulted in the arming of the Kosovo Liberation Army [KLA]. In the spring of 1999, Albania ceded control over its airspace to the NATO forces bombing Serbia. Exactly when Albania became a base for the KLA is not clear, but during the most recent strife, it became quite clear that the KLA were free to operate quite openly in Albania.

Given Greek claims on Albanian territory, Albania should not be supporting either the secession of Kosovo or attempting to annex it. Clearly, Greece and Serbia present the most severe threats to Albania, so it makes sense that it supports separatists within Serbia, but Macedonia could have been Albania's ally against the twin menaces they face. Instead, Albania has risked a good relationship with Macedonia due to the plight of Albanians in Macedonia.

Bulgaria was first to recognize Macedonia. It has tried to help develop Macedonia's economy to bypass Greece's stranglehold. Bulgaria considers Macedonian to be a dialect of Bulgarian, and that Macedonians are ethnically Bulgarian. This does lead to some conflict between the two countries, but there are groups within Macedonia that want it to be annexed to Bulgaria. This view of Macedonia as ethnic kin produces predictions that dovetail with realist ones. Macedonia is both kin and potential ally against the greater threats of Greece and Serbia, so support for Macedonia and opposition to Greece does not discriminate between realist and ethnic political explanations. Vulnerability cannot explain Bulgaria's policies because its groups at risk are not separatist, so Bulgaria is not very constrained.

Applying the Competing Arguments

Because of the complexity of this conflict, it is harder to apply some of the hypotheses developed in chapter 2. Since Bosnian separatists were seceding from Bosnia as it seceded from Yugoslavia, it is less than clear who are the separatists and who are the host states from the standpoint of supporting international norms. Likewise, the relative power of the various actors is hard to determine because the different actors inherited parts of Yugoslavia's military and economic capabilities. Even understanding the ethnic ties in play here is not simple since there are a variety of identities that might matter.

Applying Realism

To consider realist arguments, we need to assess which countries posed the most significant security threats to whom. Before war broke out in 1991, Yugoslavia did not pose a dangerous threat to its neighbors, nor was it a significant ally of anyone. Since Yugoslavia was not a part of NATO or the Warsaw Pact, no country depended upon it for their security. Once the Berlin Wall fell, Yugoslavia played an even lesser role, as countries in the region focused on the intentions of the United States and NATO. Still, Yugoslavia was stronger than many of its neighbors and certainly was more threatening than any one of its constituent republics. The Yugoslav army was stronger than anything Slovenia, Croatia, Bosnia, or Macedonia could throw at any external enemy. None of the separatist republics had a significant ability to engage in offensive military actions or to intervene in the politics of neighboring states, even to throw support to separatist movements, with the possible exception of Macedonia. However, as discussed above, Greece's reactions were not those a realist would predict.

Consequently, at the outbreak of the conflict, most states, particularly Yugoslavia's neighbors, should have supported separatists that would weaken Yugoslavia's ability to pose a threat. This expectation is partially met by nearly all states within the region: Albania, Austria, Bulgaria, Hungary, and Italy. These states supported some of the separatist republics, but did not support every seceding republic. Realism cannot account for this inconsistency. Austria, Hungary, and Italy supported the separatist movements, Slovenia and Croatia, that could pose the most significant threat if they successfully seceded. Slovenia and Croatia had the most modern and developed economies, and they were the closest to these supporters. On the other hand, helping such states might create potential friends and a buffer zone between Serbia on one side and Austria and Italy on the other. Realists would argue that as long as the enemy's capabilities decline, the effect on intentions is relatively unimportant. Still, the following question goes unanswered: why did these countries give much less support Macedonia and Bosnia as this would weaken Serbia further, as well as lessen Croatia's ability to pose a threat?

Relative threat cannot account for the reactions of the more powerful states, as none of the actors within the conflict posed any kind of threat beyond the region. Realists cannot not make determinate predictions about American, British, French, German, or Russian foreign policy toward Yugoslavia, because the Balkans mattered much less to these countries in 1991 than they did in 1914. Since none of the major powers had committed to the defense of Yugoslavia or of any of its component republics, none were motivated by the potential loss of other allies if they did not come to the aid of one or more Yugoslav republics. Outside actors were not tied to each as if they were in 1914.[158]

During the conflict's second stage, realists would expect that neighbors would generally support Serbia's enemies as Serbia inherited most of the Yugoslav Armed Forces, and therefore presented a greater threat than the other republics. Further, since Serbia was actively supporting separatism in its neighbors, it was viewed as having hostile intentions. Again, support for the seceding republics was more selective than realism would have predicted, as Austria, Hungary, and Italy were much less supportive of Bosnia and Macedonia than they were of Slovenia and Croatia. Most puzzling is that none of these countries gave significant assistance to separatists within Serbia. Instead of supporting the Hungarians of Vojvodina, Hungary limited its support for the anti-Serb coalition, essentially considering their kin to be hostages held by Serbia. Likewise, support for the Albanians of Kosovo was much less than one would expect, given the threat Serbia presented.

Realists would argue that alignment decisions would also depend upon other adversaries within the region, and that states might choose to align with certain former Yugoslavia republics against these other enemies. Romania may have supported Serbia, or at least, been ambivalent about Serbia because Romania may feel more threatened by Hungary because of their tense relationship over the condition of ethnic Hungarians residing in Romania. Likewise, Greece may have supported Serbia because they faced one or more common foes — Turkey and perhaps Bulgaria and Macedonia. However, even these alignment choices are in large part based on histories and politics of ethnic ties and enmities — Hungarians versus Romanians, Greeks versus Turks, and the like.

TABLE 5.1 Realism and Yugoslavia's Disintegration

Country	Power Relative to Yugoslavia/ Serbia	Which State or Group Is Threat	Neighbors of Yugoslavia	Predicted Policy	Actual Policy
Albania	Weaker	Yugoslavia, then Serbia	Yes	Support all seceding from Yugoslavia	**Supported Albanians in Kosovo** *and Macedonia*
Austria	Weaker	Yugoslavia, then Serbia	Yes	Support all seceding from Yugoslavia	**Supported Croatia and Slovenia***
Bulgaria	Weaker	Yugoslavia, then Serbia	Yes	Support all seceding from Yugoslavia	**Supported Macedonia and Serbia's enemies**
France	Stronger	No security threats	No	Indeterminate	Supported Yugoslavia, then Serbs, then Bosnia
Germany	Stronger	No security threats	No	Indeterminate	Supported Croatia and Slovenia
Greece	Weaker, Stronger than Serbia	Turkey, Macedonia	Yes	Support enemies of Turkey, Oppose Macedonia	**Support for Serbs; Oppose Macedonia**
Hungary	Weaker	Yugoslavia, then Serbia	Yes	Support all seceding from Yugoslavia	**Support for Croatia and Slovenia,*** *changing to ambivalent*
Iran	Stronger	No security threats	No	Indeterminate	Supported Bosnia
Italy	Stronger	Yugoslavia	Yes	Support all seceding from Yugoslavia	**Supported Croatia and Slovenia***
Romania	Stronger	Hungary	Yes	Indeterminate	Ambivalent, Neutral
Russia	Stronger	No security threats	No	Indeterminate	Support for Yugoslavia, then Serbs
Turkey	Stronger	Yugoslavia then Serbia, Greece	No	Support Bosnia, Macedonia	**Supported Bosnia, Macedonia**
U.S.	Stronger	No security threats	No	Indeterminate	Ambivalence, changed to supported Croatia, Bosnia

*Indicates that country did not support Bosnia or Macedonia
Bold indicates correct predictions
Italics indicates incorrect predictions

Overall, realism, with its focus on power and security, can explain some of the policies states followed during the conflict. However, realism cannot provide clear predictions about what actors outside the region might do, as they faced no clear threat. Further, states made choices about which separatist movements to support, and their selective support, including efforts by Albania, Austria, Hungary, and Italy poses challenges for realist arguments.

Vulnerability and International Organizations

If fears of vulnerability motivate states, vulnerable states would have followed consistent policies. Such states would have supported Yugoslavia's territorial integrity and then the integrity of its constituent republics once Yugoslavia's disintegration was a *fait accompli*. The United States, perhaps more than any other country, took such a stand, supporting Yugoslavia's unity until it was no longer possible, and then supporting Bosnia's territorial integrity for most of the conflict. Of course, vulnerability cannot account for this, since the U.S. faces no significant secessionist threats. Great Britain and France, who have experienced some separatism (Northern Ireland and Scotland, and Corsica respectively), supported Yugoslavia's integrity, but quickly accepted various plans to partition Bosnia. Russia backed the Bosnian Serbs despite its secessionist conflict in Chechnya and potential ones elsewhere. Of the thirteen observations in this case, vulnerability predicts four wrongly out of six, is indeterminate in six, and cannot really address Romania's policies, either. The norm of territorial integrity did not bind states as they supported the secessionist movements they liked and opposed those that they did not like.

However, the timing of the European Community's recognition policy suggests one constraint that the various actors felt: they did not want to set a precedent that might encourage the Soviet Union's disintegration.[159] After the coup in August 1991, the Soviet Union fell apart, and, consequently, fears of encouraging such an outcome no longer restrained Germany nor the rest of the EC.

Did the involvement of international organizations limit external support for the various secessionists? Most clearly, the United Nations arms embargo, which the North Atlantic Treaty Organization enforced, decreased the amount of arms reaching Bosnia and Croatia, though arms continued to flow. Yet, the United States condoned arms transfers from Iran through Cro-

TABLE 5.2 Vulnerability and Yugoslavia's Disintegration

Country	Vulnerability	Vulnerability Predictions	Actual Policy
Albania	High	Support for Yugoslavia, then new states	*Supported Albanians in Kosovo and Macedonia*
Austria	Low	No Prediction	Supported Croatia and Slovenia
Bulgaria	Low	No Prediction	Supported Macedonia and Serbia's enemies
France	High	Support for Yugoslavia, then new states	*Supported Yugoslavia, then for Serbs, then Bosnia*
Germany	Low	No Prediction	Supported Croatia and Slovenia
Greece	Low	No Prediction	Supported Serbs; Oppose Macedonia
Hungary	Low	No Prediction	Supported for Croatia and Slovenia, changing to ambivalent
Iran	High	Support for Yugoslavia, then new states	**Supported Bosnia**
Italy	High	Support for Yugoslavia, then new states	*Supported Croatia and Slovenia*
Romania	High	Support for Yugoslavia, then new states	Ambivalent, Neutral
Russia	High	Support for Yugoslavia, then new states	**Supported Yugoslavia,** *then Serbs*
Turkey	High	Support for Yugoslavia, then new states	Supported Bosnia and Macedonia*
U.S.	Low	No Prediction	Ambivalence, changed to Supported Croatia, Bosnian Muslims

* Indicates that initial support ran counter to vulnerability, but subsequent support for their integrity supports the vulnerability hypothesis.
Bold indicates correct predictions
Italics indicates incorrect predictions

atia to Bosnia despite its membership in both NATO and the UN's Security Council. Still, the arms embargo impeded the United States, as domestic actors wanted to give more assistance to the Bosnians. Significantly, international organizations themselves supported certain separatists, enabling them to continue their fight or maintain their holdings. The introduction of UN peacekeepers into Croatia essentially ratified the Serb conquest of one-third of Croatia, which Croatia altered forcefully in August 1995. The expanding UN role in Bosnia from providing food and medicine to guaranteeing safe areas was significant in maintaining the Bosnian regime and its ability to separate from Yugoslavia. Of course, one can interpret this as support for an existing state as it fought off separatists (the Bosnian Serbs).

Apart from direct assistance or blocking such support, international organizations also served as forums for supporters of various separatists. Because of hard bargaining over the EC integration project, Germany could leverage the entire European Community into recognizing Slovenia and Croatia. Without the European Community and the coinciding dispute concerning the Maastricht accords, other members might not have recognized the seceding republics. Of course, the EC also strengthened Greece as it sought to prevent Macedonia's recognition. This particular international organization did not consistently support secessionists or host states. The United Nations enhanced Russia's ability to support the Bosnian Serbs by opposing expansion of UN intervention. The United States and its allies were only able to use force extensively once decisionmaking was moved from the UN to NATO in the summer of 1995, cutting Russia out of the loop. Therefore, international organizations mattered as they constrained some states and empowered others. Still, no international organization could develop a consistent policy during the crisis due in part to the complexity of the conflict (groups seeking to secede from seceding republics), and in part to bargaining among member nations, which generated the international organizations' policies.

Besides stressing international organizations, neoliberal arguments consider reciprocity to be an important influence on states' behavior. Reciprocity suggests that a previous history of cooperation will lead to continued cooperation, while a past of conflict would lead to more conflict. How does this play out in the international relations of Yugoslavia's disintegration? Germany had a previous relationship of cooperation with Yugoslavia, but was the first to support Slovenia and Croatia. Certainly, within the European Community, ongoing efforts to develop a common foreign policy caused its members to cooperate with each other over the crisis. Bitterness over Germany's assertiveness and the EC's failed efforts has diminished the likelihood of future foreign policy cooperation. On the other hand, while the West and Russia were creating a variety of cooperative efforts in other issue areas, such as arms control, trade, and financial assistance, cooperation during the Yugoslav conflict was less consistent. Despite the increasing web of interactions between the United States and Russia, cooperation during the Yugoslav wars was difficult at best, as Russia tended to support Serbia, while the U.S. tended to support Bosnia. The most damning evidence for reciprocity arguments is that the efforts at international cooperation were inconsistent, as the various external actors cooperated and conflicted with each other. While resentments developed, states did not reciprocate the past moves of the other external actors.[160]

Applying Ethnic Ties

The theory of ethnic politics and foreign policy predicts that domestic political imperatives motivate states, and that states give support to the side with which the important constituencies had ethnic ties or against the side with whom the relevant supporters had ethnic enmities. This conflict is complex, in part, because there are multiple ethnic identities at work: religious, racial, and linguistic. The Slovenes and the Croats are primarily Catholic. The Serbs are primarily Orthodox. Bosnia is multiethnic, but the Muslim community has dominated the government, and its enemies defined Bosnia as an Islamic movement, so we can interpret support given to Bosnia as support for the Muslims. Macedonia consists of both Muslim Albanians and orthodox Macedonians, but the latter govern Macedonia. Most frequently, the various identities reinforce each other, as Albanians speak a different language than Serbs or Macedonians and follow a different religion as well. Where the identities do not reinforce each other, elites create distinctions. Much of the region's population is Slavic, but the Serbs were relatively successful in defining themselves as Slavs and the Bosnians as "Turks." In general, we expected states with Catholic constituencies to support Slovenia and Croatia, states with Muslim constituencies to support Bosnia, and states with Orthodox constituencies to support Serbia. Likewise, states with Slavic populations should support the Serbs more than the Bosnian Muslims or the Albanians. Because Slavic populations and Orthodoxy tend to coincide, states characterized by these populations should be less confused and more consistent than others.

As Table 5.3 illustrates, these expectations were fulfilled, and the theory

TABLE 5.3 Ethnic Politics and Yugoslavia's Disintegration

Country	Ethnic Ties To:	Ethnic Competition	Ethnic Politics Predictions	Actual Policy
Albania	Albanians in Kosovo and Macedonia	High	Support Albanians in Kosovo and Macedonia	**Supported Albanians in Kosovo and Macedonia**
Austria	Slovenes, Croats	High	Support Croatia and Slovenia	**Supported Croatia and Slovenia**
Bulgaria	Enmity with Serbs, Ties with Macedonians	High	Support Macedonia and Serbia's enemies	**Supported Macedonia and Serbia's enemies**
France	Croats, Slovenes	Low	Support Croatia and Slovenia	*Supported Yugoslavia, then Serbs, then Bosnia*
Germany	Croats, Slovenes	High	Support Croatia and Slovenia	**Supported Croatia and Slovenia**
Greece	Ties with Serbs, Enmities with Macedonia	High	Support Serbs; Oppose Macedonia	**Supported Serbs; Opposed Macedonia**
Hungary	Ties to Croats, Enmities with Serbs	High	Support Croatia and Slovenia	**Supported Croatia and Slovenia**, *changing to ambivalent*
Iran	Muslims	High	Support Bosnia	**Supported Bosnia**
Italy	Croats, Slovenes	High	Support Croatia and Slovenia	**Supported Croatia and Slovenia**
Romania	Serbs	High	Support Yugoslavia then Serbia	*Ambivalent, Neutral*
Russia	Serbs	High	Support Yugoslavia then Serbia	**Supported Yugoslavia, then Serbs**
Turkey	Muslims	High	Support Bosnia	**Supported Bosnia, Macedonia**
U.S.	weak to all sides	Low	Ambivalence or neutrality	**Ambivalence**, *changed to supported Croatia, Bosnia*

Bold indicates correct predictions
Italics indicates incorrect predictions

of ethnic politics and foreign policy provided the most accurate predictions of the three competing explanations. Croatia's and Slovenia's most energetic supporters were countries where politicians relied significantly on the Catholic vote. However, not all Catholic countries gave support to these two republics, as many stayed out and France assisted Serbia at times. Orthodox countries, including Greece and Russia, tended to support Serbia and the Bosnian Serbs. Muslim countries were among the distant states to get involved, giving diplomatic and military assistance to the Bosnian government. Of the thirteen countries examined, ten acted in ways predicted by the theory of ethnic politics and foreign policy. Only France, Romania, and the United States behaved in unexpected ways, if one focuses narrowly on ethnic ties alone. France supported Yugoslavia and then Serbia against the Catholic Slovenes and Croats, although France's positions were not consistent during the Bosnian conflict. Romania's largely Orthodox population suggests that Romania would have supported Serbia, but instead, Romania policy vacillated between ambivalence and neutrality due to Western pressures to support sanctions. Domestic politics permitted Romanian leaders to play a lesser role in this conflict, since they could focus the attention of their supporters on more salient ethnic issues, particularly the Hungarian minority in Romania and the irredentism toward Moldova. Ethnic politics predicts the initial ambivalence of American foreign policy, as no leader depended solely or crucially on voters with ties to one combatant. What the theory of ethnic politics and foreign policy cannot readily predict or explain are the more active and interventionist steps the U.S. took later in the conflict, including bombing the Serbs to the bargaining table.

The theory of ethnic politics and foreign policy also makes predictions about the behavior of the combatants, as they try to identify themselves in ways that maximize domestic and international support. The Serbs and Croats went to great efforts domestically and internationally to define their fight as one between Western Civilization and Islamic fundamentalism. The Serbs also sought to define the conflict as one between Slavs and "Turks." The former strategy could play well in Western Europe, while the latter was aimed at Russia. These strategies mattered, as important actors in the West emphasized the Islamic-Christian division in the conflict, weakening support for Bosnia.[161] The Serb emphasis on their Slavic identity was a tactic to gain Russian support, and it armed Russian nationalists with more criticisms of the Yeltsin regime. The Bosnian government was left in an awkward position. Emphasizing Islam as a binding force would alienate Serbs and

Croats who still supported it, and such a strategy would alarm the West, while attracting support from the Islamic states. Ultimately, Bosnia tried to have it both ways, as it appealed to support from the Middle East and elsewhere at the same time, it reemphasized its secular identity. The Macedonians were stuck, as they could not identify themselves as anything but Macedonians for their domestic audience, no matter what Greece demanded.[162] The Macedonia-Greece conflict illustrates the dynamics and dilemmas leaders face because ethnic ties and political competition create very strong incentives and constraints.

Clearly, the leaders of the seceding republics knew that their identity mattered for both domestic and international audiences, and were quite careful in trying to emphasize those aspects that would lead to greater support. Once again, though, it becomes clear than any effort to define oneself not only attracts support but also enemies. The efforts of the Serbs to define the conflict as a religious one, including the destruction of mosques, attracted Russian assistance, but also caused other states to give more aid to the Bosnian government.

Summary

The previous case studies suggested that vulnerability was a poor predictor of foreign policy, that realism was somewhat better although often indeterminate, and that ethnic politics accounts better for the behavior of states than the competing explanation. This chapter indicates that these findings hold true today, for both developed democracies and states undergoing transitions to democracy.

While ethnic politics explains many actors' policies better than vulnerability or realism, it is also important to note that ethnic politics also provides a better explanation of international relations of Yugoslavia's demise than simply the "Clash of Civilizations" or affective motivations.[163] If either the Clash thesis or the affective argument was correct, then all Orthodox states would have supported Serbia, all Muslim states would have supported Bosnia, and all Catholic countries would have supported Croatia. Other ethnic identities came into play, so that Bulgaria opposed both Greece and Serbia, despite the dominance of Orthodox Christianity in each. Likewise, Romania should have strongly sided with Serbia, but did not. Similarly, France did not strongly support Croatia at the outset, as its politicians did not rely strongly on appeals to Catholic voters. Where politicians did require such support, such as Austria and Italy, they gave much more support to Croatia. While no Muslim country gave serious support to Serbia, not all Muslim countries gave material assistance to Bosnia.

Finally, it is important to note that ethnic politics is not new, as the reactions of outsider actors to the Yugoslavia conflict were quite similar to how states behaved toward the Congo Crisis and the Nigerian Civil War. Leaders supported those with whom their constituents had ethnic ties, opposed those with whom a history of ethnic enmity was shared, and were ambivalent or neutral if ethnic ties existed with more than one side.

6 Quantitative Analyses of Ethnic Conflict's International Relations

In the previous chapters, studies of secessionist crises indicate that ethnic politics more consistently and more powerfully conditions states' behavior than the other explanations. However, one could wonder how significant these results are or whether they apply beyond secessionist conflicts to other kinds of conflicts. This chapter, by using data from the case studies and from the Minorities at Risk [MAR] Datasets, addresses these concerns.

First, simple cross-tabulations indicate which factors produce significant correlations using data from the case studies in the preceding chapters. Second, basic trends in international support of ethnic groups in the 1990s suggest that fears of precedents, an expectation of the vulnerability thesis, were not well placed. Third, the MAR data allows us to determine which groups are more likely to receive support, telling us something about the competing hypotheses. Finally, I evaluate whether particular kinds of states are more likely to support ethnic groups at risk. Because the ethnic ties approach is difficult to operationalize with the available data, the clearest findings of the analyses do more to challenge vulnerability and realist arguments than to lend support to the ethnic ties argument.

The Findings of the Case Studies

To be clear, any statistical findings from the case studies have limited value, since there are relatively few cases and their selection was not random.

However, I did not choose the cases according to the existence of ethnic ties, but focused instead on which countries took an active role. In the tables in this section, I use the data from the case studies to determine the relationships between various factors and the foreign policies of states. For the actual foreign policy, I use the foreign policy of each state for most of the crisis. For instance, Belgium would be coded as supporting secessionists during the Congo Crisis since it supported Katanga for almost the entire conflict. In essence, the following tables summarize the tables from chapters 3, 4, and 5.

It is impressive that table 6.1 indicates that ethnic ties are highly correlated (.678) with states' foreign policies.[1] Even without considering political competition, ethnic ties serve as an excellent predictor of the foreign policies of states toward secessionist conflicts.

Similar cross-tabulations indicate that realist hypotheses do not hold well across the cases. Table 6.2 indicates that neighbor states do not behave any differently than non-neighbors, while, table 6.3 indicates that relative power does not seem to have a clear impact on states' reactions toward secessionist crises.

Later in this chapter, I develop indicators for the relative power of states for the multivariate analyses. Here, I simply compare each state's power in the case studies to the host state and code each external actor as relatively weaker or stronger than the host state. Table 6.3 suggests that relative power, by itself, does not say much about what states were likely to do.

Since relative power, proximity, and other factors are components of threat, we need to consider how the various components together correlate

TABLE 6.1 Ethnic Ties and Foreign Policy

Actual Foreign Policy	Secessionists	Both	Host State	Neither
Supported Secessionists	18	1	1	0
Supported Both (Ambivalence)	0	2	1	1
Supported Host State	2	0	15	0
Neither (Neutrality)	0	1	0	1

Pearson Chi square of 59.36, Cramer's V of .678

TABLE 6.2 Neighbors and Foreign Policy

Actual Foreign Policy	Does Potential Supporter Neighbor the Host State?	
	No	Yes
Supported Secessionists	13	7
Supported Both (Ambivalence)	3	1
Supported Host State	14	3
Neither (Neutrality)	1	1

Pearson Chi square of 1.892, Cramer's V of .210

TABLE 6.3 Relative Power and Foreign Policy

Actual Foreign Policy	Relative Power of Potential Supporter Compared to Host State	
	Weaker	Stronger
Supported Secessionists	10	10
Supported Both (Ambivalence)	1	3
Supported Host State	9	8
Neither (Neutrality)	2	0

Pearson Chi square of 3.037, Cramer's V of .266

with foreign policy. I develop an indicator of overall threat by subtracting the level of threat a separatist group presents to the outside actor (0 for none, 1 for moderate, 2 for high) from level of threat posed by the host state. Then I subtract 1 if the outside actor is stronger than the host state (so the host is less threatening), and add 1 if the host state is adjacent to the outside actor. This indicator ranges from zero to four, but is truncated in the cross-tabulations with the three highest levels of threat collapsed into one column.

TABLE 6.4 Threats and Foreign Policy

Actual Foreign Policy	Level of Threat Posed by Host State		
	Weak	Moderate	High
Supported Secessionists	6	6	8
Supported Both (Ambivalence)	2	2	0
Supported Host State	11	4	2
Neither (Neutrality)	0	1	1

Pearson Chi square of 8.857, Cramer's V of .321

I find even weaker correlations if I do not collapse it. Table 6.4 provides slightly better results.

Thus, in each test of the realist argument, there are weak relationships or none at all between realist variables and the foreign policies of states. Because this project initially focused on the other two arguments, I did not pick cases that would either support or challenge the realist approach so selection bias, while still a possibility, is not as problematic.

The vulnerability argument fared worst of all. Using the coding rules developed in chapter two and applied in the case studies, I simply code each

TABLE 6.5 Vulnerability and Foreign Policy

Actual Foreign Policy	Is Potential Supporter Vulnerable to Separatism	
	No	Yes
Supported Secessionists	5	15
Supported Both (Ambivalence)	2	2
Supported Host State	5	12
Neither (Neutrality)	1	1

Pearson Chi square of 1.377, Cramer's V of .179

actor as vulnerable to separatism or not and then cross-tabulate with the foreign policy of each state in each conflict. As table 6.5 indicates, vulnerability served as a poor predictor of how states reacted to the secessionist crises studied.

Together, these tables indicate that the findings of each of the case studies are consistent with the others. Ethnic ties are related to what countries do, realist variables are less helpful predictors of foreign policy, and that vulnerability frequently mis-predicts outcomes. Of course, the relationships may simply be artifacts of the selection of cases and of observations. Further, studying only secessionist crises omits most ethnic groups. To determine whether any of the three competing explanations applies more broadly, we need to examine the entire universe of ethnic conflict.

Trends in the International Relations of Ethnic Conflict

Only one of the three competing approaches makes strong assertions about the international relations of ethnic conflict over time — the vulnerability approach. Vulnerability theorists claim that precedents matter, and that if norms are violated, then the regime is likely to collapse, leading to greater support for ethnic groups.[2] The precedents set by the international recognition of the former Soviet Republics, Slovenia, Croatia, Bosnia, the Czech Republic, Slovakia, and Eritrea should not only have encouraged more groups to secede,[3] but also caused the breakdown in boundary norms worldwide. Given the number of secessionist movements that gained international support and became independent countries between 1991–1993, according to this logic, we should see an explosion in support for ethnic groups after 1993.

Using data collected by the Minorities at Risk project,[4] we can consider whether patterns of international support changed during the 1990s. Before discussing the coding of international support and presenting the 1990s patterns, I need to be clear about why I chose to use this dataset and what it contains.[5] The Minorities At Risk Dataset, Phase III, is currently the state of the art for ethnic conflict-related datasets. No other dataset currently in existence contains as much information about as many groups. While its focus on groups and on the domestic politics of ethnic conflict makes it harder to assess relationships between groups and external actors, the dataset provides enough information to test some of our ideas about the international relations of ethnic conflict.

MAR has as its unit of analysis individual ethnopolitical groups. The dataset includes only politically salient ethnic groups. Specifically, minorities "at risk" are defined as those ethnic groups that gain from or are hurt by systematic discriminatory treatment compared to other groups in the society; and/or groups that are the basis for political mobilization for the promotion of the group's interests. The dataset contains information for 275 groups. Groups are included if they meet the following criteria. Only groups in countries with 1995 populations larger than half a million; groups with populations of larger than one hundred thousand, or, if fewer, if the group exceeds one percent of at least one state's population are included. Groups are counted separately if they reside in more than one country as they meet the more general population criteria; and if the group is not an advantaged majority (advantaged minorities and disadvantaged majorities are included).[6]

The MAR raw data codes the level of support each ethnic group receives and from whom. Two sets of dependent variables can be created from this data: one set uses groups as the unit of analysis to consider what causes groups to receive support, and the other uses each potential supporter as the unit of analysis. For the former, I have developed two measures for inter-

TABLE 6.6 Coding Intensity of Support

---

0   No Support Received

1   Ideological Encouragement, Diffuse Support, Other Unspecified Support

2   Non-Military Financial Support, Access to External Communications, Markets, Transport, including the Hosting of Nonviolent Exile Organizations

3   Funds for Military Supplies, Provision of Military Equipment, Military Training in Exile, Advisory Military Personnel, Peace-keeping Observers, Sanctions Against Host Regime*

4   Blockades, Interdiction Against Regime, Cross-border Sanctuaries, Rescue Missions in Country, Cross-Border Raids in Support of Dissidents, Active Combat Units in Country.

---

*This last kind of support, sanctions against host, is included in the update of MAR for 1996, 1997, and 1998.

---

national support for each group: breadth and intensity. Breadth refers to how many countries supported a particular ethnic group. Intensity refers to the highest level of support a group receives from any one state.

Table 6.6 indicates the various forms of support countries might give to an ethnic group, and indicates how support is coded by level of intensity. While these are MAR labels, I have coded intensity of support in order of increasing cost, risk of war, and efficacy. For example, according to the MAR data, in 1994–95, Armenia gave Azerbaijan's Armenians military equipment and supplies, as well as access to external communications, markets, and transport. In addition, Russia gave them funds for military supplies and advisory military personnel. This group receives a score of 2 for the number of countries giving support, and a score of 3 for highest level of support (advisory military personnel).[7]

There are three shortcomings in this data. It is important to note that the data sheets have only four places to mark the countries giving support to a particular group and the level of support given, so with a few exceptions, the maximum number of supporters is four. This clearly leads to some undercounting, but only ten groups have at least four supporters in 1998, the highest year. Therefore, the actual effect of this coding problem should be quite small.[8] Second, some of codesheets lacked information about international support, so the total number of observations ranges from 251 to 267.[9] Finally, the data in the first half of the 1990s was collected by two-year periods and yearly in the latter half.

To consider vulnerability theorists' claims about precedents and norm violations, I graphed the frequencies of breadth and intensity of support received by groups throughout the 1990s: these graphs are displayed in figures 6.1 and 6.2. They indicate that there was no explosion in support for ethnic groups at risk. Groups did not get support from more states, nor did the intensity of support increase over time.

A different way to assess changes throughout the decade is to chart the changes in mean breadth and intensity of support. As figure 6.3 illustrates, very little changed in the levels of support groups received throughout the 1990s.

To directly consider the pattern of change throughout the decade, I subtracted the 1990–91 breadth and intensity data from the equivalent 1998 data. Figure 6.4 illustrates the frequencies of changes in breadth and intensity in the 1990s.

Figure 6.4 indicates that roughly as many groups lost support as gained it through the decade, and that most groups received the same level of

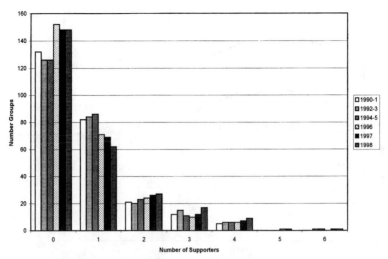

FIGURE 6.1 Trends in Breadth of Support Groups Received, 1990s

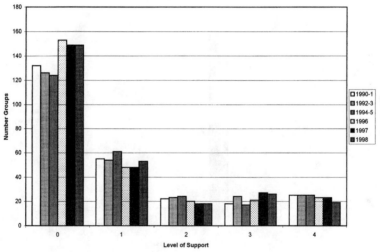

FIGURE 6.2 Trends in Intensity of Support Groups Received, 1990s

support at the beginning and at the end of the 1990s. The distribution in the figure appears to be distributed normally. This suggests that international support is stable, despite apparent changes in respect for international boundaries or the newfound desire to value the norm of self-determination

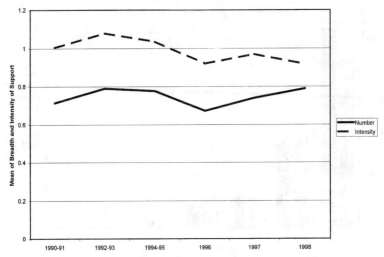

FIGURE 6.3 Mean Breadth and Intensity of Support Groups Received, 1990s

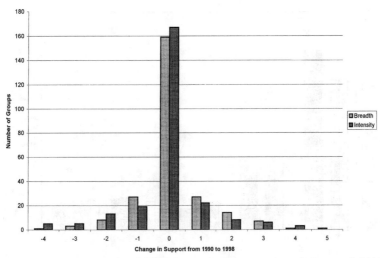

FIGURE 6.4 Changes in Breadth and Intensity of Support Groups Received, 1990s

over the norm territorial integrity. This should surprise vulnerability theorists. Assistance to the Baltic Republics, Eritrea, Slovenia, Croatia, Bosnia, Macedonia, and the division of Czechoslovakia between 1991 and 1993 should have challenged the boundary regime.[10] These attacks upon the norm of territorial integrity should have led to a cascade of support for groups.

Using the same raw data, I developed two other variables where the unit of analysis is the potential supporting country (for all countries with a population over one million): breadth and intensity. Intensity again ranges from zero to four, but the number of groups a state supports ranges from zero to thirty-seven countries, with the United States supporting the most groups. In the figures, I use data from three periods: 1990–91, 1994–95, and 1998.

Figure 6.5 indicates that more states gave support to ethnic groups as the decade progressed, but it is not clear that a trend exists. Figure 6.6 suggests that the intensity of support states gave did not change much throughout the decade. The biggest change is in the number of states that gave the second highest level of support. This may be due to a change in coding from the 1994–95 data to the 1998 data, as the Minorities At Risk project began to code sanctions against the regime as a relatively intense form of support (see table 6.6).

Again, I determined the mean levels of support as well as subtracting the 1990–91 indicators from the 1998 data to determine what kinds of changes took place throughout the 1990s, producing figures 6.7 and 6.8.

Figure 6.7 shows a slight increase in the mean number of groups countries supported, but very little change in the intensity of support states gave. As Figure 6.8 indicates, there was no systematic change in behavior. The frequencies again resemble a normal curve. If the vulnerability claims were correct, then we should see more states giving support to more groups and probably more intense support over time, but this is simply not the case.

What do these trends say about the other two competing approaches? For realism, these results may be unexpected. If states respond to relative power and to threats, then the collapse of some relatively strong and threatening states, and the creation of many weak states, should have led to some change in the patterns of international support. However, we see no such change over time. Still, the absence of a significant trend does not seriously challenge realism, as some states became relatively stronger while others weakened, washing each other out.

The stability in international support for ethnic groups does not challenge the theory of ethnic ties and foreign policy. If the leaders of a state start supporting a group, they are unlikely to change this policy, as the imperatives of domestic politics—ethnic ties and the composition of their constitu-

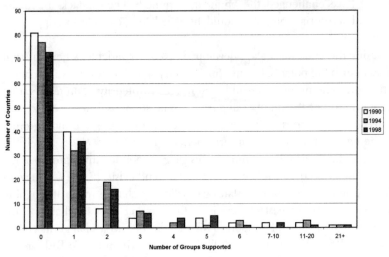

FIGURE 6.5 Trends in Number of Groups States Supported, 1990s

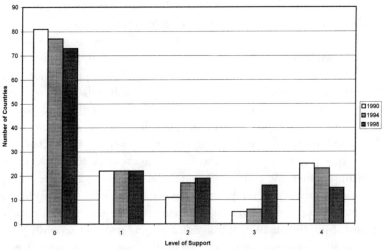

FIGURE 6.6 Trends in Intensity of Support Given by States, 1990s

ency—are unlikely to change in any systematic way. Of course, as groups engage in conflict, their cause becomes more important in the domestic politics of other states. As groups end their conflicts, their plight becomes

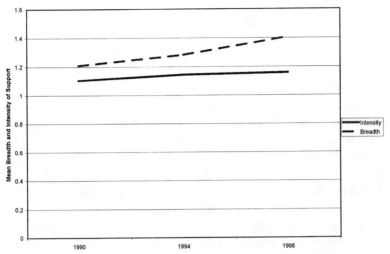

FIGURE 6.7 Mean Breadth and Intensity of Support States Gave, 1990s

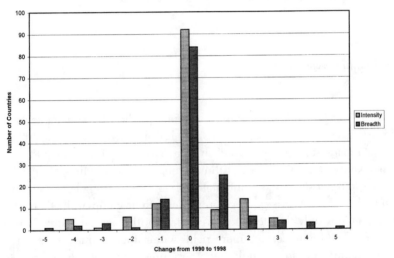

FIGURE 6.8 Changes in Breadth and Intensity of Support States Gave, 1990s

less salient elsewhere. Therefore, changes in group conflict may cause some change in international behavior. Tracking this relationship might be a useful direction for future research.

Which Ethnic Groups Receive Foreign Assistance?

There are four ways to assess quantitatively the international relations of ethnic conflict. Why do some groups get more support than others? Why do some states give more support than others? How are ethnic conflicts different from other conflicts? Why do some dyadic relationships matter while others do not? This chapter addresses only the first two approaches, as analysts have generally followed the third approach,[11] and the fourth approach is currently impossible with existing data.[12] In this section, I consider why some groups receive broader and more intense support than others, and in the subsequent section, I consider what attributes of states increase their likelihood of supporting ethnic groups in conflict.

First, I draw out testable hypotheses from the competing arguments. Some of these will come straight from chapter 2, while the dataset facilitates additional tests. Second, I discuss how I operationalize the concepts, using almost entirely Minorities at Risk data. Third, I present multivariate analyses to assess which group attributes influence the assistance they receive.

Testable Hypotheses

Vulnerability   While this argument generally predicts that vulnerable states are less likely to support separatism, a logical implication of this approach is that separatist groups are less likely to receive international support than other kinds of ethnic groups. Ethnic groups with such aims are greater threats to other states and to international norms governing boundaries because they seek to revise existing boundaries. Ethnic groups with other kinds of aspirations only threaten the government of the country within which they reside. Groups seeking more rights within their political system and groups competing for control of the government pose less of a threat to international norms and to the political stability of other countries.[13] Further, the vulnerability argument focuses on the development of a norm of territorial integrity,[14] which applies to the question of separatism and does not have direct implications for other kinds of ethnic conflict. Therefore,

H1: *Separatist groups are less likely to have many supporters and are less likely to receive intense support.*

A second implication of vulnerability is that states may be deterred from helping groups residing in highly vulnerable states. If states are concerned about the consequences of supporting an ethnic group, then they should be most concerned about supporting ethnic groups in states already characterized by a high degree of separatist activity. Supporting such a group is more likely to lead to the disintegration of the state, perhaps endangering regional stability. Therefore, if a state is compelled by whatever reason to give support, it will give relatively modest support. On the other hand, a group is more likely to receive support if its host state faces no other secessionist threats, since the likelihood of a spiraling of conflict beyond the immediate state is less likely. Thus,

H2: *Groups in highly vulnerable states are less likely to have many supporters and less likely to receive intense support.*

Third, states may be inhibited from supporting an ethnic group if it resides in a particularly troubled area. If a group resides in a country where the neighboring states are confronting separatist groups, then the danger of conflict spilling over is a significant risk. The heart of the vulnerability argument is that regional security concerns caused African states to support a prohibition against supporting secession.

H3: *When a host state neighbors states facing separatism, ethnic groups within the host state are less likely to have many supporters and less likely to receive intense support.*

Fourth, we should consider whether African ethnic groups are less likely to receive external assistance. Because the vulnerability argument was created with Africa in mind, we should test whether groups in Africa are treated differently than groups elsewhere. Vulnerability theorists would expect groups in Africa to receive less support due to the norm of territorial integrity that the Organization of African Unity established in 1964.

H4: *Ethnic groups in Africa are less likely to receive support than groups elsewhere.*

Power   If states ordinarily balance power by allying with weaker states and by mobilizing their resources (internal balancing), then it makes sense that weakening the strong states would also improve one's security. If an adversary has to fight or contain ethnic groups within its boundaries, then it will have fewer resources available to challenge other states. Further, if the supported ethnic group secedes, then the adversary loses territory, population, and perhaps even significant economic resources, thus lessening the adversary's relative power.

H5: Groups in stronger states are more likely to receive broad support and more likely to receive intense support.

However, some realists might make the opposite prediction — that ethnic groups in weaker states are more likely to receive broad and intense support. States may avoid supporting ethnic groups in more powerful states, as this is a relatively risky course of action. The powerful host state is more capable of reacting strongly, thus deterring states from supporting ethnic groups. Offensive realists argue that states are opportunistic and choose those strategies most likely to improve their situation.[15] Supporting ethnic groups within a more powerful adversary may not be worthwhile since the costs imposed on the enemy may not be as significant as the potential response. Instead, states may be more willing to support ethnic groups in weaker states because such states cannot respond. The example of Bangladesh is instructive, since India was already stronger than Pakistan, but still decided to divide its weaker adversary.

H6: Groups in weaker states are more likely to receive broad support and more likely to receive intense support.

Ethnic Politics   The first test of the impact of ethnic politics upon foreign policy is to those states where the ethnic group's kin has power. When an ethnic group has kin ruling a neighboring state,[16] we should expect that state to help the ethnic group. Because the kin dominates the state, we should expect the support to be intense.

H7: If a neighboring state is dominated by an ethnic group's kin, then that group is likely to receive external support, and that support is more likely to be intense.

The case studies indicate that the identities at stake matter. Therefore, we ought to consider whether the ethnic identity of a group shapes the amount of international support a group gets.[17] Identities vary in how widely they are shared. Clan or tribal identity is less likely to involve people in other states because such an identity is not shared very widely. Religion is perhaps the most widely shared identity, since many religions have adherents around the world. Consequently, events in Jerusalem matter to Jews in the United States, Muslims in Indonesia, and Catholics in Latin America. Religious identities overlap international boundaries much more so than linguistic groups and clans. If ethnic politics influences foreign policy, then we should expect groups that have ties to more people in more states to get broader support than those having ties to fewer people in fewer states.

To test this argument, we need to focus on what ethnically differentiates the group in question from the rest of the society. Many identities may help to identify an ethnic group, but only the differences between itself and its adversary are going to mobilize potential supporters elsewhere. If a group is of the same religion as those it is fighting, then religious identity is unlikely to cause outside actors to assist the group, as they will have ties to both sides. Only if the group is of a different religion will the religious affinities attract outside assistance.[18] Groups that are differentiated by a broader ethnic identity are more likely to appeal to the constituents of politicians in other states than groups identified by a narrower ethnic identity.

H8: *Groups defined by religion or race are more likely to get broader support.*

H9: *Groups defined by language are less likely to receive broad support.*

Identities may also vary in how intensely they are felt, but it is not clear *a priori* that a particular kind of identity like language might be felt less intensely than religion by individuals outside of the conflict. Therefore, the hypotheses make no predictions about whether particular kinds of identities will shape the intensity of external support.

B. Data Analysis

These analyses focus on two dependent variables. Breadth refers to the number of states supporting a particular group. Intensity refers to highest level of support given to a group by at least one state. I discussed the coding of these variables earlier in this chapter on pages 158–60.

The raw data was available for the periods 1990–91, 1992–93, 1994–95, 1996, 1997, and 1998. I present analyses of data from 1990–91, 1994–95, and 1998, so that we can see whether the dynamics changed throughout the 1990s.

Table 6.7 presents the indicators used to test each hypothesis. A few require more explanation. To test the realist arguments, we need a measure of power. Correlates of War data proved helpful in developing an indicator for relative power. Using data on each country's military personnel, military expenditure, energy use, production of iron and steel, and urban and total

TABLE 6.7 Hypotheses and Related Indicators

	Hypothesis	MAR indicator
H1	Separatist groups are less likely to have many supporters or to receive intense support.	SEPX, recoded as SEPARTSM to indicate actively separatist groups.
H2	Groups in highly vulnerable states are less likely to have many supporters or to receive intense support.	OTHSEPX, coded from SEPX: how many other groups in host state are actively separatist?
H3	When a host state neighbors states vulnerable to separatism, ethnic groups within the host state are less likely to have many supporters or to get intense support.	NRSEPX, from SEPX: how many separatist groups exist in adjacent states?
H4	Ethnic groups in Africa are less likely to have many supporters or to get intense support.	REGION variable, coded as dichotomous: is group in sub-Sarahan Africa or not?
H5	Groups in stronger states are more likely to receive broader support and to receive intense support.	POWER90 for 1990–91; POWER92 for 1994–95, 1998
H6	Groups in weaker states are more likely to receive broader support and intense support.	POWER90 for 1990–91; POWER92 for 1994–95, 1998
H7	If ethnic group's kin dominates a neighboring state, then that group is more likely to receive support and to receive intense support.	IDOMSEG, from Phase I and updated for 1990s.
H8	Groups defined by religion or race are more likely to broad support.	RACE, BELIEF
H9	Groups defined by language are less likely broad support.	LANGFMI: see below
C1	Does the type of host state's government matter?	REGTYP90 for 1990–91, REGTYP94 for 1994–95, REGTYP98 for 1998
C2	Does the conflict's level of violence influence outside actors?	REB89 for 1990–91, REB93 for 1994–95, REB 97 for 1998

population, I developed an indicator of each country's power relative to the rest of the world. The actual equation for country x would be:

power of x relative to the world = [(military personnel of x/world total) + (military expenditure of x/world total]/2 + [(energy use of x/world total) + (x's production of iron and steel/world total)]/2 + [(x's urban population/world total) + (x's total population/world total)]/2 /3.

That is, the military, economic, and population components are each averaged,[19] and then the categories are averaged.[20] The numbers result in a ranking similar to what common intuitions are of the great powers, middle powers, and the rest of the world.[21] Since the dataset's unit of analysis is the ethnic group, the variable POWER90 indicates the relative power of each ethnic group's host state in 1990. I use POWER92 for the remaining analyses since there was simply too much missing data to create new indicators for each subsequent period. This should not be too problematic since neither the relative power of countries nor evaluations by states of their adversaries' relative power probably changed after 1992 as they did after the fall of the Soviet Union. While the power indicators may not be perfect measures,[22] the criteria used for the rankings provide a good basis for assessing relative capabilities. If states tend to balance power, we should expect groups in states with high POWER rankings to get more support than groups in states with lower rankings. We expect the opposite if the predatory nature of international politics plays a greater role.

The Minorities At Risk dataset contains indicators for inter-group differentials between the ethnic group and the majority or typical group. These variables range from 0 where no socially significant differentials exist to 2 with substantial differentials. The dataset contains indicators for racial distinctions[23] and religious cleavages. For linguistic differences, I use data from *Ethnologue*[24] that codes groups by common supersets.[25] The data is coded from one to twenty with twenty reflecting groups whose language is considered identical to that of the comparison group. For the analyses, we divide one by the language family score to put more weight on greater differentials.[26] We expect groups who are distinct due to race or religion to receive more support than groups distinguished by language.

Two control variables are also included in the analysis to deal with potential alternative explanations. First, given the importance of regime type in today's foreign policy debates, regime type is included to control for the impact of the type of political system within which an ethnic group resides. Do ethnic groups within democracies get more or less support than ethnic groups in authoritarian systems? The indicator comes from Polity98 data.[27] Specifically, I created the indicator by subtracting the autocracy score from democracy score, so groups with high regime type values reside in highly democratic states.

Second, very violent conflicts may be more likely to attract external attention due to greater media attention, greater refugee flows, and/or greater humanitarian concern. On the other hand, Patrick Regan argues that states intervene less in more violent conflicts because of the higher risks and lower probabilities of success, so including rebellion allows us to test his argument as well.[28] The rebellion indicator reflects the intensity of the conflict from none to local rebellions to guerrilla warfare to protracted civil war. Since the dataset contains yearly values for rebellion in the 1990s, I use the preceding year. The logic here is that conflict attracts attention, so that states should react to past events. If we used rebellion scores from the same year as the dependent variable, it makes it harder to distinguish whether rebellion attracts external support or that external support exacerbates ethnic conflict.[29]

I performed poisson regressions with robust standard errors (to control for heteroskedasticity)[30] for the periods 1990–91, 1994–1995, and 1998 when analyzing the factors shaping the breadth of support groups received since the dependent variable is essentially a counting of separate events.[31] For the analyses of intensity of support, I performed ordered probits with robust standard errors (to control for heteroskedasticity) for the same periods since the dependent variables are ordinal. I report these results in table 6.8.

To determine the robustness of these results, I performed several additional tests. First, I reran the analyses using only the variables that were significant in the first set to determine whether the initial results were caused by interactions among significant and insignificant variables, and these results are reported in table 6.9.

As table 6.9 indicates, very little changes, as nearly all of the significant findings from the complete analyses are significant in the reduced model, and the variance that is accounted for by the model is reduced only slightly. The notable exceptions are: the existence of other separatists in the same state, whether a group is separatist, and whether the group resides in Africa. Given that these variables were significant in only one or two analyses in table 6.8, their insignificance in table 6.9 is hardly surprising. Second, I reran the analyses in table 6.8 excluding Eastern Europe or the former Soviet

TABLE 6.8 Group Characteristics' Impact on Breadth and Intensity of Support

Argument	Variables	1990–1991 Breadth	1990–1991 Intensity	1994–1995 Breadth	1994–1995 Intensity	1998 Breadth	1998 Intensity
Ethnic Politics	Racial Differences	.11	.08	.11	.20**	.004	−.01
	Linguistic Differences	−.17	−.17	.02	−.35	.14	−.09
	Religious Differences	.03	.06	.03	.02	.06	−.02
	Does Ethnic Kin Dominate Adjoining State?	.37*	.41**	.50**	.64***	.52**	.46**
Vulnerability	African States	−.17	−.10	−.02	−.31	−.45**	−.54**
	Is Group Separatist?	.65**	.29	.32*	.12	.03	−.07
	Other Separatist Groups in Host State	−.12**	−.08	−.02	−.06	.03	−.01
	Separatists in Nearby States	.08**	.07**	.04**	.06**	.02	.06**
Realism	Relative Power of Host State	−.03	−.01	.03	−.01	.01	−.04
Control Variables	Regime Type	−.04**	−.03**	−.03**	−.03**	−.04**	−.04**
	Rebellion	.07	.15**	.11**	.33**	.16**	.34**
	N	186	186	201	201	227	227
	Wald Chi²	99.26	48.14	90.47	91.29	95.55	90.70
	Prob > chi²	.0000	.0000	.0000	.0000	.0000	.0000
	Log likelihood	−196.33	−211.09	−215.09	−217.53	−244.23	−235.35
	Pseudo R²	.1320	.1021	.1065	.1789	.1484	.1893

Breadth results are produced by poisson regressions, intensity values are produced by ordered probits.

* p < .1

** p < .05

TABLE 6.9 Group Characteristics' Impact on Breadth and Intensity of Support, Significant Variables Only

Argument	Variables	1990–1991		1994–1995		1998	
		Breadth	Intensity	Breadth	Intensity	Breadth	Intensity
Ethnic Politics	Race				$.17^{**}$		
	Does Ethnic Kin Dominate Adjoining State?	$.58^{**}$	$.46^{**}$	$.54^{**}$	$.83^{**}$	$.58^{**}$	$.72^{**}$
Vulnerability	African States					$-.69^{**}$	$-.31$
	Is Group Separatist?	$.59^{**}$		$.26$			
	Other Separatist Groups in Host State	$-.08$					
	Separatists in Nearby States	$.07^{**}$	$.06^{**}$	$.05^{**}$	$.06^{**}$		$.06^{**}$
Control Variables	Regime Type	$-.03^{**}$	$-.02^{**}$	$-.02^{**}$	$-.02^{**}$	$-.03^{**}$	$-.03^{**}$
	Rebellion		$.20^{**}$	$.10^{**}$	$.29^{**}$	$.20^{**}$	$.25^{**}$
	N	209	207	225	224	238	237
	Wald Chi^2	67.48	40.76	71.85	83.73	81.49	93.47
	Prob > chi^2	.0000	.0000	.0000	.0000	.0000	.0000
	Log likelihood	−225.01	−231.70	−239.30	−245.75	−262.06	−244.28
	Pseudo R^2	.1034	.1003	.0995	.1591	.1368	.1498

Breadth results are produced by poisson regressions, intensity values are produced by ordered probits.

* p < .1
** p < .05

cases to see if the newly independent states and the conflicts within them biased the results. I found that no consistent pattern of new results emerged from this, although power gained significance in the 1990–91 analysis of breadth of support, and that separatism lost significance in 1994. Given that Russia has eleven different ethnic groups in the dataset and is one of the more powerful countries in the world, it is not surprising that dropping these cases influences relative power's significance.

I also performed tests for collinearity. I regressed all of the independent variables on each other, and found no high r-squares. I also performed bivariate correlations, and none of the independent variables are correlated at more than the .600 level. Moreover, I performed the same analyses in table 6.8 but used regression techniques rather than probit, allowing me to calculate the variance inflation factors. These tests produced no "vifs" close to the level of multicollinearity.

Because probit does not produce easily interpreted coefficients, I have used CLARIFY, a program written for STATA.[32] This program uses simulations to produce probabilities and allows the user to see what happens when the values of particular variables change. Tables 6.10–6.14 present the results from various simulations.[33]

Findings

The first important finding is that there are relatively few differences between the various models. Most variables have coefficients of similar size, direction, and significance regardless of whether the dependent variable is the number of supporters or the highest level of support received and regardless of the period studied. Two variables produce significantly different results across the three periods: the separatism of groups and whether groups are located in Africa. The most consistently significant relationships are: the presence of dominant ethnic kin nearby, the existence of separatism in nearby states, and violence with more support, and regime type with less support.

1. Ethnic Ties   The quantitative analyses suggest that ethnic ties matter, although not as clearly as hoped. The existence of a neighboring state dominated by a group's ethnic kin has the expected relationships. The hypotheses focusing on ethnic identities did not produce any significant relationships

TABLE 6.10 Probabilities of Significant Variables Influencing Each Group's Breadth of Support, 1990–91

We hold everything constant at the minimum value except regime type and relative power held constant at the mean value, but:	Change in Probability that Number of Supporters = 0	Change in Probability that Number of Supporters = 1	Change in Probability that Number of Supporters = 2	Change in Probability that Number of Supporters = 3	Change in Probability that Number of Supporters = 4 or more
If the group changes from having no **kin dominating a nearby state** to having such kin reign nearby,	−10.2%	5.4%	3.5%	1.0%	.2%
If the group becomes **actively separatist,**	−19.4%	8.7%	7.3%	2.6%	.8%
If a group's host does not **border states facing active separatist movements** changes to one bordering states facing the maximum,	−50.3%	3.2%	18.7%	14.1%	13.0%
If the **number of other separatist movements** changes from none to max,	15.5%	−11.2%	−3.6%	−.6%	−.1%
If the host state changes from **most authoritarian to most democratic,**	20.8%	−11.4%	−6.9%	−2.0%	−.5%

TABLE 6.11 Probabilities of Significant Variables Influencing Each Group's Intensity of Support, 1990–91

We hold everything constant at the minimum value except regime type and relative power held constant at the mean value, but:	Change in Probability that Intensity of Support = 0	Change in Probability that Intensity of Support = 1	Change in Probability that Intensity of Support = 2	Change in Probability that Intensity of Support = 3	Change in Probability that Intensity of Support = 4
If the group changes from having no **kin dominating a nearby state** to having such kin reign nearby,	−14.8%	5.5%	3.4%	2.3%	3.6%
If the group becomes **actively separatist**,	−10.8%	3.9%	2.4%	1.6%	2.9%
If a group's host does not **border states facing active separatist movements** changes to one bordering states facing the maximum,	−51.4%	4.2%	8.8%	8.7%	29.7%
If the host state changes from **most authoritarian to most democratic**,	21.3%	−8.8%	−4.8 %	−3.0%	−4.9%
If the conflict moves from **no violence to protracted civil war**,	−38.7%	6.7%	7.7%	6.8%	17.6%

TABLE 6.12 Probabilities of Significant Variables Influencing Each Group's Breadth of Support, 1994–95

We hold everything constant at the minimum value except regime type and relative power held constant at the mean value, but:	Change in Probability that Number of Supporters = 0	Change in Probability that Number of Supporters = 1	Change in Probability that Number of Supporters = 2	Change in Probability that Number of Supporters = 3	Change in Probability that Number of Supporters = 4 or more
If the group changes from having no kin dominating a nearby state to having such kin reign nearby,	−14.6%	7.5%	5.2%	1.5%	.3%
If the group becomes actively separatist,	−8.5%	4.9%	2.8%	.7%	.1%
If a group's host does not border states facing active separatist movements changes to one bordering states facing the maximum,	−22.8%	9.0%	9.0%	3.5%	1.3%
If the host state changes from most authoritarian to most democratic,	13.7%	−7.8%	−4.5%	−1.1%	−.3%
If the conflict moves from no violence to protracted civil war	−24.1%	9.1%	9.6%	3.9%	1.4%

TABLE 6.13 Probabilities of Significant Variables Influencing Each Group's Breadth of Support, 1998

We hold everything constant at the minimum value except regime type and relative power held constant at the mean value, but:	Change in Probability that Number of Supporters = 0	Change in Probability that Number of Supporters = 1	Change in Probability that Number of Supporters = 2	Change in Probability that Number of Supporters = 3	Change in Probability that Number of Supporters = 4 or more
If the group changes from having **no kin dominating a nearby state** to having such kin reign nearby,	−16.9%	6.2%	3.7%	5.3%	1.7%
If the group changes from located elsewhere to being in **Africa,**	15.7%	−8.5%	−3.2%	−3.3%	−.7%
If a group's host does not **border states facing active separatist movements** changes to one bordering states facing the maximum,	−46.0%	5.0%	8.2%	19.3%	13.5%
If the host state changes from most **authoritarian to most democratic,**	26.5%	−10.2%	−5.6%	−8.0%	−2.6%
If the conflict moves from **no violence to protracted civil war**	−64.4%	−8.6%	3.9%	23.7%	45.4%

TABLE 6.14 Probabilities of Significant Variables Influencing Each Group's Intensity of Support, 1998

We hold everything constant at the minimum value except regime type and relative power held constant at the mean value, but:	Change in Probability that Intensity of Support = 0	Change in Probability that Intensity of Support = 1	Change in Probability that Intensity of Support = 2	Change in Probabiliy that Intensity of Support = 3	Change Probability that Intensity of Support = 4
If the group changes from having **no kin dominating a nearby state** to having such kin reign nearby,	−16.9%	a6.2%	3.7%	5.3%	1.7%
If the group changes from located elsewhere to being in **Africa,**	15.7%	−8.5%	−3.2%	−3.3%	−.7%
If a group's host does not **border states facing active separatist movements** changes to one bordering states facing the maximum,	−46.0%	5.0%	8.2%	19.3%	13.5%
If the host state changes from **most authoritarian to most democratic,**	26.5%	−10.2%	−5.6%	−8.0%	−2.6%
If the conflict moves from **no violence to protracted civil war**	−64.4%	−8.6%	3.9%	23.7%	45.4%

except race with intense support in 1994. Therefore, we cannot say with confidence that the particular identity of a group causes it to get more or less support. Given that the ethnic ties argument is inherently dyadic and that there may be multiple identities in play (as the case studies suggested), this finding is only moderately troublesome for the theory of ethnic politics and foreign policy.

The existence of a nearby state dominated by a group's kin strongly influenced breadth and intensity of support a group receives. A group with kin dominating a nearby state is at least 10 percent more likely to receive support (depending on which analysis in tables 6.10–6.14 we consider) and even more likely to receive intense support. This suggests that the power of kin matters, as more powerful kin significantly increase the likelihood of groups receiving assistance.

To provide an additional test of this intuition, I ran analyses with a dummy variable in place of the dominant kin indictor for whether a group was Roma or not instead of the measure for dominant kin nearby. Since the Roma are discriminated and disenfranchised nearly everywhere they exist, we should expect them to be unable to push their host states into supporting their kin elsewhere. In all of the analyses, Roma were significantly less likely to receive any support.

In sum, the quantitative analysis suggests that ethnic politics may influence the international relations of ethnic conflicts. Kin nearby matter, at least when they dominate a state, and groups are much less likely to receive support if their kin are powerless, as the Roma tests suggest. In most ethnic conflicts, multiple identities exist and which ones are salient depends on the efforts of the various actors to define the conflict. Given this dynamic and perceptual character of identity, it is not surprising that the findings for ethnic identities were not statistically significant.

2. *Vulnerability* While the various ethnic politics hypotheses produced more mixed results than expected, the data analyses seriously challenge the vulnerability argument. Two significant findings—a group's separatism and whether its host state bordered separatist conflicts elsewhere—had coefficients in the opposite direction from what a vulnerability theorist would expect. The coefficients of the African host state indicator pointed in the "right" direction for nearly all of the analyses, but consistently fell short of statistical significance except in 1998. Other separatism in the same state produced coefficients with the expected direction, but fell short of statistical significance except for breadth of support in 1990–91.

Separatist groups were significantly more likely in 1990–1991, rather than less likely, to receive widespread support than other kinds of groups. In 1990–91, such groups were 19 percent more likely to receive support (table 6.10) and 7 percent more likely to receive intense assistance (two or greater, table 6.11) than nonseparatist groups. The vulnerability hypothesis suggests that if states obeyed international norms, then separatist groups should receive less support, so we should have found significant negative coefficients. Consequently, we must question the core vulnerability hypothesis.

An even more striking finding that table 6.9 indicates is that being near a separatist group has more causal weight than being separatist. The variable for groups in a less vulnerable region, where no neighboring states are confronting separatism, consistently had the largest impact on the dependent variables of breadth and intensity (tables 6.10–6.14). Further, this variable increases the likelihood of widespread support more than any other with the possible exception of the level of violence. Groups near states fighting their own separatist conflicts are at least 14 percent more likely to receive assistance from more than two states. Such groups were at least 25 percent more likely to receive the most intense forms of assistance (three or four, according to tables 6.11 and 6.14).

The only support the vulnerability argument receives is that African states were less likely to receive support in 1998. Because this result is significant only for that year, it is not clear what to make of this result. Given that African states should have received less support earlier in the decade when the norm of territorial integrity was less challenged, it is not clear that African groups received less support in 1998 because of international norms or something else.

In sum, the vulnerability argument, when faced with evidence, is found wanting. None of the four hypotheses performed as a vulnerability theorist might expect. Instead, separatism and being near other separatists increased the likelihood of receiving any support, improved the chances of receiving wider support, and enhanced the odds of gaining intense support. Consequently, these analyses raise important questions about the conventional wisdom that vulnerability and international norms deter support for separatist movements. The analyses found that many of the vulnerability beliefs are not grounded in state behavior.

3. *Realism*   The analysis produced inconsistent, small correlations between relative power and the dependent variables. This suggests that neither defensive realism nor offensive realism is always correct. It may be the case

that the mixture of security-seeking and greedy states in the international system produced the mixed results.[34] Perhaps these states cancel each other out in the statistical analysis. The fact that the relative power variable did not provide significant findings may not challenge realism's essence. It does suggest that we need to have a clearer idea of either the balance of security-seeking and greedy states in the world or a clear statement of under what conditions will a state be greedy or not. The weakness of these results is a startling contrast to the analyses below focusing on the characteristics of potential supporters, where relative power seems to matter a great deal.

4. Regime Type and Rebellion   The two control variables both were significantly correlated with whether a group received greater support or not. Groups in authoritarian regimes were consistently more likely to receive broad and intense external support, generally 20 percent more likely to receive assistance. This may support arguments suggesting that the justness of the cause might matter. Because ethnic groups in the most authoritarian regimes have few options for settling their problems besides separation, they may receive more sympathy.

Rebellion was strongly related to breadth and intensity of international support, except in 1990–91. Tables 6.10–6.14 indicate that this variable had the strongest impact on foreign assistance groups received. The problem is interpreting these results, as international support may spur a group to engage in more violent efforts, or a violent civil war may gain more international intention than other groups. Further work is required to clarify the causal relationship between violence and external assistance.

Which States Support Ethnic Groups at Risk?

A different approach is to consider which characteristics of states influence their willingness to support ethnic groups at risk. While the theory of ethnic politics and foreign policy does not imply clearly specific attributes of states that might cause them to support more groups or give more intense support, the other approaches do make such predictions. For the vulnerability theorist, states that are hosts to separatists should be the least likely to give assistance to ethnic groups, given their precarious situations at home. Likewise, realists would argue that relative power ought to matter—that states with greater interests and capabilities are likely to be involved in more ethnic conflicts than other states. Below, I delineate testable hypotheses for each argument. After operationalizing the competing claims, I discuss the multivariate analyses to determine which characteristics of states correlate with broader and more intense assistance to ethnic groups.

Testable Hypotheses

1. Vulnerability   The vulnerability argument provides the most straightforward hypotheses. States that are vulnerable to separatism should be inhibited from supporting ethnic groups elsewhere, as they would not want to face retaliation or set unfortunate precedents. The more separatist groups a state faces, the more inhibited it is likely to be. Therefore,

H1: The more separatist groups inhabit a state, the less likely that state is to support many groups, and the less likely it is to give intense assistance.

If the vulnerability of states causes them to cooperate, then states in regions characterized by separatism should be less likely to support ethnic groups. If a state's neighbors confront separatism, then that state should fear the spread of such clashes. Even if the conflict itself does not cross international boundaries, it is still likely to have a negative impact on neighboring states, including the possibility of economic sanctions against one or more of the combatants, refugee flows, among other "externalities."

H2: States neighboring highly vulnerable host states are less likely to give support to many groups or to give intense support.

Third, we should consider whether African states are less likely to support ethnic groups. Because the vulnerability argument was created with Africa in mind, we should test whether norms and common interests inhibit Africa states. They should be particularly less likely to give intense support since that would greatly challenge the boundary regime and risk retaliation.

H3: African states are less likely to support many groups or to give intense support.

2. Power   The obvious test for realism is whether more powerful states are more or less inclined to support ethnic groups. Offensive realists would assert that powerful states are more likely to support ethnic groups in other states, given their predatory nature. Defensive realists might suggest that supporting ethnic conflict might be a weapon for weak states to wield. Ultimately, they would probably argue that because more powerful states have more interests and more capabilities (by definition), they are more likely to intervene around the world in the domestic politics of other states.

H4: *More powerful states are more likely to give support to many groups and to give intense support.*

3. Ethnic Politics   Given the nature of the theory of ethnic politics and foreign policy and the available data, it is hard to test the impact of ethnic identity on foreign policy. Ethnic tie is an inherently dyadic concept, so it is hard to apply if the unit of analysis is an individual state. Further, the data currently available is limited. However, there is one possible test—do states with Muslim majorities behave differently from other states? Two of the case studies raise this question. In both case studies where religion was a major cleavage, Islamic countries tended to give intense support. In the 1990s, there have been a number of intense ethnic wars where one side has been predominantly Muslim or characterized as such, including Armenia-Azerbaijan, Bosnia, Chechnya, Kosovo, and Sudan to name just a few. Given that leaders of many states with Muslim majorities encountered strong pressure from religious competitors, we should expect that such leaders would try to disarm their opposition by supporting Muslims in conflict elsewhere. Further, those states where leaders are using Islam as a source of legitimacy should also support their religious kin in other states.[35]

H5: *States with Islamic majorities are more likely to give support to many groups and to give intense support.*[36]

Data Analysis

Like the previous set of analyses, the analyses in this section focus on the breadth and intensity of support, but here the unit of analysis is the potential supporter rather than the ethnic group. The dataset includes all countries having a population greater than one million. The raw data for the dependent variables was available for the periods 1990–91, 1992–93, 1994–95, 1996, 1997, and 1998. I present analyses of data from 1990–91, 1994–95, and 1998 since only one independent variable in this study varied throughout the period—regime type. Because of missing data, relative power again is coded for 1990 and 1992 only, but I must use the 1992 relative capabilities data for the 1994 and 1998 analyses.[37]

Table 6.15 summarizes the hypotheses and the indicators developed to test the competing arguments. I have included one control variable: regime

TABLE 6.15 Hypotheses and Related Indicators

	Hypothesis	Indicator
H1	The more separatist groups inhabit a state, the less likely that state is to support many groups or to give intense assistance.	SEPX, recoded as SEPARTOT, counting the number of actively separatist groups in each state.
H2	States neighboring highly vulnerable host states are less likely to give external support to many groups or to give intense support.	NRSEPX, from SEPX: how many active separatist groups exist in adjacent states?
H3	African states are less likely to assist many groups or to give intense support.	REGION variable, coded as dichotomous: is state in Africa?
H4	More powerful states are more likely to give support to many groups or to give intense support.	POWER90 for 1990–91 POWER 92 for 1994–95, discussed earlier in this chapter.
H5	States with Islamic majorities are more likely to give support to many groups or to give intense support.	MUSMAJ from CIA World Factbook data, if population of state is 50% or more Muslim
C1	Does the type of host state's government matter?	REGTYP90 for 1990–91 REGTYP94 for 1994–95 REGTYP98 for 1998

type. Do democracies or authoritarian regimes give more support to ethnic groups? I have included this for a couple of reasons. First, regime type seemed to matter for the previous set of analyses, so it would be interesting to determine whether the type of political system affected who gives support, in addition to who receives it. Second, ongoing debates in the field of foreign policy analysis have focused much attention on regime type as an important influence on state behavior.[38]

Again, I performed poisson regressions for the analysis of breadth and ordered probits for the intensity of support, with each analysis configured with robust standard errors (to deal with heteroskedasticity)[39] for the periods 1990–91, 1994–95, and 1998 since the dependent variables are ordinal. These results are reported in table 6.16.

To determine the robustness of these results, I performed several additional tests.[40] First, I reran the analyses using only the variables that were significant in the first set, and these results are reported in table 6.17.

As table 6.17 indicates, there are no changes, as all of the significant findings from the complete analyses are significant in the reduced model. The variance for which the model accounts is reduced only slightly in the case of breadth and more significantly in the intensity analyses. Second, specifying the vulnerability hypothesis differently by considering simply whether a state contains at least one separatist group only weakens the significance of the positive correlations, without changing any of the more consistent findings. I also reran the analyses without the United States, an outlier in both level of support and relative power. I found a few changes in the results: being vulnerable to separatism was more significant in 1990–91 without the U.S.; being near separatists became significantly and positively related to breadth of support in 1990–91 and 1994–95; and that power was less significant in 1990.

I, again, use CLARIFY to make clear the impact of the significant variables, and the CLARIFY results are illustrated in table 6.18–6.23, focusing on effect of the significant indicators on the breadth and intensity of support states gave.

Findings

The analyses of potential supporters' characteristics suggest that vulnerability arguments do not have empirical support, but that power influences

TABLE 6.16 Analyses of Potential Supporters

Argument	Variables	1990–1991		1994–1995		1998	
		Breadth	Intensity	Breadth	Intensity	Breadth	Intensity
Ethnic Ties	Muslim Majority	1.28**	.57*	1.01**	.45	1.15**	.53*
Vulnerability	African State	−.50	−.04	−.48*	.13	−.13	−.04
	Number of Separatist Groups in Potential Supporter	.11	.30**	.21**	.23**	.14**	.06
	Separatists in Nearby States	.03	.10**	.03	.09**	.03	.07**
Realism	Relative Power	.21**	.09	.19**	.09	.21**	.07*
Control Variable	Regime Type, Democracy 10	.01	−.03	.003	−.02	.04**	.01
	N	118	118	132	132	137	137
	Wald Chi²	166.55	31.09	258.31	22.10	793.13	20.05
	Prob > chi²	.0000	.0000	.0000	.0012	.0000	.0027
	Log likelihood	−155.78	−130.57	−171.80	−154.32	−189.57	−176.96
	Pseudo R²	.4835	.1428	.4390	.1112	.4522	.0621

Breadth results are produced by poisson regressions, intensity values are produced by ordered probits.

* p < .10
** p < .05

TABLE 6.17 Analyses of Potential Supporters, Significant Variables Only

Argument	Variables	1990–1991 Breadth	1990–1991 Intensity	1994–1995 Breadth	1994–1995 Intensity	1998 Breadth	1998 Intensity
Ethnic Ties	Muslim Majority	1.26**	.54**	.72**		1.14**	.60**
Vulnerability	African States			−.54**			
	Number of Separatist Groups in Potential Supporter		.21**	.23**	.22**		
	Separatists in Nearby States		.08**		.10**	.17**	.08**
Realism	Relative Power	.25**		.19**		.21**	.08**
Control Variable	Regime Type, Democracy 10					.03*	
	N	128	143	141	144	137	141
	Wald Chi^2	651.89	19.92	548.35	20.62	870.62	16.88
	Prob > chi^2	.0000	.0002	.0000	.0000	.0000	.0007
	Log likelihood	−175.06	−163.40	−184.97	−174.23	−191.76	−181.40
	Pseudo R^2	.4437	.0728	.4179	.0646	.4458	.0586

Breadth results are produced by poisson regressions, intensity values are produced by ordered probits.

* p < .10

** p < .05

TABLE 6.18 Probabilities of Significant Variables Influencing Numbers of Groups States Supported, 1990–1991

	Change in Probability that Number of Groups Supported = 0	Change in Probability that Number of Groups Supported = 1	Change in Probability that Number of Groups Supported = 2	Change in Probability that Number of Groups Supported = 3	Change in Probability that Number of Groups Supported = 4 or more
We hold everything constant and at their minimum value except regime type and power which are held at their mean values:					
If the state changes to one that has a **Muslim majority,**	−42.2%	−9.1%	14.7%	16.4%	18.6%
If a state with the least **power** changes to a state at the mean,	−5.4%	2.3%	2.2%	.8%	.2%

TABLE 6.19 Probabilities of Significant Variables Influencing Intensity of Support States Gave, 1990–1991

	Change in Probability that Highest Intensity of Support = 0	Change in Probability that Highest Intensity of Support = 1	Change in Probability that Highest Intensity of Support = 2	Change in Probability that Highest Intensity of Support = 3	Change in Probability that Highest Intensity of Support = 4
We hold everything constant and at their minimum value except regime type and power which are held at their mean values:					
If the state changes to one that has a **Muslim majority**,	−20.9%	4.8%	3.9%	2.4%	9.8%
If a state facing no **separatist threat** changes to facing the maximum,	−56.8%	−5.4%	1.8%	2.8%	57.7%
If a state does not **border states facing active separatist movements** changes to one bordering states facing the max,	−61.5%	−6.6%	2.1%	3.1%	62.9%

TABLE 6.20 Probabilities of Significant Variables Influencing Numbers of Groups States Supported, 1994–1995

We hold everything constant and at their minimum value except regime type and power which are held at their mean values:	Change in Probability that Number of Groups Supported = 0	Change in Probability that Number of Groups Supported = 1	Change in Probability that Number of Groups Supported = 2	Change in Probability that Number of Groups Supported = 3	Change in Probability that Number of Groups Supported = 4 or more
If the state changes to one that has a **Muslim majority**,	−35.2%	−1.7%	15.3%	12.3%	15.7%
If the state changes to one that is in **Africa**,	14.2%	−7.4%	−5.1%	−1.4%	3.1%
If a state facing no **separatist threat** changes to facing the maximum,	−46.2%	−14.2%	11.9%	16.9%	26.6%
If a state with the least **power** changes to a state at the mean,	−4.4%	1.9%	1.8%	.6%	.1%

TABLE 6.21 Probabilities of Significant Variables Influencing Intensity of Support States Gave, 1994–1995

We hold everything constant and at their minimum value except regime type and power which are held at their mean values:	Change in Probability that Highest Intensity of Support = 0	Change in Probability that Highest Intensity of Support = 1	Change in Probability that Highest Intensity of Support = 2	Change in Probability that Highest Intensity of Support = 3	Change Probability that Highest Intensity of Support = 4
If a state facing no **separatist threat** changes to facing the maximum,	− 51.3%	a − 1.8%	6.1%	4.8%	42.2%
If a state does not **border states facing their own active separatist movements** changes to one that is,	− 58.7%	− 3.5%	6.1%	5.4%	50.7%

TABLE 6.22 Probabilities of Significant Variables Influencing Numbers of Groups States Supported, 1998

We hold everything constant and at their minimum value except regime type and power which are held at their mean values:	Change in Probability that Number of Groups Supported = 0	Change in Probability that Number of Groups Supported = 1	Change in Probability that Number of Groups Supported = 2	Change in Probability that Number of Groups Supported = 3	Change in Probability that Number of Groups Supported = 4 or more
If the state changes to one that has a **Muslim majority,**	−39.0%	−6.2%	15.5%	15.1%	13.9%
If a state facing no **separatist threat** changes to facing the maximum,	−33.1%	−3.3%	13.4%	11.8%	10.6%
If a state with the least **power** changes to a state at the mean,	−5.0%	2.0%	2.0%	.7%	1.8%
If state changes from **most authoritarian** to **most democratic,**	−24.0%	10.2%	9.4%	3.4%	1.0%

TABLE 6.23 Probabilities of Significant Variables Influencing Intensity of Support States Gave, 1998

We hold everything constant and at their minimum value except regime type and power which are held at their mean values:	Change in Probability that Highest Intensity of Support = 0	Change in Probability that Highest Intensity of Support = 1	Change in Probability that Highest Intensity of Support = 2	Change in Probability that Highest Intensity of Support = 3	Change in Probability that Highest Intensity of Support = 4
If the state changes to one that has a **Muslim majority,**	−20.2%	1.8%	4.8%	6.2%	7.5%
If a state does **not border states facing active separatist movements** changes to one bordering states facing the max,	−48.1%	−3.9%	3.2%	11.8%	37.0%
If a state with the least **power** changes to a state at the mean,	−1.9%	.4%	.6%	.5%	.4%

the breadth of support, if not its intensity. These tests do not say much about ethnic politics because of the difficulty of operationalizing the argument, but the religious composition of potential supporters seems to matter.

In the 1990s, vulnerable states were not less likely to support ethnic groups, but in four of the six tests significantly more likely. Where vulnerability was statistically significant, it had a large impact on outcomes—vulnerable states are at least one-third more likely to assist ethnic groups elsewhere and give more intense support. This finding contradicts the conventional wisdom. Given that both vulnerable states are more likely to receive support (table 6.8) and more likely to give assistance to groups, perhaps the darker side of vulnerability carries the day. That is, mutual vulnerability encourages, rather than inhibits, states to support separatists elsewhere as there may be benefits to country A for supporting groups in other countries first before they do to country A. Of course, this may lead to retaliation and ongoing conflict. This perhaps has characterized the relationships of many countries, including, for example, Ethiopia and Somalia, Sudan and Uganda, India and Pakistan, among others. This finding suggests that reciprocity may be producing mutual conflict, rather than cooperation, but a dyadic analysis would help determine this.

Another finding that contradicts the vulnerability logic is that states are more likely to support ethnic groups at risk if they live in a dangerous neighborhood. Such groups are at least 37 percent (table 6.23) more likely to give the most intense support than states in the least volatile regions. This finding further undermines the vulnerability hypothesis, as states apparently may be unafraid of conflict spilling over.[41] Likewise, African states were not significantly less likely to help ethnic groups at risk, except in 1994–95, despite the norms the OAU has established. Further, nearly all groups that African states supported in the 1990s reside in Africa.[42] Thus, these analyses leave little doubt that vulnerability, however defined, poorly predicts foreign policy.

Relative power mattered a great deal, as the stronger states supported many more groups than weaker states. Even if one removes the United States and Russia from the analysis, as they are two of the most powerful states and are the two most frequent supporters of ethnic groups, relative power still significantly increases the odds of broad support. Powerful countries have more ability to support ethnic groups, and, apparently, feel less constrained by international norms or pressures from other states. This finding suggests that the international system is a predatory environment, where the strongest do what they will. However, as tables 6.18–6.23 indicate the difference in the probability of the weakest state supporting a number of ethnic groups is not very different from the average state. On the other hand, the difference between the weakest and the strongest is huge (although not presented in the tables). These findings do not really say much about the relative merits of offensive and defensive realism, since both approaches could have predicted this outcome.

Relative power's significance here does not undermine the ethnic politics argument unless the stronger states do not support ethnic kin elsewhere, but oppose them. The United States, Great Britain, and France stand apart from most as they are the only states to support more than two ethnic groups yet have obvious ethnic ties to none.[43] The U.S. consistently supported more than twice as many groups as the next most active supporter, but much of this assistance was in the form of election monitoring, human rights assessments, and the like. Great Britain, France, Belgium, and the Netherlands tended to take sides in their former colonies' conflicts. The other powerful countries tended to support their ethnic kin. Three-quarters of the groups Russia assisted had ethnic ties to Russia. Of the six groups China helped, four were ethnically Chinese. More than half of the groups India supported had ethnic ties to important domestic constituencies. Germany supported Germans in Kazahkstan, and South Korea supported Japan's Koreans. In sum, relative power supplements ethnic politics rather well, as stronger states tend to intervene more, taking the side of ethnic kin if they exist, or intervening anyway for other reasons.

States with majority Muslim populations helped significantly more states and gave significantly more intense assistance than other states. This finding suggests that neither the Nigerian Civil War nor the Bosnian conflict is unique. Leaders dependent upon Islamic groups support Muslims at risk in other states. Even if Iran is dropped from the analysis, the finding is still significant and roughly of the same magnitude. While Iran supported at least eleven predominantly Islamic groups, Malaysia, Saudi Arabia, and Turkey all supported at least four. While this finding does not say much about other ethnic ties, it clearly suggests that religious ties influence foreign policy.

Conclusions

Together, this chapter's quantitative analyses support the findings from the case studies: vulnerability is overrated; relative power matters but not as clearly as usually asserted; and ethnic politics, though hard to test given the available data, shapes how states react to ethnic conflict in other states. The analyses and figures also demonstrate that the dynamics revealed in the case studies apply to more than just secessionist crises and beyond 1960s Africa.

Vulnerability hypotheses fail every test in this chapter. The cross-tabulations of the case studies findings show no correlation between vulnerability and support for either host states or secessionists. The figures of trends and changes in the 1990s (figures 6.1–6.8) show no systematic changes in support states gave or groups received, which contradicts an approach that focuses on precedent-setting. In both sets of multivariate analyses, none of the significant findings were in the direction vulnerability theorists would expect. There simply was no empirical support for the vulnerability theorists' claims in the 1990s. One could argue that these findings are the result of the breakdown in the international regime, and that pre-1990s studies would provide different findings. However, two of the case studies are from the 1960s, and they are similar to statistical analyses—vulnerability does not inhibit foreign policy.

Realist accounts fare somewhat better. The cross-tabulations gave little support to realist hypotheses. The figures of 1990s trends cannot really say much about realism since realism makes no claims about precedents or the passage of time. The multivariate analyses of group characteristics indicate that states are not significantly more likely to support groups in relatively powerful or relatively weak states. There are two possible ways to account for this. Either states are a mix of defensive positionalists and power maximizers and, therefore, they cancel each other out. Or the monadic nature of this analysis prevents us from determining the power of each supporter relative to each group's host state. The second set of multivariate analyses focusing on potential supporters (the state as the unit of analysis) strongly suggests that relative power matters a great deal, even if we control for the strongest state's (the U.S.) exceptional behavior. Stronger states are more likely to support more ethnic groups and more likely to support them intensely, despite the American tendency to give less intense forms of support. It is hard to tell, however, whether stronger states are engaging in predatory behavior or have more kin abroad due to colonial legacies (which would include Russians in the former Soviet Union).

The results suggest that the findings of the qualitative chapters are not the product of case selection, but of the tendencies of states to support their ethnic kin. The cross-tabulations indicate that ethnic politics influences foreign policy. The analyses of group characteristics suggest that ethnic politics play an important role in the international relations of ethnic conflict. Groups with dominant ethnic kin nearby were more likely to receive intense support. In the analysis of supporters, religion played a strong role, as states with Islamic majorities tended to give more intense assistance and more help to more groups than other states. The challenge to the theory of ethnic politics and foreign policy in the quantitative analyses was not finding contradictory results, but simply developing good indicators for the theory.

Overall, this chapter strengthens the conclusions derived from the previous chapters. Each argument performed as well or as badly in the statistical analyses as it did on the case studies. Realism is correct in arguing that power matters, but it is not very clear how it matters. Vulnerability serves as a poor predictor in both case studies and in quantitative analyses. Ethnic politics was somewhat more elusive in the quantitative analyses, but the various tests indicate that ethnic ties influence foreign policy, just as the qualitative analyses suggested. Further, this chapter has shown that ethnic politics accounts for the international relations of all kinds of ethnic conflict more consistently than relative power and much more powerfully than vulnerability. In the next chapter, I draw out the implications of these findings both in policy and theoretical debates.

Appendix to Chapter 6

Groups Dataset (mostly Minorities At Risk data)

Indicators	N	Min	Max	Mean	Std. Deviation
Breadth of Support Received, 1990–91	251	0	4	.72	.95
Breadth of Support Received, 1994	250	0	6	.78	1.02
Breadth of Support Received, 1998	263	0	6	.79	1.13
Intensity of Support Received, 1990–91	251	0	4	1.01	1.34
Intensity of Support Received, 1994	250	0	4	1.04	1.33
Intensity of Support Received, 1998	263	0	4	.91	1.28
Racial Differences	274	0	3	1.08	1.14
Linguistic Differentials	249	.05	1	.60	.40
Religious Differentials	274	0	3	1.38	1.32

Groups Dataset *(continued)*

Indicators	N	Min	Max	Mean	Std. Deviation
Group is Dominant in Adjoining State	267	0	1	.26	.44
Number of Segments of Group Nearby	275	0	4	1.34	1.26
Is Host State in sub-Saharan Africa?	267	0	1	.24	.43
Is a Group Actively Separatist?	267	0	1	.34	.47
How Many Other Groups in Same State are Separatist?	267	0	7	1.18	1.83
How Many Groups in Adjacent States are Separatist?	266	0	21	4.06	4.19
Host State's Relative Power, 1990	234	.01	16.47	1.76	3.69
Host State's Relative Power, 1992	261	.01	16.28	1.48	3.15
Host State's Regime type, 1990	226	−10	10	.50	7.37
Host State's Regime type, 1994	244	−10	10	2.76	6.71
Host State's Regime type, 1998	263	−10	10	2.66	6.44
Rebellion Index for 1989	271	0	7	.96	1.97
Rebellion Index for 1993	272	0	7	1.06	1.97
Rebellion Index for 1997	268	0	7	.86	1.82

Supporters Dataset

Indicators	N	Min	Max	Mean	Std. Deviation
Intensity of Support Given, 1990	144	0	4	1.10	1.53
Intensity of Support Given, 1994	145	0	4	1.14	1.50
Intensity of Support Given, 1998	145	0	4	1.16	1.41
Number of Groups Supported, 1990	144	0	32	1.21	3.31
Number of Groups Supported, 1994	145	0	25	1.28	2.94
Number of Groups Supported, 1998	145	0	37	1.41	3.64
Is State in sub-Saharan Africa?	145	0	1	.28	.45
Is the population majority Muslim?	145	0	1	.21	.41
Number of Actively Separatist Groups	144	0	7	.60	1.18
Number of Actively Separatist Groups Nearby	144	0	21	2.98	3.63
Regime Type, 1990	122	−10	10	.89	7.78
Regime Type, 1994	136	−10	10	3.20	6.88
Regime Type, 1998	141	−10	10	2.97	6.77
Relative Power, 1990	128	.01	16.47	.77	2.20
Relative Power, 1992	141	.00	16.93	.71	2.03

7 Findings, Future Directions and Policy Dilemmas

As Yugoslavia disintegrated, states debated which sides to support and to recognize, causing scholars to wonder whether the international norms of boundary maintenance were obsolete. Because of the failure of the conventional wisdom to anticipate or explain the international relations of Yugoslavia's demise, we are tempted to ignore the past and consider each ethnic conflict either as a unique event or as a harbinger of escalating identity conflicts—the "Clash of Civilizations."[1] Instead, this book suggests that the past was poorly understood, and that revisiting it is helpful for understanding today's conflicts. Rather than proving that there is something new going on, this book demonstrates the continuities in states' reactions to ethnic conflict. Ethnic politics shapes the foreign policies of many states, causing them to take competing sides, making international cooperation difficult, although not impossible.

In this chapter, I first compare the case studies to consider what they shared in common and what caused them to differ. Indeed, one puzzle remains to be explored. If international norms and vulnerability did not cause states to support the territorial integrity of the Congo and Nigeria, why did most states support the host states in these conflicts? Second, I address a limitation of the case studies—I only address secessionist crises—by reviewing the quantitative analyses and suggesting case selection strategies for future research. As I revised this book, a "new" war broke out in the former Yugoslavia—the Kosovo conflict. I examine this conflict briefly as readers may have questions that are unanswered by chapter 5 and to demonstrate this study's relevance for more recent events. Then, the chapter develops the book's implications for larger theoretical controversies and for future research. I conclude by suggesting some policy implications—particularly how to facilitate cooperation among states that disagree.

Comparing the Case Studies

Ultimately, vulnerability is least helpful in understanding the international relations of ethnic conflict, that realism, while indeterminate, properly highlights the role of powerful states, and that ethnic politics best explains state behavior toward ethnic conflicts.

Vulnerability

One of the most consistent findings across the case studies was that states that were vulnerable to ethnic conflict and separatism supported secessionists. Belgium, Congo-Brazzaville, the Federation of Rhodesia and Nyasaland, and South Africa all supported Katanga despite facing severe ethnic conflict at home. With the exception of Portugal, all of Biafra's most significant allies were dealing with potential or ongoing separatist disputes. The Yugoslav conflicts are more confusing since separatist republics became host states resisting their own secessionist movements. Still, vulnerability theorists should be surprised that Italy supported Croatia and Slovenia's recognition, Russia helped the Bosnian Serbs, Iran was so eager to help Bosnia, and Albania has been so helpful to the Kosovars.

Vulnerability theorists might argue that most states helped the Congo and Nigeria, that most states supported Yugoslavia's territorial integrity until its disintegration was already accomplished, and that most states supported each republic in its efforts to maintain its borders. Since vulnerability does not inhibit states, why did most states help the Congo and Nigeria and oppose Biafra and Katanga? The case studies suggest that this was essentially an accident of history—the ethnic definition of these two conflicts. Most African states supported the Congo because it was defined as a racial conflict and as a dispute between Pan-Africanism and neoimperialism. Because many African states relied on Pan-Africanism as part of a civic nationalism, and because all newly independent countries feared the former colonial powers and the white minority regimes of Southern Africa, Katanga's appeal to whites and its ties to white interests made foreign policy decisions easy for most actors. Likewise, the religious definition of the Nigerian Civil War caused most African states to support Nigeria, as most African states had large Muslim populations. Only those states with relatively small Muslim populations assisted Biafra. If outsiders had viewed either conflict as purely tribal, then much of the continent probably would not have cared all that much. Or, the norms set up by the Organization of African Unity [OAU] might have mattered more. By paying attention to the role of ethnic politics in the past, we ought to be less surprised by how states reacted toward the Yugoslav conflict.

Defenders of the conventional wisdom would assert that the United Nations and OAU played crucial roles in the major African secessionist crises, while the UN and the North Atlantic Treaty Organization [NATO] significantly influenced the course of Yugoslavia's decline. Involvement by international organizations is a common attribute among the three conflicts studied here. While this may be a product of case selection, vulnerability theorists are right in emphasizing the importance of international organizations during these conflicts. The UN defeated Katanga, the OAU facilitated Nigeria's victory, and the UN and NATO helped to end the wars in Croatia and Bosnia. These and other organizations made it harder to abet the secessionists by creating resolutions supporting the host states and, in the case of Yugoslavia, enforcing an arms embargo.

However, these efforts did not emerge out of any autonomous international organization, but out of the wrangling and bargaining among states that disagreed with each other. The Congo Crisis and the Bosnian conflict are quite similar in that international organizations in each conflict gradually escalated their involvement, eventually taking one side and supporting it with force. While these organizations were responding to events, states defined these responses. India and African states threatened to withdraw troops from the UN force in the Congo if they did not aggressively act against Katanga. Ultimately, it was the possibility of having to use force to facilitate the withdrawal of UN peacekeepers that compelled the United States to bomb the Bosnian Serbs and help bring them to the Dayton negotiations. Further, while international organizations raised the costs of supporting secessionists, they did not prevent those states that were bent on supporting separatists from doing so.

Finally, one last aspect of the vulnerability argument needs to be addressed: specific reciprocity.[2] The notion is that cooperation begets cooperation, as states reciprocate each others' behavior. Of course, reciprocity also means that conflict causes more conflict. This notion may explain why some states supported secession while others did not. Those states having a history of conflict with the host state supported the separatists. Therefore, it should not be surprising that the white minority regimes of Africa supported Biafra and Katanga, or that the Ivory Coast supported Biafra. However, reciprocity-based arguments have a hard time explaining Congo-Brazzaville's support of Katanga, Tanzanian and Zambian assistance to Biafra, or German and Italian support of Slovenia and Croatia (since both had good relations with Yugoslavia throughout the 1980s). That the U.S. and Russia could cooperate with each other on a variety of issues but conflict over Yugoslavia suggests that cooperation can be quite specific — to some interactions but not others. Likewise, the inability of the European Community to cooperate during this conflict suggests that reciprocity has limits. Overall, vulnerability analysts overestimate the level of cooperation, as very hard bargaining and strong disputes among the outside actors characterized the international relations of each dispute. Cutting Russia and the UN out of the decisionmaking process made decisive action in Yugoslavia in 1995 and again in Kosovo in 1999 possible. Western countries facilitated cooperation by refusing to co-operate with those who would disagree.

Realism

To apply realism to this study, I extended Stephen Walt's balance of threat theory by adjusting offensive capability to include the ability to support ethnic groups within the host state and by including in perceived intentions the apparent willingness of a state to do so.[3] The biggest difficulty in applying this approach to the case studies was weighing the various components of threat. Frequently, the various elements pointed in different directions. How should a relatively weak state facing little offensive threat behave compared to a stronger state perceiving hostile intentions? Realism was frequently indeterminate, as outsiders were not significantly threatened.

The second problem was coding intentions and perceived intentions. Walt admits that "Determining intentions is not easy. Accordingly, political leaders often seek shortcuts to identify friends and foes. One approach is to focus on the domestic characteristics of potential partners in order to ally with those whose beliefs or principles resemble one's own."[4] Walt has no theory about which domestic characteristics might matter, but as I applied balance of threat theory to the cases, the ethnic politics of countries seemed to determine which states were perceived to have nasty intentions. Katanga's reliance on white settlers caused African countries to view it as threatening, while Lumumba's Pan-African nationalism caused South Africa and the Federation of Rhodesia and Nyasaland to view his regime as a threat. South Africa and Rhodesia supported Biafra as Nigeria was a powerful state ruled by Black Africans. If race was not part of the threat calculation, then these two countries would probably have viewed each other as potential threats rather than as allies against the rest of Africa. In the Yugoslav case, for each state, there were many potential allies and adversaries, so perceived intentions were crucial for determining with which states and groups to side. Bulgaria could have helped Serbia, but chose to support Macedonia. Greece viewed Macedonia as its enemy, despite Macedonia's powerlessness. Romania viewed Hungary as its most significant threat despite Yugoslavia's and then Serbia's military power.

However, relative power plays an important role in the international relations of ethnic conflicts. As case studies suggest and as the analysis of potential supporters proves, powerful countries are likely to get involved in more ethnic conflicts than other states. The United States, the Soviet Union/ Russia, People's Republic of China, France, and Great Britain were usually involved, and their policies mattered, shaping who won and who lost. Stronger countries tended to get involved for three reasons. First, the conflict took place in a former colony or near former colonies. Belgium, Britain, and France were major players in the Congo Crisis; and Britain, France, and Portugal influenced the Nigerian Civil War, largely through their former or current colonies. Second, these countries had ethnic ties with or ethnic enmities toward one of the combatants and were unafraid of defying the others. Germany's ties with Croatia and Slovenia significantly shaped its policies, as the bond between Russia and Serbia caused Russia to support Serbia more than it might have.

Third, in the absence of ethnic ties, great powers became involved in these conflicts as part of competition for influence. The Soviet Union used the Congo Crisis to challenge the United Nations and threaten American influence in Africa, and the U.S. responded to this challenge by creating a friendlier regime and then helping to defeat the secessionist movement. Both countries supported Nigeria against Biafra because failing to do would alienate more African countries than it would attract. Interestingly, China supported Biafra through Tanzania and Zambia, as this served the perfect opportunity to oppose both Soviet and American interests. During the Yugoslav conflict, the United States was motivated to intervene, in part, to maintain credibility within its alliance. Therefore, balancing behavior does take place in ethnic conflicts, but ethnic politics frequently, though not always, determines against whom a state is balancing.

Finally, relative power significantly shapes the outcomes of ethnic crises. Eventually, both the U.S. and the Soviet Union opposed Katanga, and Katanga was crushed. Great Britain, the Soviet Union, and the United States supported Nigeria, allowing Nigeria to defeat Biafra. While European states tried to cooperate to settle the Yugoslav conflicts, American leadership brought the Bosnian Croats and the Bosnian government together, leading to greater pressure placed on the Serbs. Combined with American assistance for Croatia's August 1995 offensive and the American-led NATO bombing campaign, these efforts brought the combatants to Dayton and to an enduring, if imperfect, peace in Bosnia.

The Theory of Ethnic Politics and Foreign Policy

Ethnic politics proved to be a better predictor of states' foreign policies toward ethnic crises than the two other approaches. The identities at stake shaped which countries took which sides during each of the crises studied here. In a few countries, leaders defied the narrow predictions produced by ethnic ties, but in most of these situations, ethnic politics still influenced foreign policy. In this section, I briefly review the importance of ethnic ties, considering alternative means for dealing with ethnic politics and variations in political competition before addressing the centrality of each conflict's ethnic identification.

Ethnic ties and enmities served as the most accurate predictor of foreign policy in the case studies. In the Congo Crisis, ethnic ties predicted the initial policies of twelve of the thirteen states studied, although both Belgium and the United States changed their foreign policies over time. Even if one considers those two countries as failed predictions, ethnic ties predicted correctly 77 percent of the observations. Ethnic ties predicted correctly fourteen of seventeen countries' policies toward the Nigerian Civil War (82%). Even in 1990s Europe, ethnic ties predicted the initial foreign policies of eleven of thirteen states (85%), although two, the United States and Hungary, deviated from the predicted policies over time. The exceptions in each case tended to prove the rule. Low competition or alternative ethnopolitical strategies tended to produce the "unexpected" policies or policy changes by Belgium, Congo-Brazzaville, the United States in the Congo Crisis, Tanzania, Ethiopia, and Senegal during the Nigerian Civil War, and France, Romania and the U.S. toward Yugoslavia's disintegration.

The theory of ethnic politics and foreign policy does not anticipate alternative strategies for dealing with ethnic conflict, so Belgium's, Congo-Brazzaville's, and Romania's behavior were surprising. Belgian behavior changed, in part, because a different party came to power based on an ideology and not on ties to Belgium's glory. This facilitated less support for Katanga. Congo-Brazzaville's leadership used money to buy off ethnic opposition, and conditioned its foreign policy accordingly by selling it. Romanian leaders cared a great deal about Romanian nationalism, but focused their efforts on more salient ethnic conflicts—toward Hungarians at home and Romanians in Moldova.

Variations in political competition allowed some politicians to act contrary to the predictions of ethnic ties. The United States was able to take a much more assertive role in the Congo Crisis after the Cuban Missile Crisis had buttressed President Kennedy from right-wing opposition. In the Yugoslav conflict, President Clinton was able to move from an ambivalent foreign policy to strongly supporting Bosnia because the ethnic kin of the combatants were not very powerful politically in the U.S, with the notable exception of Greek-Americans. Ethiopia's Emperor was able to side against Biafra in part because he faced no real opposition for Christian support at home. They had no exit option at the time. Finally, France did not actively support the Catholics in Slovenia and Croatia because President Mitterand did not rely on Catholics for political support, and because he was in his last term in office. Because political competition matters here, the theory of ethnic politics and foreign policy is distinct from Huntington's Clash of Civilizations, which assumes that states will act according to civilization identity regardless of political incentives or constraints.[5]

In each conflict, multiple identities coexisted, but a particular perception of the identity at stake developed each time. While the conflict's history and the combatants' composition mattered, so did the efforts of the actors themselves. The theory of ethnic politics and foreign policy expects leaders to attempt to define their identities to maximize domestic and international support. In each crisis, leaders of the separatists and of the host states competed to define the conflict in ways that would favor their side. Tshombe of

Katanga defined the dispute as one between anti-communism versus communism, appealing to the West and to white minority regimes in southern Africa. Lumumba and his successors identified the cleavage as one between Black Nationalism and Pan-Africanism on one side and neocolonialism and white minority regimes on the other. Biafran leaders tried to define the conflict as a religious one to mobilize domestic and international support, while Nigeria tried to characterize the crisis as an internal one, downplaying the role of religion. Bosnian leaders tried to have it both ways, appealing to Islamic countries for support while trying to maintain its multiethnic identity for both Western and domestic audiences. Serbs and Croats undermined these efforts by defining the Bosnian government as one controlled by Islamic fundamentalists. All of these attempts to characterize each conflict were important elements of strategies to gain more support domestically and internationally. These groups and their host states believed that outsiders would react based on perceived ethnic ties, so they went to great efforts to emphasize particular identities.

Most actors generally saw the Congo Crisis as a racial conflict between a group influenced by white settlers and European interests on one side and Black nationalists and Pan-Africanism on the other. Instead of arguing whether the Lunda or the Baluba were most deserving of support, leaders and followers argued that the white settlers deserved support or opposition, depending on whether they allied with or against the white minority regimes of southern Africa. Biafra's attempt to identify itself as an oppressed religious minority worked—states relying on Christian constituents were more likely to support Biafra. However, this identity also worked against Biafra, as predominantly Islamic states strongly assisted Nigeria. The same dynamic played out in Yugoslavia. The Serb efforts to define the conflict as one between Christianity, particular Orthodoxy, and Islam, gained some support from Orthodox countries, particularly Greece and Russia, but also caused the Islamic world to help Bosnia. Any broad identity a group chooses creates not only potential supporters but also potential adversaries. Leaders of separatist groups must take care, and consider whether the gains are greater than the losses, if they are strategic in attempting to shape their group's identity.[6]

One complication that arose in the course of this study is that leaders of multiethnic coalitions frequently develop civic nationalisms to bind their constituents together. This is a logical strategy, but makes foreign policy predictions more difficult since the content of civic nationalism varies and does not have the obvious implications that ethnic nationalisms generally have.[7] For instance, Belgian nationalism, at a time of rising linguistic divisions, was a necessary tool for heterogeneous parties to maintain their unity. The events in the Congo caused Belgian nationalism to resonate in a particular way—opposition to Lumumba and favoritism toward his enemies, especially Tshombe and Katanga. The importance of Pan-Africanism in several states' civic ideologies shaped their reactions to the Congo Conflict. Likewise, the content of Zambia's civic nationalism mattered when it reacted to Nigeria's civil war. Analysts generally perceive civic nationalisms to lead to more peaceful and cooperative foreign policies.[8] Nevertheless, the case studies, particularly Belgium's role in the Congo, suggest that we must take seriously the possibility that the content of a non-ethnic nationalism may cause a state to be less acquiescent to international pressures.

Summary of the Case Studies

Ethnic politics consistently provided better predictions and more accurate explanations than either vulnerability or relative power. Relative power performed better than vulnerability as it helped to explain, in part, why the stronger powers got involved and how they tended to shape the course of events, even if it did not always readily predict which side a state would take. Vulnerability not only failed to predict the behavior of less vulnerable states, but usually the strongest supporters of each separatist movement were themselves vulnerable to secessionism. One could argue that the selection of cases and observations may have produced these particular results, if one ignores or downplays the quantitative analyses in chapter 6.

Can We Apply the Findings More Generally

Do the findings of the case studies apply beyond these cases and beyond secessionism to other kinds of ethnic conflicts? The quantitative analyses of the Minorities at Risk [MAR] data aimed to disarm criticisms about case selection and generalization. Chapter 6 indicates that the conventional wisdom that vulnerability inhibits support for ethnic groups has a poor empirical foundation, as it failed every test. Not only were vulnerable states *more* likely to give intense assistance to ethnic groups in other states, but separatist

groups were *more* likely to receive such help as well. The international relations of ethnic conflict did not change much throughout the 1990s.
Groups generally received as much support in 1998 as they did in 1990, and
states gave as much assistance at the end of the decade as they did at the
beginning. These trends, or lack thereof, cause us to question claims about
precedent setting that are so important to vulnerability arguments.

Relative power produced mixed results, as groups in powerful states were
no more likely to receive support as groups in less powerful states. However,
stronger states were much more likely to get involved in other countries'
ethnic conflicts, even if one controls for the United States and Russia. This
suggests that states may be predatory, as offensive realists suggest, but more
work is needed. The motivations of the more powerful states may not focus
on gaining power. American involvement in ethnic conflicts in the 1990s
seems to have been motivated by humanitarianism, while Russia intervened
most frequently on behalf of Russians in the "Near Abroad."

Given the dyadic nature of the theory of ethnic politics and foreign policy,
it was hard to test given the available data. Strikingly, one characteristic of
ethnic groups increases the likelihood of receiving support: whether ethnic
kin dominate a neighboring state. In the study of potential supporters' characteristics, whether a country had a Muslim majority significantly influenced
its chances of giving assistance to a number of groups. Clearly, more work
is required to test the role of ethnic politics in the international relations of
ethnic conflict. Given the relational nature of the argument, future research
ought to consider analyzing the universe of state-group dyads.

Kosovo: Déjà vu All Over Again

If there is one thing the conflict in Kosovo in 1999 proved, it is that
achieving multilateral cooperation to manage ethnic conflicts can be very
difficult. Perhaps the most crucial obstacle to successful cooperation has
been the diverging preferences of the states involved. This book began by
arguing that advocates for particular conflict management techniques overlook the problem of getting states to cooperate. The Kosovo conflict has
become quite complex because the countries involved have not agreed
about the methods or goals of intervention. While an agreement was finally
reached between the outside actors and Serbian leader Slobodan Milosevic,
implementation of the agreement has been problematic. The appearance of

Russian troops at the Pristina airport, which denied the British peacekeepers use of it as a base of operations, should not have been that surprising. Domestic politics within most states, and ethnic politics in quite a few, explains why states have not easily found a common position toward the conflict.

This conflict has, besides Serbia itself, affected Albania and Macedonia most directly. Each has had to bear the burden of hundreds of thousands of Kosovo's Albanians who either fled from or were expelled by Serbia's armed forces and paramilitary groups.[9] Albania was much more willing to assist the Kosovars in their escape and in their fight than Macedonia. Albania essentially donated its airspace, its ports, and tracts of land to NATO to facilitate its bombing of Serbian armed forces. The Kosovo Liberation Army [KLA] openly used Albanian territory as a base for training new recruits and as a sanctuary from Serb attacks. While Serbia's forces occasionally crossed into and shelled Albanian territory in pursuit of the KLA, raising the costs Albania paid for supporting its kin, these bases were crucial for the KLA's survival. Clearly, the ethnic ties between the refugees from Kosovo and the people of Albania help to explain Albania's enthusiasm for the KLA.[10]

Macedonia was much less cooperative with NATO, despite the presence of more than ten thousand NATO troops. The Macedonians insisted that the refugees be moved to other countries rather than settling in Macedonia even if only temporarily. Macedonia occasionally blocked its border with Kosovo, depriving the refugees of food and shelter. It even resorted to bussing refugees during the night to neighboring countries.[11] The major difference between Albania and Macedonia is that increasing the Albanian population of Macedonia threatens its political stability, while Albanians run Albania. The exact number of ethnic Albanians in Macedonia was and still is contested, but dealing with this large minority preoccupied the Macedonian government. Efforts to incorporate ethnic Albanians and their political parties in the governing coalition have prevented Macedonia from exploding into ethnic conflict, but the flood of new refugees was perceived as a threat to ethnic peace. Ironically, heavy-handed efforts to deal with the refugee crisis may have alienated ethnic Albanians as much as the refugees' presence alienated nationalist Macedonians.

Ethnic politics influenced other actors as well. This conflict worsened relations between Russia and NATO, as Russian nationalists as well as moderate sections of the Russian population considered the solution of NATO bombing to be worse than the problem of ethnic cleansing. Politicians in parliament demanded that Russia give military assistance to Serbia. President Boris Yeltsin, facing his own impeachment, railed against NATO, but also pushed Russia to the forefront by having former Prime Minister Viktor Chernomyrdin serve as mediator.[12] By trying to elicit some concessions from NATO, Yeltsin hoped to disarm Russian nationalists.

The Patriarch of the Russian Orthodox Church flew to Serbia while it was being bombed and had his picture taken not only with leaders of the Serbian Orthodox Church but also with Slobodan Milosevic. This suggests that important actors within Russia perceived the Serbs to be their religious brethren. Meanwhile, it is not clear whether Russia's nationalists really cared about Serbia, or merely found NATO's use of force against a "Slavic brother" to be a convenient tool for attacking Yeltsin.[13] What is clear is that all politicians perceive this issue to matter domestically and acted accordingly.[14] Obviously, Russian decisionmakers had legitimate concerns about an alliance created to fight the Soviet Union using force against a political system over a human rights problem. Still, the politics of the issue seemed to have revolved around Russian nationalism.[15]

Ukraine faced an important dilemma. Its Russian-speaking population sided with the Serbs in polls, while Ukrainian speakers were supportive of NATO.[16] As a result of ethnic ties existing with both sides of the conflict, the Ukraine's foreign policy has been described as "fence-sitting."[17] Taking a strong stand either way would have alienated one important faction or the other, particularly with elections on the horizon. Contributing troops to a UN-sponsored, NATO-dominated peacekeeping force would satisfy both sides, but doing anything else might be politically dangerous.

Coalition management has significantly shaped German policy toward Kosovo. A key player in the conflict, Germany was less willing to consider the use of ground troops than other countries, particularly Britain. While left-center parties have taken power in both countries recently, a critical difference is that Britain's Labour Party needs no coalition partners, while Germany's Social Democrats rely on the Green Party to rule.[18] The Green Party, traditionally quite opposed to the use of force, was initially willing to go along with bombing, but lost enthusiasm for that. German public support waned as the bombing continued without much progress at the negotiating table. This stands in contrast to public support for assertive German foreign policy toward Croatia and Slovenia in 1991.

American and British efforts have not been motivated by ethnic ties, as neither country's leaders relies on Orthodox Christians or Muslims for their positions. Instead, two motivations were: the fear of the conflict spreading to involve Greece and Turkey in a war over Macedonia; and regret that little was done to save Bosnia. Further, in negotiations before this latest outbreak of violence, the U.S. and its NATO allies had promised to use force if Serbia did not sign the agreement negotiated at Rambouillet, France. Thus, alliance credibility was a major impetus for U.S. policy toward the Balkans in 1999 as it was in 1995.

Finally, as some last evidence that ethnic ties shape peoples' preferences, it should be noted that the initial protests of the bombing in countries around the world were by Serb emigrés. Serbs in Austria, Australia, and the U.S. protested NATO's bombing of Serbia. In Sweden, Greeks, Russians, and Syrians joined Serbs in protesting NATO actions.[19] Romanian Orthodox priests were among the protestors in Bucharest, carrying signs saying "The Romanian and Serbian peoples are brothers."[20] While ethnic ties cannot explain every foreign policy, it is a good predictor for peoples' and states' foreign policy preferences toward ethnic conflicts.

Implications for Foreign Policy Analysis and International Relations Theory

While the aim of this book was to challenge the conventional wisdom about boundary maintenance and the international politics of ethnic conflict, it has implications for broader debates in foreign policy analysis and international relations theory. Specifically, the theory of ethnic politics and foreign policy and the findings are relevant to three distinct debates. First, this research suggests that we need to consider more seriously a neglected aspect of diversionary foreign policy—the choice of target.[21] Second, the findings here emphasize that the resurgence of domestic approaches to state preferences is well aimed. Third, this work challenges the claim that international organizations and norms restrain states as much as frequently argued.

The foundation of most diversionary theories of foreign policy is the social psychological dynamic that conflict with an "out-group" unifies an "in-group."[22] Morgan and Bickers point out that translating this from social groups to states is complicated, because "some will feel greater kinship with groups in other countries than with other domestic groups."[23] They go on then to focus on how the in-group's coherence influences the likelihood of using foreign policy as a diversion from domestic problems. Morgan and

Bickers overlook how group kinship to outsiders might determine which groups, states, and conflicts are suitable or likely targets for diversionary foreign policies. This element, the choice of target, is largely missing from the logic and the analyses of diversionary theory. In part, the quantitative nature of much of this work makes it difficult for scholars to focus on likely targets and easier to focus on popularity of the leaders, changes in the economy, and other factors. Only recently have studies started to take into account whether the opportunity for diversion exists. That is, do external actors deny a vulnerable politician by following accommodative foreign policies?[24] This starts to get us toward the consideration of targets, but not close enough.

Still, there may be more than one potential target for diversionary foreign policy, so why would a leader focus on one conflict and not another? This book suggests that the preferences of politicians' supporters probably matter, even for non-ethnically defined policies and disputes. This book shows that the interests of constituents and the foreign policies of states are related, at least toward ethnic conflicts. It demonstrates that the content of a state's nationalism, civic or ethnic, shapes which states are seen as threats and which actors are worthy of support. Together, constituent preferences and the content of the state's nationalism (partly produced by politicians' strategies) influence which sides states take in ethnic conflicts elsewhere. This may play out for other kinds of policies and conflicts. For instance, Argentina's generals targeted the Malavinas/Falkland Islands because of its place in Argentinean nationalism, not merely because it was nearby. There were weaker neighbors to attack, but perhaps none were quite as likely to work domestically.[25] Future work in the field of diversionary foreign policy should consider the identities of the potential targets and the preferences of swing groups or essential coalition partners to determine whether and how preferences affect policy.

Recently, scholars have argued that we ought to study domestic sources of international cooperation.[26] This book provides strong evidence that this is the appropriate path for future research. The assumption of common interests in boundary maintenance, while intuitively appealing and matching the rhetoric of African politicians, fails to account for states' behavior. Instead, the pressures of political competition meant that the interests of particular constituents mattered. Leaders supported the side with which their constituents had ethnic ties, and generally had a difficult time when their supporters had ties to both sides of a conflict. If constituents' preferences mattered less, then the common interests of states might have mattered more, but this was simply not the case. Both the cases and the quantitative analyses leave little doubt that the common interest in boundary maintenance did not constrain states as much as previously believed.

However, these findings do not mean that liberal international relations theory is misguided, only that the neoliberal institutional variant assumes too much. Moravcsik is correct in emphasizing the priority of preferences for understanding international cooperation and conflict. "States first define preferences—a stage explained by liberal theories of state-society relations. Then they debate, bargain or fight to particular agreements—a second stage explained by realist and institutionalists (as well as liberal) theories of strategic interaction."[27] In this study, politicians frequently developed civic nationalisms, used ethnic identities for domestic political gain, or were compelled to develop ethnically defined policies by their constituents. These efforts determined their general foreign policy preferences: support or oppose Pan-Africanism, assist or hinder potential allies of white minority regimes, help or hurt Christian secessionist movements in Africa, assist Muslims under attack in Europe, or support Orthodox groups. This book generally does not focus on outcomes—why groups win or lose—produced by interstate bargaining. The pattern of preferences, Moravcsik asserts, determines whether there will be a conflict, but not necessarily who wins, and so other factors then come into account. Clearly, in two cases, American interests greatly influenced outcomes, as the U.S. influenced the UN's behavior in the Congo and NATO's use of force against the Bosnian Serbs. Arguing that domestic politics determines preferences and that American behavior determined who wins or loses does not mean that international organizations and norms are irrelevant. In each conflict, international organizations served as essential forums for bargaining, as facilitators of multilateral intervention, and as agents empowering weaker countries. Actors bargained within international institutions and outside of them. The particular organization determined which countries were relatively more influential. Moving decisionmaking for using force in Bosnia from the UN Security Council to NATO in mid-1995 made the bombings in August and September 1995 possible by excluding Russia and China. More recently, the resistance of the U.S. and its NATO allies to submit to UN resolutions addressing the Kosovo conflict clearly demonstrates that international organizations matter, and that the outcomes are likely to be different if the negotiating table moves to another institution. Thus, scholars ought to pay more attention to "forum-shopping," as this behavior might reveal how the structures of international organizations shape outcomes, even if the outcome is that one institution is avoided in favor of others.

International organizations shaped the likelihood and substance of multilateral intervention. The OAU made it easier for outside states to stay out of Nigeria's Civil War by claiming that it was already being handled. In the other two cases, international organizations passed resolutions and sent military forces that shaped the outcomes. The UN forces defeated the Katangans, and NATO helped bring the Serbs to the bargaining table. The nature of each intervention evolved over time due to the pulling and hauling of different states with competing visions of what the institution should do. Although the U.S. was the most powerful actor in each conflict, it responded to the lobbying efforts of others. African states helped Kennedy to perceive Katanga to be the problem. Similarly, Britain and France blocked American desires to "lift and strike" against the Bosnian Serbs while their troops were at risk.

International organizations, perhaps most importantly, increased the influence of weaker states. African countries serving on the UN Security Council wrote resolutions that influenced the use of force. Additionally, African states used their troop contributions as bargaining chips. If the UN force was not used as they wished, they would withdraw their troops, which they eventually did. This enhanced India's influence once it became the major source of UN troops in the Congo. Again, Great Britain and France essentially held a veto over American foreign policy toward Bosnia, as long as their troops were at risk. In sum, international organizations were important in each conflict, but states determined what these institutions did. The combination of and conflict between states with competing preferences shaped how international organizations behaved.

International norms play a lesser role than usually argued. The norm of territorial integrity did not seem to inhibit states motivated by ethnic politics. Perhaps leaders of other states, without ethnic ties or facing little competition, supported the host state or stayed out of the conflict due to respect for the state's territorial integrity. However, in the case studies, it is quite clear that the states that had the most to gain from the territory norm were also equally likely to support secessionists (and in the quantitative analyses, such states were more likely to do so), despite the risk of setting unfortunate precedents that might weaken the boundary regime.

This finding does not necessarily challenge the idea that norms matter in international relations for two reasons: the existence of competing norms and the Yugoslav case, in particular, may not be a fair test of international norms. Because the norm of territorial integrity competes with the norm of self-determination and frequently with human rights norms, such as the prohibition against genocide (Biafra and Kosovo), two things might happen. A state might respect a different norm, so violations of the territorial norm may not indicate that a state ignores norms in general. Then, we must ask why states respect one norm and not another. Domestic politics might help explain that. The second possibility is that the conflict between two or more norms allows states to consider other factors, so domestic political concerns may become more important in such cases. The Yugoslavia conflict is an unfair test of the role of norms since it was less clear how they should apply, particularly after Slovenia and Croatia broke free. Should states support the territorial integrity of Yugoslavia or of its constituent republics? Obviously, this study raises questions about whether norms constrain foreign policy as much as frequently asserted, and future work needs to consider how seriously norms inhibit states in other issue areas.

Future Research

This book is clearly not the last word on the subject. The case studies do not address other kinds of ethnic conflicts, although the quantitative analyses do. The ethnic politics argument is inherently dyadic, so it is difficult to test it through monadic quantitative analyses. Economic arguments have generally been ignored, as the focus has been on the conventional wisdom in the issue area—vulnerability—and the dominant theoretical approach to international relations—realism.

This book only considers secessionist crises, so the question remains as to whether the theory of ethnic politics and foreign policy applies to other kinds of ethnic conflicts. Groups seek not only independence, as many desire autonomy or control over the government. For instance, the conflicts in the Great Lakes region of Africa (Burundi, Rwanda, the Congo) are largely about who controls the government. The quantitative analyses suggest that the findings of the cases apply more broadly. Still, future research should consider how and why countries react to rebellions (Angola, Rwanda) and toward severe discrimination (the Roma of Europe and Indigenous peoples around the world). For instance, it would be interesting to compare how states have related to India's nonsecessionist groups to how outsiders have reacted toward groups trying to secede from India.

The quantitative analyses consider the characteristics of states and of groups, but the theory of ethnic politics and foreign policy like some of its competitors, is inherently dyadic. That is, they focus on the relationship between two actors. The best-known dyadic question today is whether democracies fight with each other. Most of the studies of this question have used as their unit of analysis dyads—the pairing of two states, and considering whether both are democratic or not.[28] For the study of ethnic conflicts, it makes sense to study all the possible combinations of possible supporters (states) and possible groups to be supported (groups). Because we have good data on approximately 275 groups with the Minorities At Risk dataset and 145 states, we could collect information about almost 40,000 dyads. We could then test whether ethnic ties themselves influence the likelihood of support, and compare whether religious or linguistic ties are more likely to influence support. Such a study could also address the relevance of relative power more directly as the power of the state compared to the group in question's host state can be considered directly. It could also address whether states within the same region as the ethnic group behave the same as states outside the region. A dyadic study could also address the effects of joint democracy and of economic interdependence, allowing us to consider two liberal arguments. Such a study was not performed for this book because the costs were too prohibitive for an initial study. Now that we know that there is something to the ethnic politics argument and now that we understand the limitations of monadic analyses of ethnic conflict's international relations, it is clearer that investing in a dyadic study is worthwhile.

The third direction for future research is to consider whether economic arguments provide better explanations of states' behavior toward ethnic conflicts. Gibbs asserts that the economic ties of states' leaders shaped their reactions to the Congo Conflict.[29] I did not examine such claims at any length, because it would significantly increase the length of the book and complicate the discussion of the case studies. Future work could directly compare economic arguments against ethnic politics approaches now that the conventional wisdom has been sufficiently debunked.

Implications for Policy

Clearly, this study indicates that getting states to cooperate will be difficult since they are likely to disagree about outcomes of ethnic conflicts—which group should give up what to settle the conflict. This finding produces several policy directions: stay out of ethnic conflicts entirely, define them toward narrow identities to limit outside interference, or use conflict management techniques that require as little cooperation as possible. There is another possibility that must be addressed as well. If a state strongly prefers one side, then it should identify the conflict in ways that maximize support for its favorite combatant.

If ethnic conflicts are so difficult to manage, then perhaps countries that do not have a stake should simply stay out of them. While states without ties might be the best choices of mediating, peacekeeping, and the like, it might make sense for them to stay out if the disputes among other outside actors make any intervention impossible to succeed. The cases suggest otherwise, as cooperation was difficult but not impossible. Eventually, in each crisis, a consensus developed among most states (though not all), and states gave significant support to implement the consensus.

The second possibility is that states can try to redefine the conflict as one characterized by relatively narrow identities. If successful, this would lessen the domestic political pressures leaders felt, and allow them to cooperate more easily. Most states would have cared much less about the Congo Crisis or the Nigerian Civil War, if they had been defined solely as tribal conflicts. Domestic politics would have compelled few leaders to take strong stands toward the Yugoslav conflict had it been purely defined by linguistic cleavages. Of course, the challenge is to identify a conflict differently from how others might perceive it. This is unlikely if the combatants actively identify themselves as members of broader groups, such as members of particular religious or racial groups. It is also difficult if other states are attempting to identify the conflict according to broader identities. While membership in particular international organizations may facilitate the efforts of some states to define a conflict,[30] redefining a conflict is quite difficult.

Alternatively, if one cannot influence the identities in play but still wants to influence the conflict, unilateral strategies or those needing only a few actors are best. The threat to use force might still work, if the state or states making such threats are not operating through an international organization and if the states possess enough military power to intimidate whichever actor they desire. Mediation could still work as long as others do not interfere. The provision of outside security guarantees might still help if others do not undermine the credibility of the assurances.[31] Arms embargoes, economic sanctions, and other strategies that require multilateral cooperation are less likely to work if states cannot cooperate.

Finally, for states less interested in simply resolving a conflict and preferring that one side wins, the optimal strategy may be to emphasize a particular identity. If one definition of the conflict might lead to more support for the favored group and less for the other combatant, then emphasizing that definition should help the group attract external support and minimize assistance for the other. During the Congo Crisis, Ghana and others quite energetically attempted to define the conflict as one between Black Nationalism and neocolonialism. This resonated not only in Africa but in much of the Asia as well. Efforts by various actors inside and outside of Nigeria to define the Biafran conflict as a humanitarian conflict may have prolonged the conflict. Serbia and Croatia's efforts to define the Bosnian conflict as a religious war boomeranged, as Islamic states gave significant assistance to Bosnia and pushed the West to support the Bosnians more aggressively. Again, defining conflicts is not easy, as the ethnic composition and histories of the combatants shape perceptions, but the existence of multiple identities permits such efforts.

Ultimately, this study suggests that getting international cooperation to manage ethnic conflicts is quite difficult.[32] While states can eventually reach an agreement about what to do, the product of international organizations and of multilateral intervention is likely to leave most sides dissatisfied and may not be terribly efficient. In both the Congo Crisis and Yugoslavia's wars, much bargaining, blaming, criticism and failure occurred, pushing international organizations to escalate their interventions. Future studies of international management of ethnic conflicts should consider the cooperation problem more directly, especially since the obstacles to international cooperation will shape which conflict management techniques are eventually applied.

Notes

Chapter 1

1. Bienen 1995 addresses and criticizes these fears.
2. Herbst 1992.
3. Herbst 1989 and Jackson and Rosberg 1982, among others.
4. Fearon and Laitin (1999) assert that external support may be an integral part of the decision of potential rebels to engage in conflict.
5. Allen 1996, Cigar 1995, Cohen 1998, Donia and Fine 1994; Gutman 1993, Honig 1997, Rieff 1995, and Stiglmayer 1994.
6. Weiner 1996, 12.
7. Dowty and Loescher 1996, 47.
8. Ibid.
9. Weiner 1996, 8.
10. Dowty and Loescher 1996, 49.
11. For this debate, see Pape 1997, Elliot 1998.
12. Watts 1997, 225.
13. *New York Times*, Sept. 29, 1993, A11.
14. Various authors make claims in favor or against these kinds of contagion arguments in Lake and Rothchild 1998. In that volume and elsewhere, I argue that ethnic conflict is not as contagious as usually argued, but I mention the possibility here since fears of contagion increase the relevance of ethnic conflict, even if such fears are unfounded.
15. Walter 1997.
16. Harvey 1997.

17. Chopra and Weiss 1995.
18. Kaufmann 1996a, 1996b, 1998. For another view on partition, see Byman 1997.
19. Davies and Gurr 1998.
20. Stedman 1997.
21. The distinction between conflicts over the dispute versus how to enforce the peace agreement is similar to the bargaining problem that Fearon (1998) discusses.
22. See chapter 5.
23. Moravcsik 1997. I see this book as fitting into Moravcsik's definition of liberalism even while the arguments and findings will undermine some of the assertions of neoliberal institutionalism.
24. Coser 1956, 87.
25. Since Jack Levy's excellent review of this literature (1989), there has been a resurgence of interest considering this question, including James and Hristoulas 1994; Morgan and Bickers 1992; Miller 1995; Smith 1996; Gelpi 1997; Leeds and Davis 1997; and Clark 1998.
26. Moravcsik 1997.
27. Herbst's (1989) argument is explicitly based on Keohane's neoliberal institutionalist theory (1986).
28. Herbst 1989; Jackson and Rosberg 1982; Jackson 1990.
29. Ultimately, only two of these theories are in direct competition—vulnerability and ethnic politics cannot both be true. However, the imperatives of power and security (realism) may supplement or interact with either of the two other approaches. For the sake of clarity, I present the three approaches as competing. In the conclusion, I discuss how some of the dynamics predicted by each approach may interact.
30. Mayhew 1974. As this first assumption suggests, this argument is rational choice theoretic. I assume that politicians are rational actors, choosing policies that are best for ensuring their political survival in the short run.
31. The varying impact of political competition is important because it separates this argument from more simplistic arguments focusing on the power of nationalism. Chapter 2 will draw out the distinction between the theory of ethnic politics and foreign policy and the nationalism arguments.
32. For example, see Buchheit 1978; Foltz 1991; Herbst 1989; Jackson and Rosberg 1982; Jackson 1990; Neuberger 1986; and Touval 1972.
33. Nakarada 1991. Ironically, much progress has been made in settling many of these conflicts, despite the successful Yugoslav secessions, including Northern Ireland.
34. Indeed, several realists have changed their focus from conventional realist concerns like deterrence and military doctrine to ethnic conflicts, including Kaufmann 1996a 1996b, 1998 and Posen 1993a, 1993b, 1996.

35. Vasquez 1997.
36. Walt 1987.
37. Heraclides 1991, Huntington 1993.
38. The focus on secessionist crises is explained toward the end of chapter 2.

Chapter 2

1. Zartman 1966, 109.
2. I do not deal explicitly with irredentism here, though the argument can be applied to irredentism, Saideman 1998a.
3. Touval 1972, 33.
4. Ibid., 34.
5. Saideman 1998a.
6. Jackson and Rosberg 1982; Jackson 1990.
7. Jackson and Rosberg 1982, 17.
8. See for the Grotian approach, Bull 1977.
9. Emphasis is added, Jackson and Rosberg 1982, 18.
10. Suhrke and Noble 1977, 13–14. For a more thorough critique, see Kamanu 1974.
11. Keohane 1986.
12. Herbst 1989, 680.
13. Ibid., 687.
14. Ibid., 689–690.
15. Keohane 1986.
16. Herbst 1989, 689.
17. Keohane 1986, 27.
18. Ibid., 24. One of the main criticisms of neoliberal institutionalism is the tendency to assume the preferences of state, particularly the desire to cooperate. Moravcsik (1997) recently developed a liberal theory of international politics that focuses directly on preference formation.
19. Herbst 1989, 685.
20. Ibid., 690.
21. Ibid.
22. Olson 1965.
23. Herbst 1989, 689.
24. I address whether ethnic conflict is contagious in Saideman 1996, Saideman 1998b, Ayres and Saideman 2000, and Saideman and Ayres 2000.
25. James 1988; James and Oneal 1991; James and Hristoulas 1994; Levy 1989; Morgan and Bickers 1992; Miller 1995; Smith 1996; Gelpi 1997; Leeds and Davis 1997; and Clark 1998.

26. It may also vary according to leaders' propensity to engage in risky behavior. I am indebted to Pat James for pointing this out.
27. I am grateful to Jack Snyder for pointing out the dark side of vulnerability.
28. Nakarada 1991. See also Lukic and Lynch 1996, chapter 13; and Steinberg 1993, 34, 61.
29. See chapter 5.
30. Heraclides 1991, 207.
31. This is not meant as a criticism of Heraclides since developing a theory was probably not a goal, but that we are left without any realist theories of ethnic conflict's international relations.
32. Increasingly, realists are paying attention to ethnic conflict, but thus far, have focused on applying realism to ethnic conflicts themselves, but not the international relations surrounding such crises. For instance, see Kaufmann 1996a, 1996b, 1998; Posen 1993a.
33. Fareed Zakaria (1992) was perhaps the first to make clear this division within realism.
34. Colin Elman (1996) and Kenneth Waltz (1996) argue about whether neorealism can be a theory of foreign policy. Regardless of whether Waltz convincingly argues that neorealism is limited in its application, the practice of IR scholarship has been to develop neorealist predictions for the behavior of individual states.
35. The focus on balancing, whether it is balancing power or threat, is an essential argument within the realist canon, as Vasquez (1997) convincingly argues, regardless of whether one agrees with his assessment of realism as a degenerating research program.
36. Walt 1987. I have chosen to use Walt's work as the basis for a realist approach to the international relations of ethnic conflict since his approach is perhaps the clearest realist theory of foreign policy. Walt (1992), moving beyond alliances, also applies his balance of threat framework to the international relations of revolutions. Thus, applying Walt's argument to the international relations of ethnic conflict should not be that much of a stretch.
37. Walt 1987, 22.
38. Waltz 1979.
39. Walt 1987, 24.
40. Walt 1992, 333.
41. Walt 1987, 23.
42. Also, see Bueno De Mesquita 1981.
43. Ibid., 25.
44. Ibid., 25–26.
45. A different approach to the problem of threat and conflict is the notion of policy distance. Bruce Bueno De Mesquita (1981) argues that policy distance

is a useful concept for identifying potential friends and enemies. Policy distance measures how much two states agree or disagree on a variety of issues. Bueno De Mesquita measures policy distance through the alliances states join. Erik Gartzke (1998) uses different measures, focusing on UN votes, to measure whether states' preferences converge or conflict, arguing that democracies are less likely to go to war because their preferences tend not to be in conflict. The notion, then, is that states are less likely to have conflicts with states that largely agree with them, and are more likely to have disputes with states that pursue largely disagree with them. The potential application here is that states ought to be less likely to support secessionist movements in those states having a smaller policy distance (that are largely in agreement with each other) and more likely to support such groups in states with which many policy differences exist. I do not apply it in this book for two reasons. First, the data requirements can be quite steep. Second, there is a larger theoretical problem: what causes states to have narrow or wide policy distances? These can be caused by regime type (Oneal and Russett 1999), the realist variables that Walt emphasizes, or ethnic ties.

46. Ironically, this may suggest a similar outcome as the vulnerability argument. A state may be deterred from supporting secessionism if the possibility of others responding in kind is a serious threat to a state (I am grateful to Lisa Martin for suggesting this irony). However, we will assume here that the states are not be deterred, since that hypothesis is already being tested under the vulnerability rubric. If vulnerability inhibits foreign policy, then we could return to this point to consider whether the causal process is a neoliberal or realist one. For an important discussion of anticipated reactions, see Nagel 1975.

47. David 1991.

48. Prominent examples include Mearsheimer 1994/95, Schweller 1996, and Labs 1997.

49. Schweller 1996, 91.

50. Labs 1997, 12.

51. Ibid.

52. Ibid., 13, fn. 39.

53. Roy (1997) makes a similar argument, but defines both the question and the answer somewhat differently.

54. For the classic discussion of this assumption applied to democracies, see Mayhew 1974. It is assumed here that elites in nondemocracies will behave similarly, as the costs of losing one's office are probably greater in authoritarian regimes, Ames 1987.

55. Hirschman 1970.

56. For a rational choice theoretic explanation of why followers care about ethnic identities, see Hardin 1995. Also, see Breton 1995; Bates, de Figueiredo and Weingast 1998; Kuran 1998; and de Figueiredo and Weingast 1999.

57. Rothschild 1981, 2.
58. For the examples of the primordial approach, see Geertz 1963 and Stack 1981, 1997. For the opposing instrumental approach, see Brass 1991. For moderate approaches that inspire the view of ethnicity presented here, see Horowitz 1985; Laitin 1986; and Rothschild 1981.
59. Davis and Moore 1997.
60. Henderson 1997.
61. Carment and James 1995, 1997.
62. Horowitz 1985, especially chapter 4.
63. Roy (1997) and Carment and James (1996) make similar arguments, focusing on ethnic ties, but conceptualize them somewhat differently than I do.
64. Young 1976. Perhaps the best example of ethnic enmity has been Greece hostility towards Macedonia—see chapter 5.
65. See Gagnon 1994/95 for a discussion of Slobodan Milosevic's efforts to use events in Kosovo and other parts of Yugoslavia to redefine the political context away from economic issues.
66. Since politicians may anticipate public opinion, what appears to be a top-down, elite use of ethnicity may actually be a bottom-up situation where the pressure from the masses is the driving force, even if it is only potential pressure. I am grateful to Barbara Harff for pushing me on this.
67. For a discussion of civic versus ethnic nationalisms, see Snyder 1993, 1999.
68. Das Gupta 1989; Heimsath 1965.
69. My focus on domestic political competition, rather than international imperatives, is one factor that distinguishes my approach from that of Carment, James and Rowlands 1997.
70. Jacobsen 1988.
71. Heraclides 1991; Huntington 1993.
72. The role of political competition in this argument also suggests that the distinction between affective and instrumental explanations of the international relations of ethnic conflict (Heraclides 1993, Carment 1993) is a false dichotomy. These works suggest that ethnic ties refers to emotional linkages, and that instrumental explanations focus more on rational, strategic motives. There are three problems with this distinction: politicians may be quite rational, as I argue, in considering the ethnic ties of their constituents; constituents may be quite instrumental as leaders' support for ethnic kin elsewhere may serve as a measure of sincerity on ethnic issues at home; and the instrumental category contains all other possible explanations, including realist, neoliberal institutionalist, and Marxist explanations.
73. Chapter 6 addresses how ethnicity is operationalized in the quantitative analyses.
74. Saideman 1997, Saideman and Dougherty 2000.

75. Gurr and Haxton 1996. Fifty-three states contain actively separatist movements in the 1990s according to the Minorities at Risk dataset, so vulnerability is most likely to constrain about 36% of states.
76. Ibid.
77. Mill 1950; Meckstroth 1975.
78. For using most likely cases to evaluate theory, see Eckstein 1975.
79. In qualitative analyses, random selection may be problematic, King, Keohane, and Verba 1994, 124–128.
80. Jackson 1992, 7; and Herbst 1992, 20.
81. Herbst 1989; Jackson and Rosberg 1982.
82. The promise of economic resources might attract foreign support, rather than ethnic ties, so that the selection of cases might introduce some bias. Specifically, secessionists that do not have economic resources do not get foreign support. Because this study focuses on the vulnerability argument, I am biasing the cases in favor of that approach (most likely cases), rather than other theoretical arguments.
83. Lijphart 1975; King, Keohane, and Verba 1994, 117.
84. Geddes 1990; King, Keohane and Verba 1994.
85. Such as France's involvement in the Congo Crisis and the Soviet Union's during the Nigerian Civil War.
86. I used the Minority At Risk Project's (1999) coding of separatism to check my accuracy.
87. The details of the MAR dataset are discussed in chapter 6.
88. For an excellent discussion of precedent setting, see Kier and Mercer 1996.

Chapter 3

1. Brecher and Wilkenfeld (1997) code the conflict as lasting from July 1960 to February 1962. While there is no problem with the starting date of the conflict, the United Nations forces defeated the Katangans in early 1963, so my discussion of the conflict addresses the policies of countries from the time Katanga chooses to secede to when it ceases to exist.
2. Jackson 1992, 7.
3. The Congo changed its name to Zaire in 1971 and has only changed back with the successful rebellion in May 1997. The focus of this chapter is on the 1960s crisis, so I do not address the ongoing conflict between President Kabila and the rebels supported by Rwanda and Uganda.
4. Spaak 1971, 358.
5. Hoskyns 1965, 81.
6. Ibid., 140.

7. Ibid., 99.
8. Ibid., 114–116.
9. Ibid., 116.
10. Gerard-Libois 1966, 17–23. Also, see Young 1965.
11. Gerard-Libois 1966, 25–26.
12. Ibid., 43–44.
13. Ibid., 7.
14. The provision was written so that multiparty coalitions would be encouraged even if some parties gained majorities in seats in the provinces, Gerard-Libois 1966, 63–83.
15. This tribal conflict has also been ignored by most analysts of this crisis. Only those focusing purely on the domestic politics of the Congo address this issue.
16. Good 1962, 49–53.
17. Gerard-Libois 1996, 282.
18. Schatzberg 1991, 12.
19. Weissman 1974, 69–70.
20. Hoskyns 1965, 142–43.
21. Epstein 1965, 40.
22. Weissman 1974, 71.
23. Gibbs 1991; Weissman 1974.
24. Hoskyns 1965, 140.
25. The Liberal Party's name is deceptive, as it was a conservative party, with much right-wing support. Fitzmaurice 1983, 162–168.
26. Lefever 1967, 29; Helmreich 1976, 395.
27. Fitzmaurice 1983, 50.
28. Ibid., 114.
29. Ibid., 60.
30. Gourevitch 1979.
31. Johansson 1984, 56–58.
32. Vanderlinden 1989, 119.
33. A counterfactual example suggests that if the conflict in the Congo were a linguistic one between Flemish- and French-speaking areas, then Belgian foreign policy would have been very ambivalent. For a recent discussion of counterfactual reasoning, see Tetlock and Belkin 1996.
34. Hoskyns 1965, 85.
35. Helmreich 1976, 395.
36. Hoskyns 1965, 140–141.
37. Linguistic conflict may have existed between the Lunda and the Baluba, but Tshombe did not portray his secessionist movement as being of a particular linguistic (or other ethnic) identity.
38. Hoskyns 1965, 250.

39. Spaak 1971, 378.
40. Ibid., 367.
41. Ibid., 369–70.
42. Ibid., 374.
43. The assassination of Lumumba and subsequent changes in Congolese politics suggests that Belgium, among others, may have been doing exactly that—creating a more favorable government for the West.
44. Gerard-Libois 1966, 236.
45. Epstein 1965, 122.
46. Welensky, 1964, 214.
47. Wood 1983, 824.
48. Ibid., 960.
49. Ibid., 986.
50. Spiro 1963, 424.
51. Ibid., 417.
52. Gauze 1973, 126.
53. Lefever 1967, 118; Gauze 1973, 133.
54. Hoskyns 1965, 187.
55. Gauze 1973, 89.
56. Ibid., 104.
57. Ballard 1966, 295.
58. Ibid., 249.
59. Gauze 1973, 125.
60. Karis 1963, 533; and Potholm 1970, chapter 4.
61. Barber 1973, 86.
62. Hoskyns 1965, 80; Nkrumah 1967, 16.
63. Ghana's was the fifth largest contribution, as measured in man-months, Lefever 1967, 228.
64. Gerard-Libois 1966, 196.
65. Nkrumah 1967, 111.
66. Smock and Smock 1975, 229–230; Nkrumah 1970, 74.
67. Smock and Smock 1975, 226.
68. Ibid., 233–234.
69. Apter 1964, 308.
70. Nkrumah 1970, 85.
71. Smock and Smock 1975, 235.
72. For an extended discussion of Nkrumah's use of foreign policy for domestic political purposes, see Hyde 1971.
73. Mohan 1969, 381.
74. Nigeria was only behind India and Ethiopia, as measured in man-months, Lefever 1967, 228.

75. Ohaegbulam 1982, 106.
76. Ibid., 114.
77. Ibid., 90.
78. Ibid., 14.
79. The NPC's entire support was in its own region, with no seats gained elsewhere, while the other two parties were mildly successful outside their own regions. Phillips 1964, 23.
80. Stremlau 1977, 11.
81. Ohaegbulam 1982, 60, 82.
82. Gambari 1980, 56.
83. Ohaegbulam 1982, 145.
84. Akiba (1998, 44) argues that even Federal Ministers felt compelled to criticize Nigeria's foreign policy as not being sufficiently assertive enough—that they wanted Nigeria to lead Africa.
85. Adamolekum 1977; Ingham 1990, 135–153. Also, for an excellent discussion of Toure's use of foreign policy to divert attention and political mobilization away from ethnic identities, see Riviere 1977.
86. Carment and James (1996) consider multiethnic parties as playing a two-level game (Putnam 1988), focusing on both domestic and international audiences. This differs from my approach which largely focuses on domestic incentives and constraints. Carment and James address Indian foreign policy toward a different crisis: Sri Lanka. Their logic could be applied to the Congo Crisis. However, it would mis-predict India's policies, as contrary to Carment and James's predictions—India was more focused, less constrained, and more assertive than they would expect. Moreover, they suggest that a politically constructed ideology would be too complex to determine or cause an intervention into an ethnic conflict, but that is precisely what happened in this case. They conclude by suggesting that third party intervention into ethnic conflict is likely to be uncommon—which runs counter to this book.
87. For a short background of the development of Indian democracy and the Congress party, see Das Gupta 1989.
88. Heimsath 1965, 55. Also, see Paranjpe and Thomas 1991, 167.
89. Hoskyns 1965, 293.
90. For Morocco, see Zartman 1964, and for Ethiopia, see Ayele 1977, 53–55.
91. For good discussions of Tunisia's domestic politics, see Anderson 1986 and Hopwood 1992.
92. Good 1962.
93. Overall, the U.S. paid almost 42% of the total costs, and out of the voluntary contributions, the U.S. paid $43.4 million out of the slightly more than $46 million, Lefever 1967, 200.
94. Mahoney 1983, 46. Even after Lumumba was removed from power and under arrest, the U.S. sought to eliminate him. Kalb (1982), using the U.S. Senate

Select Committee on Intelligence Activities' investigation of the CIA, details the planning of Lumumba's assassination.

95. Mahoney 1982, 54.
96. Gibbs 1991, chapter 3, 4.
97. Eisenhower 1965, 573–575.
98. Ibid., 572.
99. Weissman 1974. 63, 74–75.
100. Kennedy 1960, 126.
101. Mahoney 1982, 22.
102. Ibid., 25.
103. Ibid., 30. Emphasis is added.
104. The efforts of African states to define the conflict also influenced this perception.
105. Gibbs 1991, 122.
106. Weissman 1974, 171.
107. Mahoney 1982, 150–153.
108. O'Toole 1986, 41.
109. Lalck 1971, 148.
110. Ibid., 124.
111. Good 1962a, 55.
112. Walt 1987, 26.
113. The only evidence I have is that the Socialist party was the last one to break up along linguistic divides.

Chapter 4

1. Jackson 1992, 7; and Herbst 1992, 20.
2. Haiti recognized Biafra in the summer of 1969, apparently because Papa Doc Duvalier went to school with an Ibo who became a Biafran diplomat; see Cronje 1972, 300.
3. Heraclides 1991, 82.
4. Ibid.
5. Kirk-Greene 1971, 155.
6. Ibid., 172. Emphasis is added.
7. Ibid., 197.
8. Pope Paul VI took a strong pro-Biafran stance in this crisis, calling for cease-fires. He was the first to send a diplomatic delegation to Biafra, and called for international intervention to prevent genocide when Biafra's defeat was imminent, Stremlau 1977, 120, 367.
9. Stremlau 1977, 223.

10. De St. Jorre 1972, chapter 9.
11. Biafra wooed the predominantly Catholic states of Latin America, who were "warmly received, and discovered a strong religious sympathy that had been aroused by the Catholic Church." Whether any of these states actually gave assistance to Biafra is unclear, Stremlau 1977, 364–365.
12. Heraclides 1991, 95.
13. Chime 1969, 76.
14. For example, see Nyerere 1967, 206, and 1973, 20.
15. Nyerere 1969, 2.
16. "Tanzania Recognizes Biafra," in Kirk-Greene 1971, 207.
17. Ibid., 210–211. Those who agree with this assessment of Nyerere's motives include: De St. Jorre 1972, 198; Hatch 1976, 248; and Schwab 1971, 71.
18. Hatch 1972, 157.
19. Young 1976, 262. Emphasis is added.
20. Nyerere 1967, 263.
21. Like ethnicity, foreign policy issues were restricted from being addressed during political campaigns, Potholm 1970, 152.
22. Ferkiss, 1967, 29–33.
23. Nyerere 1969, 10.
24. Ibid., 11.
25. Johns 1977, 201.
26. For a good discussion of the difficulties of incorporating Zanzibar, see Heilman 1997.
27. Lofchie 1964, 488–489.
28. Johns 1977, 214.
29. Cited in Cronje 1972, 294–295.
30. Heraclides 1991, 97.
31. Stremlau 1977, 92.
32. Both the pre- and the post-independence constitutions called for abolishing all forms of discrimination, especially tribal and regional differentiation. See Kaunda 1967, 9–11.
33. See Kaunda 1967; Morris 1980; and Shaw 1976, 81.
34. Citing his own speech made on the day Zambia became independent, Kaunda, 1967, 91.
35. Shaw 1976, 80–81.
36. Hatch 1976, 234.
37. "Zambia Recognizes Biafra," in Kirk-Greene 1971, 221.
38. Ferkiss 1967, 33.
39. Given the animosity of many Africans in East Africa to Muslims because of the history of slavery, Zambian animists may have had ethnic enmity towards Muslims.

40. Mulford 1967, chapter 6.
41. Ferkiss 1967, 33.
42. Legum and Drysdale 1970, B499.
43. Cervenka 1972, 59, 103–104; and Melville 1979, 29.
44. Cronje 1972, 296–297.
45. Weiskel 1988, 380.
46. Ferkiss 1967, 30.
47. Wattenberg and Smith 1963, 190.
48. While Nyerere's one-party system was meant to encourage, at least at the outset, competition amongst members of TANU, the PDCI and the Ivory Coast's electoral system discouraged competition, Zolberg 1964, 264.
49. Akpan 1971, 179. Also, for a discussion of shared "the traditional fear among coastal West African leaders of greater Moslem domination from the northern hinterland," see, among others, De St. Jorre 1972, 196.
50. Legum 1971, B499. Separatist sentiment existed among the Sanwi since independence. See Thompson 1962, 281.
51. Stremlau 1977, 245.
52. Cervenka 1972, 103–104.
53. Cronje 1972, 298–299.
54. Corbett 1972, 71. Emphasis is added.
55. N.A. 1971, 328.
56. Ferkiss 1967 31.
57. De Saint-Paul 1987, 31.
58. Weinstein 1966, 111.
59. De Saint-Paul 1987, 27.
60. See De St. Jorre 1972, 219. American Jews were also persuaded that Biafra was the equivalent of Israel in Africa, Cervenka 1972, 147.
61. Legum and Drysdale 1971, A68.
62. De St. Jorre 1972, 220.
63. Heraclides 1991, 102.
64. Aluko 1981, 92.
65. Cervenka 1972, 126.
66. De St. Jorre 1972, 219.
67. Ibid., 218. These countries may have only hurt their long-term position, as one of the lessons Nigerian leaders gained from the civil war was that the white supremacist states were a threat to all black African states, not merely to their immediate neighbors. Aluko 1981, 35.
68. *Africa Confidential* 9, 17, August 23, 1968, 2.
69. Legum and Drysdale 1969, 145.
70. Ibid., 145.
71. Stremlau 1977, 103.

72. Ibid., 346.
73. Ayele 1977, 50.
74. Clapham 1969, 83; and Markakis 1974, 255.
75. Hess 1966, 479.
76. Selassie also included non-Orthodox Christians to dilute the strength of the Orthodox Church, Clapham 1969, 85.
77. Ibid., 82.
78. Hess 1966, 522. Emphasis is added.
79. One author argues that the process also worked in the opposite direction: not only did the Emperor push African unity in order to cement domestic unity, but also that the requirements of African unity required the government to play down antagonisms against Islam internally, see Clapham 1969, 84.
80. Hess 1966, 529. Also, see Hess and Loewenberg 1964, 948.
81. Ofoegbu 1975, 3.
82. Akpan 1971, 142.
83. Le Vine 1971, 175.
84. Legum and Drysdale 1969, 418. This forced the Biafrans to rely upon air transport for their arms.
85. While the cabinet consisted of several ethnic groups, the Fulani were overrepresented while most others were underrepresented, Morrison 1972, 195.
86. Kofele-Kale 1980, 214.
87. Mazrui and Tidy 1984, 77, emphasis is added.
88. Ardener 1967,299.
89. Le Vine 1963, 290.
90. N.A. 1971, 176–178.
91. Stremlau 1977, 103.
92. Cronje 1972, 291.
93. Stremlau 1977, 183–184.
94. Thompson 1972, 176.
95. It was highly likely that if Biafra won, the Western Region dominated by the Yorubas would have also seceded, leaving Hausa-dominated Northern Nigeria to be a state by itself. See Stremlau 1977, 52.
96. Ferkiss 1967, 29–33.
97. Thompson 1966, 183.
98. Charlick 1991, 10. Charlick does admit that by itself, Islam is not a sufficient force for unity in Niger as there are many different brotherhoods within the one religious group. However, aiding Nigeria would be one issue upon which all of the brotherhoods could agree.
99. De St. Jorre 1972, 219.
100. *Africa Confidential* 9, 25 (Dec. 20, 1968), 1.
101. Saideman 1998a.

102. Stremlau 1977, 274.
103. Cronje 1972, 285.
104. Stremlau 1977, 131.
105. Heraclides 1991, 99.
106. Legum and Drysdale 1970, B588.
107. Corbett 1972, 71–72.
108. Ingham 1990, 119; and Markowitz 1969.
109. For a thorough discussion Islam in Senegal's politics, see Behrman 1970. Also, see Markowitz 1970, 73–96.
110. Foltz 1964, 47.
111. Ibid.
112. Ingham 1990, 121. It is important to note that from 1966 to the mid-1970s, Senegal was a one-party system as Senghor repressed or co-opted all other parties; see N.A. 1971, 642.
113. Barry 1988, 285.
114. Stremlau 1977, 140–141. Heraclides also acknowledges the large Muslim population as a constraint on Senghor's policies toward Biafra and Nigeria, 1991, 99.
115. Ibid., 274.
116. Ibid., 279. Nigeria sought to prevent internationalization of the crisis, as it did not want external actors to interfere. After initial opposition, OAU mediation/consultation was seen as one method of keeping the UN out of the crisis.
117. Ibid., 353.
118. Legum and Drysdale 1969, B599.
119. *Africa Confidential* 10, 22 (Nov. 7, 1969), 3.
120. Morrison 1972, 334–335.
121. Fisher 1969, 622.
122. Ferkiss 1967, 30.
123. Uganda is not discussed fully here because it falls into the same general category as Sierra Leone: a relatively neutral actor in this crisis due to the conflicting religious ties of the primary constituents of the leadership of each state. However, Uganda emphasizes the point that a multireligious constituency will constrain a leader's foreign policy toward Biafra.
124. For a discussion of tribal outbidding in Uganda, see Hansen 1977; and Mazrui and Tidy 1984, 250–251. For an analysis of the role of religion in Uganda's political system, see Gingyera-Pinyewa 1978, chapter 6. For a discussion of Obote's desire for secularization, see Lockard 1980, 40–73.
125. Stremlau 1977, 131.
126. Walt 1987, 32.
127. Ibid., chapter 5.
128. See Hess 1966, 479.

Chapter 5

1. This chapter only addresses the period 1991–1995, which largely concurs with Brecher and Wilkenfeld's (1997) coding of what they consider two crises: Croatia and Bosnia. While more recent events in Kosovo lend support to the ethnic ties approach, it is too current to adequately address here, although I discuss the the international relations of the Kosovo conflict briefly in the concluding chapter.
2. The European Community became the European Union when the Maastricht Treaty was ratified in November 1993, so the European Community is the relevant actor until 1993, when the European Union replaces the EC.
3. Steinberg 1993, 27.
4. I discuss the causes of Serb irredentism in Saideman 1998a.
5. For an explanation of Yugoslavia's disintegration consistent with the theory of ethnic politics and foreign policy, see Saideman 1996, 1998b.
6. Bookman 1992, 58.
7. Snyder 1999.
8. Gagnon 1991, 21.
9. For more exhaustive accounts of the roles played by international organizations in this conflict, see Durch and Schear 1996; Burg and Shoup 1999.
10. Editors 1992, 6.
11. A third UN effort, in December 1992, deployed peacekeepers to Macedonia to prevent the spread of conflict to that republic. Interestingly, the forces were placed on Macedonia's borders with Serbia and Kosovo, but not its borders with Greece despite Greece's fears of Macedonian irredentism.
12. For a very good portrayal of this escalation, see Discovery Channel 1995.
13. Honig and Both 1996.
14. Saideman 1998a.
15. The focus here is on the complexity of identities at play. The following discussion focuses on how various identities came into play, not to provide a definitive account of what causes groups to develop particular identities. For an explanation of the dilemmas secessionists face as they develop their identities, see Saideman 1997, Saideman and Dougherty 2000.
16. Kaufman Forthcoming.
17. Ramet 1992, 27.
18. Ibid., 161.
19. Ibid., 161.
20. Poulton 1991, 22.
21. Denitch 1994, 114.
22. Zimmeran 1996, 25.
23. Rezun 1995, 152.

24. Sells 1996, chapter 2.
25. Ramet 1995a, 203.
26. Woodward 1995, 207.
27. Zimmerman 1995, 3.
28. Woodward 1995, 208.
29. Zimmerman 1995, 7.
30. Prelec 1997, 76, 82.
31. Ramet 1992, 121.
32. Kristo 1995, 432.
33. Silber and Little 1996, 83.
34. Zimmeran 1996, 117.
35. Croatia's offensives tended to coincide with the electoral schedule. Croatia attacked Serb positions in 1993 before the upcoming elections, and Tudjman called elections after his 1995 victory.
36. Donia and Fine 1994, 249. Also, see Pusic 1998.
37. Prelec 1997, 85–87.
38. For a harsh critique of the HDZ, Tudjman and the Croatian government, see Pusic 1998.
39. Bicanic and Dominis 1993, 19.
40. Cited in the New York Times, March 3, 1999.
41. "The election results read more like a census of national identities in the socialist period. The three national parties gained votes and seats almost directly proportional to individuals' choices of national identity in the 1981 census (the SDA, 33.8%; the SDS, 29.6%; and the HDZ, 18.3%), Woodward 1995, 122.
42. Friedman and Remington 1997, 94.
43. Donia and Fine 1994, 6–7.
44. Friedman and Remington 1997, 105.
45. Ibid.
46. Cohen 1995, 114.
47. Ibid., 278.
48. Poulton 1991, 43–44; Ramet 1992, 165.
49. Tupurkovski 1997, 137.
50. Danforth 1995, 144.
51. Ibid., 147–148.
52. Ibid., 155.
53. The Kosovo conflict and the refugees that it produced alarmed Macedonia, resulting in deportations of refugees, blocking them from crossing into Macedonia, and limits on the size of refugee camps. The fear apparently is that the flow of ethnic Albanians from Kosovo may upset the political balance in Macedonia, and worsen an already desperate economic situation.
54. Denitch 1994, 132.

55. Huntington 1993.
56. Lepick 1996.
57. Woodward 1995, 184.
58. Gow 1997, 159.
59. Lukic and Lynch 1996, 253.
60. Gow 1997, 159.
61. For an interesting discussion of this tendency but applied to nuclear proliferation policy, see Jabko and Weber (1999).
62. Gordon 1993, 113.
63. Kramer, 1994, 79.
64. Howorth 1994, 114.
65. For an account focusing on anti-Muslim feelings, see Sells 1996.
66. It is important to note there was some discussion about separatism in Yugoslavia setting unfortunate precedents for Romania's Hungarian minority in Transylvania, Gallagher 1995, 133; and Rezun 1995, 186.
67. Rezun 1995, 163.
68. Watts 1997, 238.
69. Gallagher 1995, 134.
70. Watts 1997, 225.
71. Tismaneanu 1997,404.
72. Dellenbrant 1994, 213.
73. Brown 1994, 189–191.
74. Nedeva 1993, 132.
75. Gallagher 1995, 235.
76. The Romanian case supports one of Morgan and Bickers's (1992) points: that external diversionary war is unnecessary and less likely when the government can divert attention and hostility toward internal groups.
77. For a critique of "Germany-Bashing," see Conversi 1998.
78. Genscher 1997, 491.
79. The timing has caused many to speculate that Germany was able to get France and/or Britain to agree to recognition in exchange for German compromises on the Maastricht Union Treaty, Maull 1995–96, 104.
80. Croat behavior since then suggests that the promises have not been kept.
81. Genscher 1997, 516.
82. Libal 1997, 99–100.
83. Schoenbaum and Pond 1996, 190.
84. Djilas 1995, 163–64.
85. Germany was roughly six times more powerful as Yugoslavia before it disintegrated and about ten times afterward, according to data discussed in chapter six.
86. Hirschman 1945.

87. Libal 1997, 105.
88. Crawford 1996, 504.
89. Ibid., 506.
90. Libal 1997, 110–11.
91. Maull 1995–96, 112.
92. Morgan 1996, 158–160.
93. Crawford (1996, 503) makes this point well.
94. Muller 1992, 153.
95. Ash 1993, 381.
96. Maull 1995–96, Morgan 1996, and Muller 1992, to name just a few.
97. Schoenbaum and Pond 1996, 190.
98. Ash 1993, 381.
99. Libal 1997 14.
100. Maull 1995–96, 103.
101. Ramet 1993, 327.
102. Maull 1995–96, 121.
103. Crawford 1996, 502.
104. Ibid.
105. Ibid., 508.
106. Muller 1992, 153.
107. Crawford 1995, 14.
108. Crawford, in a footnote (1996, 509, fn. 100), reminds us that the dominance of the two largest parties, the SPD and the CDU/CSU, was declining as their share of the votes slipped from the 1970s to the 1990 elections from more than 90% to less than 78%.
109. Genscher 1997, 512.
110. Libal 1997, 153.
111. Karp 1993, 139.
112. Urban 1997, 251.
113. Ibid., 248.
114. In one Eurobarometer poll, 72% of the Hungarians polled supported the right of Yugoslav republics to secede; cited in Cohen 1995, 235.
115. Haynes 1995, 95.
116. Szayna 1994, 29.
117. Urban 1997, 246.
118. Brown 1994, 186.
119. Urban 1997, 251–52. There still has been some cause for concern. Vojvodina's Hungarians have been drafted at greater numbers than their proportion of the population, and have suffered a disproportionate share of the casualties in Serbia's wars in Croatia and Bosnia, Gagnon 1994/95, 161.
120. Nielsson and Kanavou 1996, 15.

121. Kun, 1993, 127.

122. Urban 1997, 248.

123. Cohen 1994, 820.

124. Ibid., 822–23.

125. For example, see Cohen 1995, 262–3, 299–302; Edemskii 1996; Lukic and Lynch 1996.

126. Gow 1997, 197.

127. Gompert 1996, 136; Rezun 1995, 164.

128. Since the YPA took all of its arms and equipment with it when it withdrew, Macedonia did not possess any capability to defend itself, not to mention attacking its neighbors, Glenny 1996, 137.

129. The Badinter Commission ruled that Macedonia's name did not imply a claim on Greek territory, Lukic and Lynch 1996, 280.

130. Danforth 1995, 154.

131. Bennett 1995, 219.

132. Larrabee 1992, 41–42.

133. Woodward 1995, 358.

134. Pettifer 1996, 22.

135. Silber and Little 1996, 367.

136. It is also important to note that Greece's embargo hurt its own economy, *The Economist* September 16, 1993.

137. Müftüler-Bac 1997, 49.

138. Ullman 1996, 20.

139. Ramet 1995b, 228.

140. Poulton 1997, 198.

141. Brown 1993, 153.

142. Ibid., 152.

143. Ibid., 153.

144. For an interesting, and more than merely self-serving, discussion of the American role in the last months of the Bosnian conflict, see Holbrooke 1998.

145. Baker 1995, 635–636.

146. Burg and Shoup 1999, 200.

147. Halverson 1996, 17.

148. Holbrooke 1998, 66–68. Burg and Shoup 1999, 323–325.

149. In his address to the U.S. Air Force Academy, Clinton (1995) defined one key focus of policy towards Bosnia was "to keep the faith with our NATO allies."

150. Gompert 1996, 129.

151. Zimmermann 1996, 127.

152. In a conversation with former State Department official George Kenney, he asserted that the lobbying organizations of all three sides were inept, January 14, 1995, La Jolla, California.

153. Gompert 1996, 136.
154. Rosin 1994, 11–12.
155. Halverson 1996, 11.
156. The presence of these Islamic volunteers became a sore spot in American-Bosnian relations during and after the Dayton negotiations, Holbrooke 1998.
157. Moore 1993.
158. Christensen and Snyder 1990.
159. Baker 1995, Genscher 1997. Whether this is a reasonable fear is subject of much debate, since the Soviet Union's path toward disintegration was similar to that of Yugoslavia's—largely the product of domestic political dynamics, Saideman 1996, 1998b.
160. For an argument about reciprocity between the external and internal actors, see Goldstein and Pevehouse 1997.
161. Sells 1996.
162. Saideman and Dougherty 2000.
163. Huntington 1993, Heraclides 1991, respectively.

Chapter 6

1. Cases where ethnic enmities exist between the host state and potential supporter are coded as ethnic ties with the secessionists, and ethnic enmities exist between secessionists and the outside actor are coded as ethnic ties with the host state.
2. See chapter 2, pages 13–17.
3. The predicted explosion in ethnic conflict did not occur, as the number of new ethnic conflicts has plateaued in recent years, Gurr 2000.
4. Phase III of the Minorities At Risk dataset is available at http://www.bsos.umd.edu/cidcm/mar. I would like thank Ted Gurr, Anne Pitsch, and Deepa Khosa for their generous assistance, including provision of codesheets for international support. For more on the Minorities at Risk Project, see Gurr 1993, Gurr and Haxton 1996, Gurr 1999 and Gurr 2000.
5. The following discussion is also relevant for this chapter's subsequent analyses.
6. See Gurr 2000, chapter 1.
7. I also coded a variable for total support, which adds the highest level of support given to a group by each supporter. I have not included it in the analyses below because it is highly correlated with the other two dependent variables.
8. On several codesheets, an international organization was included as a supporter of an ethnic group, such as the Gulf Cooperation Council, Organization of Islamic Conference or the European Union. In such cases, only the countries actually listed on the codesheet were included in this analysis. This study

is intended to understand why states do what they do, which then shapes what international organizations might do. Including the policies of international organizations in the dataset would, therefore, be problematic. This might undercount the level of support for a particular group. For instance, only six countries are listed as supporters of the Bosnian Muslims (Croatia, Kuwait, Iran, Saudi Arabia, Syria and Malaysia). Further, in some cases, sub-state actors are listed as supporters, such as the Tatar Republic of the Russian Federation supporting the Abkhaz in Georgia. Since the focus of this study is why states take sides, such sub-state actors were not included.

9. The missing cases largely fall into two groups: Black minorities of Central and South America, and groups in Iran. The other groups that do not have data for international support are Germany's Turks, Guinea's Susu, Sierra Leone's Temne, Zaire's Ngbandi, Egypt's Copts, and Indonesia's Achenese. These omissions may cause some bias in the findings, but it is hard to determine whether such bias is systematic or significant.

10. Herbst 1992, Jackson 1992.

11. Carment and James 1995, 1997, Davis and Moore 1997.

12. One of my future research directions is to develop a dyadic dataset consisting of group-potential external supporter dyads to determine which relationships—ethnic ties, relative power, economic ties—influence what states do.

13. Some argue that even these kinds of ethnic conflicts can increase the probability of ethnic conflict elsewhere. For a debate about the contagiousness of ethnic conflict, see Midlarsky 1992, and Lake and Rothchild 1998.

14. Jackson and Rosberg 1982, and Herbst 1989.

15. Labs 1997.

16. The qualifier of "neighboring" is a function of the dataset. All states where the ethnic kin dominates should support the ethnic group, if this approach is correct, but the MAR dataset only codes neighboring states as being dominated by an ethnic group's kin or not.

17. Recent methodology texts implore scholars to test as many of the logical implications of their theories as possible, King, Keohane and Verba 1994 and Van Evera 1997.

18. Jonathan Fox (1997) argues that ethno-religious conflicts are more severe than other kinds of ethnic conflict, which may be the case because these conflicts attract more outside support.

19. If one of the two components of a category was missing (for instance, military personnel was missing but expenditures was available), then I used the remaining component's percentage of the world total as that category's average. If two components of one category were missing, then the entire variable was coded as missing. The data used for calculating power comes from Singer and Small 1995.

20. This is a conventional method for developing an indicator for states' relative power. I am indebted to Doug Van Belle for providing the data used to construct this indicator and suggestions on how to do it. For a similar effort to code relative power, see Bremer 1992, 322.

21. The ranking has the top ten countries in order as: the U.S., the People's Republic of China, Russia, India, Japan, Germany, the United Kingdom, France, Italy, and the Republic of Korea. India is ranked higher than it probably should be because the indicator weights heavily population size.

22. For instance, it does not contain any indicator for technological expertise.

23. Here and below are some illustrative examples of how groups were coded in the Dataset. A group not considered as racially distinct at all would be the Scots. A group that is physically distinguishable but of the same racial stock would be the Tamils in Sri Lanka. A group considered to be intermixed racially would be the Hutus and Tutsis. A group considered to be of a different racial stock would be the Europeans of South Africa.

24. A group rated as having no religious differences would be the Europeans of South Africa. A group considered as different sect but of the same religion would be Iraq's Shia. A group considered being of multiple sects not all sharing the same religion would be the Kurds of Iran. A groups considered to be of a different religion would be the Tibetans in China.

25. Grimes and Grimes 1996. I am grateful to James Fearon for providing me with this data and for help in using it.

26. A group with the least linguistic differences would be African-Americans while groups with the most differences include the Indigenous peoples of Latin America.

27. Gurr and Jaggers 1999.

28. Regan 1998.

29. Even using data from the previous year does not really control completely for the endogeneity problem, but it is a start. A time series analysis would be the best way to deal with this, but there are simply not enough time points for most of the indicators.

30. Because the distribution of the data along the dependent variable is quite skewed, I chose to use robust standard errors to address the possible impact heteroskedasticity might have.

31. For an argument about event counts, see King 1989.

32. Tomz, Wittenberg and King 1998.

33. There is not table for intensity of support in 1994–95 because the program would hang up on that analysis, and only that analysis. I have communicated with the software's creators, and we have not yet resolved this problem. This should not be too problematic, however, as the results of the CLARIFY simulations are very consistent among the various analyses.

34. Schweller 1996.
35. This discussion illustrates some of the difficulties in separating top-down from bottom-up situations. In some cases, leaders are using religion to mobilize the population, but in others, the population pushes leaders to take a strong stand on behalf of their religion.
36. Using each country's percentage of population that is Muslim produces similar results, but omits a few cases where the precise percentage was not readily available, but the minority status of the Muslims was certain.
37. Again, the data used to calculate relative power comes from Singer and Small 1995.
38. For a good discussion of the debate, see Ray 1995.
39. Again, because the distribution of the data along the dependent variable is quite skewed, I chose to use robust standard errors.
40. As on page 175, I tested for multicollinearity and found none.
41. However, this is impossible to determine here, since a state with vulnerable neighbors may actually be supporting an ethnic group in a dispute far away.
42. The only exceptions are those groups Libya supported.
43. This paragraph focuses on numbers from 1994–1995.

Chapter 7

1. Huntington 1993.
2. Herbst 1989; Keohane 1986.
3. This is not that great of stretch from Walt's latest work, 1996, 19.
4. Walt 1987, 180.
5. Huntington 1993. This approach is also distinct from Huntingon's as I do not assume that one particular identity trumps as others as he seems to do. Further, the logic of the theory of ethnic politics and foreign policy and the cases demonstrates that intracivilization conflict can be as severe as intercivilization strife.
6. Saideman 1997 and Saideman and Dougherty 2000.
7. Snyder 1993.
8. Snyder 1999.
9. One commonality between Kosovo and Bosnia has been the insertion of Arkan's Tigers, notorious (and indicted) for their atrocities in Bosnia, *New York Times*, May 25, 1999.
10. Of course, Albania largely lacked the ability to enforce its sovereignty. Although this book argues that Jackson and Rosberg's claims about vulnerability do not explain the behavior of states toward secessionist conflicts, they are quite right in pointing out how many states lack the empirical qualities of sovereignty.
11. *New York Times*, May 25, 1999.

12. *New York Times*, May 7, 1999.
13. *New York Times*, April 20, 1999.
14. However, many of Russia's Muslims opposed support for Serbia and preferred assistance for Kosovo's Albanians, *Dallas Morning News*, June 9, 1999, A18.
15. Indeed, Russian politicians have argued that Western concern about Chechnya has been hypocritical, and that the Russian use of force there is very similar to NATO's bombing of Serbia.
16. Junyk 1999.
17. Ibid.
18. The Christian Democrats have opposed a ground campaign as well, but their opposition was less threatening than the Greens. *New York Times*, May 20, 1999.
19. *New York Times*, March 29, 1999.
20. Ibid.
21. For a rare discussion of the target's relevance, see James 1988.
22. Coser 1956.
23. Morgan and Bickers 1982, 32.
24. Smith 1996, Leeds and Davis 1997.
25. Levy and Vakili 1992.
26. Gourevitich 1996, Moravcsik 1997, among others.
27. Moravcsik 1997, 544.
28. This is a simplification of these studies, but I am using this debate to clarify what could be done in this field.
29. Gibbs 1991.
30. Saideman 1995.
31. Walter 1997.
32. Other kinds of conflicts may be easier to manage because of the absence or irrelevance of ethnic ties. For a similar argument about the kind of conflict influencing the chances for successful management, see Kaufmann 1996a.

References

General

Ames, Barry. 1987. *Political Survival: Politicians and Public Policy in Latin America*. Berkeley: University of California Press.

Ayres, R. William and Stephen M. Saideman. 2000. "Is Separatism as Contagious as the Common Cold or as Cancer? Testing the International and Domestic Determinants of Secessionism." *Nationalism and Ethnic Politics* 6 (3): 92–114.

Bates, Robert H., Rui J.P. De Figueiredo, Jr., and Barry R. Weingast. 1998. "The Politics of Interpretation." *Politics and Society* 26 (4): 603–642.

Bienen, Henry. 1995. "Ethnic Nationalisms and Implications for U.S. Foreign Policy." In Charles A. Kupchan, ed., *Nationalism and Nationalities in the New Europe*, pp. 158–179. Ithaca: Cornell University Press.

Brass, Paul R. 1991. *Ethnicity and Nationalism: Theory and Comparison*. New Delhi: Sage.

Brecher, Michael and Jonathan Wilkenfeld. 1997. *A Study of Crisis*. Ann Arbor: University of Michigan Press.

Bremer, Stuart A. 1992. "Dangerous Dyads: Conditions Affecting the Likelihood of Interstate War, 1816–1965." *Journal of Conflict Resolution* 36 (2): 309–341.

Breton, Albert, et al., eds. 1995. *Nationalism and Rationality*. Cambridge: Cambridge University Press.

Buchheit, Lee C. 1978. *Secession: The Legitimacy of Self-Determination*. New Haven: Yale University Press.

Bueno De Mesquita, Bruce. 1981. *The War Trap*. New Haven: Yale University Press.

Bull, Hedley. 1977. *The Anarchical Society*. New York: Columbia University Press.

Byman, Daniel. 1997. "Rethinking Partition: Lessons from Iraq and Lebanon." *Security Studies* 7 (1): 1–32.

Carment, David and Patrick James. 1995. "Internal Constraints and Interstate Ethnic Conflict: Toward a Crisis-Based Assessment of Irredentism." *Journal of Conflict Resolution* 39 (1): 82–109.

Carment, David and Patrick James. 1996. "Two-Level Games and Third-Party Intervention: Evidence from Ethnic Conflict in the Balkans and South Asia." *Canadian Journal of Political Science* 29 (3): 521–554.

Carment, David and Patrick James. 1997. "Secession and Irredenta in World Politics: The Neglected Interstate Dimension." In David Carment and Patrick James, eds., *Wars in the Midst of Peace: The International Politics of Ethnic Conflict*, pp. 194–231. Pittsburgh: University of Pittsburgh Press.

Carment, David, Patrick James and Dane Rowlands. 1997. "Ethnic Conflict and Third Party Intervention: Riskiness, Rationality and Commitment." In Gerald Schneider and Patricia A. Weitsman, eds., *Enforcing Cooperation: Risky States and Intergovernmental Management of Conflict*, pp. 104–131. New York: St. Martin's Press.

Carter, Gwendolen M. 1963. *Five African States: Responses to Diversity*. Ithaca: Cornell University Press.

Chopra, Jarat and Thomas G. Weiss. 1995. "Prospects for Containing Conflict in the Former Second World." *Security Studies* 4 (3): 552–583.

Christensen, Thomas J. and Jack Snyder. 1990. "Chain Gangs and Passed Bucks: Predicting Alliance Patterns in Multipolarity." *International Organization* 44 (2): 137–168

Cigar, Norman L. 1995. *Genocide In Bosnia: The Policy of "Ethnic Cleansing."* College Station: Texas A&M University Press.

Clark, David H. 1998. "Rethinking the Logical Conditions of Diversionary Behavior." Paper prepared for presentation at the Annual Meeting of the *International Studies Association*, Minneapolis, MN.

Cohen, Roger. 1998. *Hearts Grown Brutal: Sagas of Sarajevo*.New York: Random House.

Coser, Lewis. 1956. *The Functions of Social Conflict*. Glencoe, IL: Free Press.

Das Gupta, Jyotirindra. 1989. "India: Democratic Becoming and Combined Development." In Larry Diamond, Juan J. Linz, and Seymour Martin Lipset, eds. *Democracy in Developing Countries, Volume Three: Asia*, pp. Boulder: Lynne Rienner.

David, Steven R. 1991. *Choosing Sides: Alignment and Realignment in the Third World*. Baltimore: Johns Hopkins University Press.

Davies, John L. and Ted Robert Gurr, eds. 1998. *Preventive Measures: Building Risk Assessment and Crisis Early Warning Systems*. Lanham, MD: Rowman & Littlefield.

Davis, David R. and Will H. Moore. 1997. "Ethnicity Matters: Transnational Ethnic Alliances and Foreign Behavior." *International Studies Quarterly* 41 (1): 171–184.

de Figueiredo, Jr., Rui J. P. and Barry R. Weingast. 1999. "The Rationality of Fear: Political Opportunism and Ethnic Conflict." In Barbara F. Walter and Jack Snyder, eds., *Civil Wars, Insecurity, and Intervention*, pp. 261–302. New York: Columbia University Press.

Dowty, Alan and Gil Loescher. 1996. "Refugee Flows as Grounds for International Action." *International Security* 21 (1): 43–71.

Eckstein, Harry. 1975. "Case Study and Theory in Political Science," In Fred I. Greenstein and Nelson W. Polsby, eds., *Handbook of Political Science, Volume 7: Strategies of Inquiry*, pp. 80–137. Reading, MA; Addison-Wesley.

Elliot, Kimberly Ann. 1998. "The Sanctions Glass: Half Full or Completely Empty." *International Security* 23 (1): 50–65.

Elman, Colin. 1996. "Horses for Courses: Why *Not* Neorealist Theories of Foreign Policy." *Security Studies* 6 (1): 7–53.

Fearon, James D. 1998. "Bargaining, Enforcement and International Cooperation. *International Organization* 52 (2): 269–306.

Fearon, James D. and David D. Laitin. 1999. "Weak States, Rough Terrain, and Large-Scale Ethnic Violence Since 1945." Paper prepared for delivery at the 1999 *Annual Meeting of the American Political Science Association*, Atlanta, GA.

Foltz, William J. 1991. "The Organization of African Unity and the Resolution of Africa's Conflicts." In Francis M. Deng and I. William Zartman, eds., *Conflict resolution in Africa*, pp. 347–366. Washington, DC: Brookings.

Fox, Jonathan. 1997. "The Salience of Religious Issues in Ethnic Conflicts: A Large-N Study." *Nationalism and Ethnic Politics* 3, 3: 1–19.

Gartzke, Erik. 1998. "Kant We All Just Get Along? Opportunity, Willingness and the Origins of the Democratic Peace." *American Journal of Political Science* 42 (1): 1–27.

Geddes, Barbara. 1990. "How the Cases You Choose Affect the Answers You Get," *Political Analysis* 2.

Geertz, Clifford. 1963. "The Integrative Revolution: Primordial Sentiments and Civil Politics in the New States." In Clifford Geertz, ed., *Old Societies and New States: The Quest for Modernity in Asia and Africa*, pp. 255–310. London: Free Press.

Gelpi, Christopher. 1997. "Democratic Diversions: Governmental Structure and the Externalization of Domestic Conflict." *Journal of Conflict Resolution* 41 (2): 255–282.

Gibbs, David N. 1991. *The Political Economy of Third World Intervention: Mines, Money, and U.S. Policy in the Congo Crisis*. Chicago: University of Chicago.

Gourevitch, Peter Alexis. 1979. "The Reemergence of 'Peripheral Nationalisms': Some Comparative Speculations on the Spatial Distribution of Political Leadership and Economic Growth." *Comparative Study of Society and History* 21 (3): 303–322.

Gourevitch, Peter Alexis. 1996. "Squaring the Circle: The Domestic Sources of International Cooperation." *International Organization* 50 (2): 349–373.

Gurr, Ted Robert. 1993. *Minorities at Risk: A Global View of Ethnopolitical Conflicts.* Washington, DC: US Institute of Peace Press.

Gurr, Ted Robert. 1994. "Peoples Against States: Ethnopolitical Conflict and the Changing World System." *International Studies Quarterly* 38 (2): 347–378.

Gurr, Ted Robert and Keith Jaggers. 1999. *Polity98: Regime Characteristics 1800–1998.* College Park, MD: Center for International Development and Conflict Management.

Gurr, Ted Robert. 1999. *Minorities at Risk Dataset.* College Park, MD: Center for International Development and Conflict Management.

Gurr, Ted Robert. 2000. *Peoples Versus States: Ethnopolitical Conflict and Accommodation at the End of the 20th Century.* Washington, DC: US Institute of Peace Press.

Gurr, Ted Robert and Michael Haxton 1996. "Minorities Report 1: Ethnopolitical Conflict in the 1990s: Patterns and Trends." College Park, MD: Center for International Development and Conflict Management.

Hardin, Russell. 1995. *One for All: The Logic of Group Conflict.* Princeton: Princeton University.

Harvey, Frank. 1997. "Deterrence and Ethnic Conflict: The Case of Bosnia-Herzegovina, 1993–1994." *Security Studies* 6 (3): 180–210.

Heimsath, Charles H. 1965. "Nonalignment Reassessed: The Experience of India." *Foreign Policy in the Sixties: The Issues and the Instruments,* eds. Roger Hilsman and Robert C. Good, pp. 47–66. Baltimore: Johns Hopkins.

Henderson, Errol A. 1997. "Culture or Contiguity: Ethnic Conflict, the Similarity of States, and the Onset of War, 1820–1989." *Journal of Conflict Resolution* 41 (5): 649–668.

Heraclides, Alexis. 1991. *The Self-Determination of Minorities In International Politics.* London: Frank Cass.

Herbst, Jeffrey. 1989. The Creation and Maintenance of National Boundaries in Africa. *International Organization* 43 (4): 673–692.

Herbst, Jeffrey. 1992. "Challenges to Africa's Boundaries in the New World Order." *Journal of International Affairs* 46 (1): 17–30.

Hirschman, Albert O. 1970. *Exit, Voice, and Loyalty: Responses to Decline in Firms, Organizations, and States.* Cambridge: Harvard University Press.

Horowitz, Donald. 1985. *Ethnic Groups in Conflict.* Berkeley: University of California.

Huntington, Samuel P. 1993. "The Clash of Civilizations?" *Foreign Affairs* 72 (3): 22–49.

Jabko, Nicolas and Steven Weber. 1998. "France's Nuclear Nonproliferation Policy in Theoretical Perspective." *Security Studies* 8 (1): 108–150.

Jackson, Robert H. 1982. *Personal Rule in Black Africa: Prince, Autocrat, Prophet, Tyrant.* Berkeley: University of California.

Jackson, Robert H. 1990. *Quasi-States: Sovereignty, International Relations, and the Third World.* Cambridge: Cambridge University Press.

Jackson, Robert H. 1992. "Juridical Statehood in Sub-Saharan Africa." *Journal of International Affairs* 46 (1): 1–16.

Jackson, Robert H. and Carl G. Rosberg. 1982. Why Africa's Weak States Persist: The Empirical and the Juridical in Statehood. *World Politics* 3 (15): 1–24.

Jacobsen, Gary C. 1988. "Running Scared: Elections and Congressional Politics in the 1980s," In Mathew D. McCubbins and Terry Sullivan, eds., *Congress: Structure and Policy,* pp. 39–81. Cambridge: Cambridge University Press.

James, Patrick. 1988. *Crisis and War.* Montreal: McGill-Queen's University Press

James, Patrick and Athanasios Hristoulas. 1994. "Domestic Politics and Foreign Policy: Evaluating a Model of Crisis Activity for the United States." *Journal of Politics* 56 (2): 327–348.

James, Patrick and John R. Oneal. 1991. "The Influence of Domestic and International Politics on the President's Use of Force." *Journal of Conflict Resolution* 35 (2): 307–332.

Kamanu, Onyeonoro S. 1974. "Secession and the Right of Self-Determination: An OAU Dilemma." *Journal of Modern African Studies* 12 (3): 355–376.

Kaufman, Stuart. Forthcoming. *The Symbolic Politics of Ethnic War: Elites, Masses, and Ethnic Violence in Post-Communist Europe.* Ithaca: Cornell University Press.

Kaufmann, Chaim D.. 1996a. "Intervention in Ethnic and Ideological Civil Wars." *Security Studies* 6 (1): 62–104.

Kaufmann, Chaim D. 1996b. "Possible and Impossible Solutions to Ethnic Civil Wars." *International Security* 20 (4): 136–175.

Kaufmann, Chaim D. 1998. "Where All Else Fails: Ethnic Population Transfers and Partitions in the Twentieth Century." *International Security* 23 (2): 120–156.

Keohane, Robert O. 1986. "Reciprocity in International Relations." *International Organization* 40 (1): 1–27.

Kier, Elizabeth and Jonathan Mercer. 1996. "Setting Precedents in Anarchy: Military Intervention and Weapons of Mass Destruction." *International Security* 20 (4): 77–106.

King, Gary. 1989. "Event Count Models for International Relations: Generalizations and Applications." *International Studies Quarterly* 33 (2): 123–147.

King, Gary, Michael Tomz, and Jason Wittenberg. 1998. "Making the Most of Statistical Analyses: Improving Interpretation and Presentation." Presented at the annual meeting of the American Political Science Association, Boston.

King, Gary, Robert O. Keohane, and Sidney Verba. 1994. *Designing Social Inquiry*. Princeton: Princeton University Press.

Kuran, Timur. 1998. "Ethnic Dissimilation and Its International Relations," in David A. Lake and Donald Rothchild, eds. *Ethnic conflict: Fear, Diffusion, and Escalation*, pp. 35–60. Princeton: Princeton University Press.

Labs, Eric J. 1997. "Beyond Victory: Offensive Realism and the Expansion of War Aims." *Security Studies* 6 (4): 1–49.

Laitin, David D. 1986. *Hegemony and Culture: Politics and Religious Change among the Yoruba*. Chicago: University of Chicago Press.

Lake, David and Donald Rothchild. eds. 1998. *Ethnic Conflict: Fear, Diffusion, and Escalation*. Princeton: Princeton University Press.

Leeds, Brett Ashley and David R. Davis. 1997. "Domestic Political Vulnerability and International Disputes." *Journal of Conflict Resolution* 41 (6): 814–834.

Legro, Jeffrey W. 1996. "Culture and Preferences in the International Cooperation Two-Step." *American Political Science Review* 90 (1): 118–137.

Levy, Jack. 1989. "The Diversionary Theory of War: A Critique." In Manus I. Midlarsky, ed., *Handbook of War Studies*, pp. 259–288. Boston: Unwin Hyman.

Levy, Jack and Lily I. Vakili. 1992. "Diversionary Action by Authoritarian Regimes: Argentina in the Falklands/Malavinas Case." In Manus I. Midlarsky, ed., *The Internationalization of Communal Strife*, pp. 118–148 London: Routledge.

Lijphart, Arend. 1975. The Comparable-Cases Strategy In Comparative Research. *Comparative Political Studies* 8 (2): 158–177.

Mayhew, David R. 1974. *Congress: The Electoral Connection*. New Haven: Yale University Press.

Mazrui, Ali A., and Michael Tidy. 1984. *Nationalism and New States in Africa: From About 1935 to the Present*. Nairobi: Heinemann.

Mearsheimer, John. 1994/95. "The False Promise of International Institutions." *International Security* 19 (3): 5–49.

Meckstroth, Theodore W. 1975. "'Most Different Systems' and 'Most Similar Systems': A Study in the Logic of Comparative Inquiry." *Comparative Political Studies* 8 (2): 132–157.

Mill, John Stuart. 1950. *Philosophy of Scientific Method*, edited by Ernest Nagel. New York: Hafner.

Miller, Ross A. 1995. "Domestic Structures and the Diversionary Use of Force." *American Journal of Political Science* 39 (3): 760–785.

Moravcsik, Andrew. 1997. "Taking Preferences Seriously: A Liberal Theory of International Politics." *International Organization* 51 (4): 513–554.

Morgan, T. Clifton and Kenneth N. Bickers 1992. "Domestic Discontent and the External Use of Force." *Journal of Conflict Resolution* 36 (1): 25–52.

Nagel, Jack H. 1975. *The Descriptive Analysis of Power*. New Haven: Yale University Press.

Neuberger, Benjamin. 1986. *National Self-Determination in Postcolonial Africa*. Boulder: Lynne Rienner Press.

Olson, Mancur. 1965. *The Logic of Collective Action: Public goods and the Theory of Groups*. Cambridge: Harvard University Press.

Oneal, John R. and Bruce Russett. 1999. "Is the Liberal Peace Just an Artificat of Cold War Interests? Assessing Recent Critiques." *International Interactions* 25 (3): 213–241.

Pape, Robert A. 1997. "Why Economic Sanctions Do Not Work." *International Security* 22 (2): 90–136.

Posen, Barry. 1993a. "The Security Dilemma and Ethnic Conflict." *Survival* 35 (1): 27–47.

Posen, Barry. 1993b. "Nationalism, the Mass Army, and Military Power." *International Security* 18 (2): 80–124.

Posen, Barry. 1996. "Military Responses to Refugee Disasters." *International Security* 21 (1): 72–111.

Putnam, Robert. 1988. "Diplomacy and Domestic Politics: The Logic of Two-Level Games." *International Organization* 42 (3): 427–460.

Ray, James Lee. 1995. *Democracy and International Conflict: An Evaluation of the Democratic Peace Proposition*. Columbia: University of South Carolina Press.

Regan, Patrick M. 1998. "Choosing to Intervene: Outside Intervention in Internal Conflicts." *Journal of Politics* 60 (3): 754–79.

Rothschild, Joseph. 1981. *Ethnopolitics: A Conceptual Framework*. New York: Columbia University Press.

Roy, A. Bikash. 1997. "Intervention Across Bisecting Borders." *Journal of Peace Research* 34 (3): 303–314.

Saideman, Stephen M. 1995. "The Relevance of International Organizations for Ethnic Conflicts: International Agenda-Setting and Domestic Political Strategies." Presented at Annual Meeting of the International Studies Association, Chicago, Il.

Saideman, Stephen M. 1996. "The Dual Dynamics of Disintegration: Ethnic Politics and Security Dilemmas in Eastern Europe," *Nationalism and Ethnic Politics* 2 (1): 18–43.

Saideman, Stephen M. 1997. "The Dilemmas of Divorce: Secessionist Foreign Policy and the Strategic Use of Identity." Presented at the Annual Meeting of the International Studies Association, Toronto, Canada.

Saideman, Stephen M. 1998a. "Inconsistent Irredentism? Political Competition, Ethnic Ties, and The Foreign Policies of Somalia and Serbia," *Security Studies* 7 (3): 51–93.

Saideman, Stephen M. 1998b. "Is Pandora's Box Half-Empty or Half-Full? The Limited Virulence of Secession and the Domestic Sources of Disintegration," in *Ethnic Fears and Global Engagement: The Spread and Management of Ethnic Conflict*, edited by David A. Lake and Donald Rothchild. Princeton: Princeton University Press.

Saideman, Stephen M. and R. William Ayres. 2000. "Determining the Sources of Irredentism: Logit Analyses of At Risk Data." *Journal of Politics* 62 (4): 1126–1144.

Saideman, Stephen M. and Beth K. Dougherty. 2000. "Secessionist Foreign Policy and the Strategic Use of Identity." Presented at the Annual Meeting of the International Studies Association, Los Angeles, CA.

Schweller, Randall. 1996. "Neorealism's Status-Quo Bias: What Security Dilemma?" *Security Studies* 5 (3): 90–121.

Singer, J. David, and Melvin Small, 1995. "National Military Capabilities Data." Modified *Correlates of War Project*, Ann Arbor: University of Michigan.

Smith, Alastair. 1996. "Diversionary Foreign Policy in Democratic Systems." *International Studies Quarterly* 40 (1): 133–154.

Snyder, Jack. 1993. "Nationalism and the Crisis of the Post-Soviet State." *Survival* 35 (1): 5–26.

Snyder, Jack. 1999. *When Voting Leads To Violence: Democratization And Nationalist Conflict*. New York: Norton Books.

Stack, Jr., John F. 1981. *Ethnic Identities in a Transnational World*. Westport, CN: Greenwood Press.

Stack, Jr., John F. 1997. "The Ethnic Challenge to International Relations Theory." In David Carment and Patrick James, eds., *Wars in the Midst of Peace: The International Politics of Ethnic Conflict*, pp. 11–25. Pittsburgh: University of Pittsburgh Press.

Stedman, Stephen John. 1997. "Spoiler Problems in Peace Processes." *International Security* 22 (2): 5–53.

Stiglmayer Alexandra. ed. 1994. *Mass Rape: The War Against Women In Bosnia-Herzegovina*, translations by Marion Faber. Lincoln: University of Nebraska Press.

Suhrke, Astri and Lela Garner Noble, eds. 1977. *Ethnic Conflict in International Relations*. New York: Praeger.

Tetlock, Philip E. and Aaron Belkin. Eds. 1996. *Counterfactual Thought Experiments in World Politics: Logical, Methodological, and Psychological Perspectives*. Princeton: Princeton University Press.

Tomz, Michael, Jason Wittenberg, and Gary King. 1998. "CLARIFY: Software for interpreting and presenting statistical results. Version 1.2." Cambridge: Harvard University.

Touval, Saadia. 1972. *The Boundary Politics of Independent Africa*. Cambridge: Harvard University,.

Van Evera, Stephen. 1997. *Guide to Methods for Students of Political Science*. Ithaca, NY: Cornell University Press.

Vasquez, John A. 1997. "The Realist Paradign and Degenerative versus Progressive Research Programs: An Appraisal of Neotraditional Research on Waltz's Balancing Proposition." *American Political Science Review* 91 (4): 899–912.

Walt, Stephen. 1987. *The Origins of Alliances*. Ithaca, NY: Cornell University Press.

Walt, Stephen. 1996. *Revolutions and War*. Ithaca, NY: Cornell University Press.

Walter, Barbara F. 1997. "The Critical Barrier to Civil War Settlement." *International Organization* 51 (3): 335–364.

Walter, Barbara F. 1999. "Designing Transitions From Civil War." In Barbara F. Walter and Jack Snyder, eds., *Civil Wars, Insecurity, and Intervention*, pp. 38–72. New York: Columbia University Press.

Waltz, Kenneth N. 1979. *Theory of International Politics*, New York: Random House.

Waltz, Kenneth N. 1996. "International Politics is Not Foreign Policy." *Security Studies* 6 (1): 54–57.

Weiner, Myron. 1996. "Bad Neighbors, Bad Neighborhoods: An Inquiry into the Causes of Refugee Flows." *International Security* 21 (1): 5–42.

Young, Crawford. 1976. *The Politics of Cultural Pluralism*. Madison: University of Wisconsin Press.

Zakaria, Fareed. 1992. "Realism and Domestic Politics: A Review Essay." *International Security* 17 (1): 177–198.

Zartman, I. William. 1964. "The Foreign and Military Politics of African Boundary Problems." In Carl Gosta Widstrand, ed., *African Boundary Problems*, pp. 79–100. Uppsala: Scandinavian Institute of African Studies.

Zartman, I. William. 1966. *International Relations in the New Africa*. Englewood Cliffs, N.J.: Prentice-Hall.

African Cases

Adamolekum, Ladipo. 1977. "The Foreign Policy of Guinea," in *Foreign Policies of African States*, Olajide Aluko ed, London: Hodder and Stoughton.

Akiba, Okon. 1998. *Nigerian Foreign Policy Towards Africa: Continuity and Change*. New York: Peter Lang.

Akpan, Ntieyong U. 1971. *The Struggle for Secession, 1967–1970: A Personal Account of the Nigerian Civil War*. London: Frank Cass.

Aluko, Olajide. 1977. *Foreign Policies of African States*. London: Hodder and Stoughton.

Aluko, Olajide. 1981. *Essays in Nigerian Foreign Policy*. London: George, Allen & Unwin,.

Anderson, Lisa. 1986. *The State and Social Transformation in Tunisia and Libya, 1830–1980*. Princeton: Princeton University Press.

Apter, David E. 1964. "Ghana." In James S. Coleman and Carl G. Rosberg, Jr. eds., *Political Parties and National Integration in Tropical Africa*, pp. 259–315. Berkeley: University of California Press.

Ardener, Edwin, 1967. "The Nature of the Reunification of Cameroon," In Arthur Hazlewood, ed., *African Integration and Disintegration: Case Studies in Economic and Political Union*, pp. London: Oxford University.

Ayele, Negussay. 1977. "The Foreign Policy of Ethiopia." In Olajide Aluko, ed., *Foreign Policies of African States*, pp.. London: Hodder and Stoughton.

Ballard, John A. 1966. "Four Equatorial States." In Gwendolen M. Carter, ed., *National Unity and Regionalism in Eight African States*, pp. 231–336. Ithaca: Cornell University Press.

Barber, James. 1973. *South Africa's Foreign Policy: 1945–1970.* London: Oxford University.

Behrman, Lucy C. 1970. *Muslim Brotherhoods and Politics in Senegal,* Cambridge: Harvard University Press.

Boubacar, Barry. 1988. "Neocolonialism and Dependence in Senegal, 1960–1980." In Prosser Gifford and Wm. Roger Louis, eds., *Decolonization and African independence*, pp. 271–294. New Haven: Yale University Press.

Cervenka, Zdenek. 1972. *A History of the Nigerian War, 1967–1970.* Ibadan, Nigeria: Onibonoje Press.

Charlick, Robert B. 1991. *Niger: Personal Rule and Survival in the Sahel.* Boulder: Westview.

Chime, Samuel. 1969. "The Organization of African Unity and African Boundaries." In Carl Gosta Widstrand, ed., *African Boundary Problems*, pp. 63–78. Uppsala: Scandinavian Institute of African Studies.

Clapham, Christopher. 1969. *Haile-Selassie's Government.* New York: Praeger.

Corbett, Edward M. 1972. *The French Presence in Black Africa.* Washington, DC: Black Orpheus.

Cronje, Suzanne. 1972. *The World and Nigeria: The Diplomatic History of the Biafran War 1967–1970.* London: Sidgwick & Jackson.

de Saint-Paul, Marc Aicardi. 1987. *Gabon: The Development of a Nation,* trans. A., F., and T. Palmer. London: Routledge.

de St. Jorre, John. 1972. *The Brothers' War: Biafra and Nigeria.* Boston: Houghton Mifflin,.

Eisenhower, Dwight D. 1965. *Waging Peace: 1956–1961,* New York: Doubleday.

Epstein, Howard M., ed., 1965. *Revolt in the Congo: 1960–64.* New York: Facts on File.

Ferkiss, Victor C. 1967. "Religion and Politics in Independent Africa: A Prolegomenon." In Jeffrey Butler and A. A. Castagno, eds., *Boston University Papers on Africa: Transition in African Politics*, pp. 1–38. New York: Praeger.

Fisher, Humphrey. 1969. "Elections and Coups in Sierra Leone, 1967." *Journal of Modern African Studies* 7 (4): 611–636.

Fitzmaurice, John. 1983. *The Politics of Belgium: Crisis and Compromise in a Plural Society* London: C. Hurst & Co.

Foltz, William J. 1964. "Senegal." In James S. Coleman and Carl G. Rosberg, Jr. eds., *Political Parties and National Integration in Tropical Africa*, pp. 16–64. Berkeley: University of California.

Gambari, I. A. 1980. *Party Politics and Foreign Policy: Nigeria Under the First Republic.* Zaria, Nigeria: Ahmadu Bello University.

Gauze, Rene. 1973. *The Politics of Congo-Brazzaville,* translated by Virginia Thompson and Richard Adloff. Stanford: Hoover Institution.

Gerard-Libois, Jules. 1966. *Katanga Secession,* translated by Rebecca Young. Madison: University of Wisconsin Press.

Gibbs, David N. 1991. *The Political Economy of Third World Intervention: Mines, Money, and U.S. Policy in the Congo Crisis.* Chicago: University of Chicago Press.

Gingyera-Pinyewa, A.G.G. 1978. *Apolo Milton Obote and His Times.* New York: NOK.

Good, Robert C. 1962. "The Congo Crisis: A Study in Postcolonial Politics." In Lawrence W. Martin, ed., *Neutralism and Non-Alignment: The New States in World Affairs*, pp. 34–62. New York: Praeger.

Hansen, Holger Bernt. 1977. *Ethnicity and Military Rule in Uganda,* Uppsala, Sweden: Scandinavian Institute of African Affairs.

Hatch, John. 1972. *Tanzania: A Profile,* New York: Praeger.

Hatch, John. 1976. *Two African Statesmen: Kaunda of Zambia and Nyerere of Tanzania.* London: Secker & Warburg.

Heilman, Bruce. 1997. "A Tale of Two Citizenships: Exclusion, Community and the Fragile Union of Zanzibar and Tanganyika." Paper presented at the Annual Meeting of the American Political Science Association, Washington, DC.

Helmreich, Jonathan E. 1976. *Belgium and Europe: A Study in Small Power Diplomacy.* The Hague: Mouton.

Hess, Robert L. 1966. "Ethiopia." In Gwendolen M. Carter, ed., *National Unity and Regionalism In Eight African States*, pp. 441–538. Ithaca: Cornell University Press.

Hess, Robert L. and Gerhard Loewenberg. 1964. "The Ethiopian No-Party State: A Note on the Functions of Political Parties in Developing States." *American Political Science Review* 8 (5): 947–950.

Hopwood, Derek. 1992. *Habib Bourguiba of Tunisia: The Tragedy of Longevity.* New York: St. Martins Press.

Hoskyns, Catherine. 1965. *The Congo Since Independence: January 1960 – December 1961,* London: Oxford University.

Hyde, Emmanuel Aryeequaye. 1971. *The Role of Ghana in the Congo Crisis: A Study of a Small State's Involvement in a Post Colonial Problem.* University of Pennsylvania: Dissertation.

Ingham, Kenneth. 1990. *Politics in Modern Africa: The Uneven Tribal Dimension*. London: Routledge.

Johansson, Rune. 1984. "Varieties of Conflict Development: Ethnic Relations and Societal Change in Belgium, Finland, and Switzerland." In Sven Tagil, ed., *Regions in Upheaval: Ethnic Conflict and Political Mobilization*, pp. 56–58. Stockholm: Esselte Studium.

Johns, David. 1977. "The Foreign Policy of Tanzania." In Olajide Aluko, ed., *The Foreign Policies of African States*, London: Hodder and Stoughton.

Kalb, Madeleine G. 1982. *The Congo Cables: The Cold War in Africa—From Eisenhower to Kennedy*. New York: MacMillan.

Karis, Thomas. 1963. "South Africa." In Gwendolen M. Carter, ed., *Five African States: Responses to Diversity*, pp. 471–616. Ithaca: Cornell University.

Kaunda, Kenneth David. 1967. *Humanism in Zambia and a Guide to its Implementation*, Lusaka: Zambian Information Service.

Kennedy, John F.. 1960. *The Strategy for Peace*, New York: Harper & Row.

Kirk-Greene, A.H.M. ed. 1971. *Crisis and Conflict in Nigeria: A Documentary Sourcebook, 1966–1970*. London: Oxford University Press.

Kofele-Kale, Ndiva. 1980. "Cameroon and its Foreign Relations." *African Affairs* 80 (319): 197–217.

Lalck, Pierre 1971. *Central African Republic: A Failure in De-Colonisation*, trans. Barbara Thomson, New York: Praeger.

Lefever, Ernest W. 1967. *Uncertain Mandate: Politics of the U.N. Congo Operation*. Baltimore: Johns Hopkins University Press.

Legum, Colin, and John Drysdale, eds. 1969. *Africa Contemporary Record, Annual Survey and Documents: 1968–1969*, London: Africa Research.

Legum, Colin and John Drysdale, eds., 1970. *Africa Contemporary Record: Annual Survey and Documents, 1969–1970*, Exeter: Africa Research.

Legum, Colin, ed. 1971. *Africa Contemporary Record: Annual Survey and Documents, 1970–1971*, Exeter: Africa Research.

Le Vine, Victor T. 1971. *The Cameroon Federal Republic*. Ithaca: Cornell University.

Lockard, Kathleen G. 1980. "Religion and Politics in Independent Uganda: Movement Toward Secularization?" InJames R. Scarritt, ed., *Analyzing Political Change in Africa: Applications of a New Multidimensional Framework*, pp. 40–73. Boulder: Westview.

Lofchie, Michael F. 1964. "Zanzibar." In James S. Coleman and Carl G. Rosberg, Jr., eds. *Political parties and National Integration in Tropical Africa*, pp. 482–509. Berkeley: University of California.

Mahoney, Richard D. 1983. *JFK: Ordeal in Africa*. New York: Oxford University Press.

Markakis, John. 1974. *Ethiopia: Anatomy of a Traditional Polity*, Oxford: Clarendon.

Markowitz, Irving Leonard. 1969. *Leopold Sedar Senghor and the Politics of Negritude*. New York: Atheneum.

Markowitz, Irving Leonard. 1970. "Traditional Social Structure, the Islamic Brotherhoods, and Political Development in Senegal." *Journal of Modern African Studies* 8 (1): 73–96.

Mazrui, Ali A. and Michael Tidy. 1984, *Nationalism And New States In Africa: From about 1935 to the Present*. Nairobi: Heinemann.

Melville, Kirsty. 1979. *The Involvement of France and Francophone West Africa in the Nigerian Civil War*, African Studies Working Papers, No. 9, Murdoch University.

Mohan, Jitendra. 1969. "Ghana, The Congo, and The United Nations." *Journal of Modern African Studies* 7 (3): 369–406.

Morris, Colin M. 1980. *Kaunda on Violence*. London: Collins.

Morrison, Donald George et al. 1972. *Black Africa: A Comparative Handbook*. NY: Free Press.

Mulford, David C. 1967. *Zambia: The Politics of Independence, 1957–1964*. London: Oxford University,.

N.A. 1971. *Africa South of the Sahara*. London: Europa Publications Ltd.

Nkrumah, Kwame. 1967. *Challenge of the Congo*, New York: International Publishers.

Nkrumah, Kwame. 1970. *Africa Must Unite*, New York: International Publishers.

Nyerere, Julius. 1967. *Freedom and unity: Uhuru na umoja, a selection from writings and speeches 1952–1965*. London: Oxford University Press.

Nyerere, Julius. 1969. *The Nigeria-Biafra crisis*. Dar es Salaam: United Republic of Tanzania.

Nyerere, Julius. 1973. *Freedom and Development: Uhuru na Maendeleo, A Selection from Writings and Speeches 1968–1973*. London: Oxford University.

O'Brien, Conor Cruise. 1962. *To Katanga and Back*. New York: Simon and Schuster.

Ofoegbu, Mazi Ray. 1975. "Nigeria and its Neighbors." *Odu* 12: 3–21.

Ohaegbulam, Festus Ugboaja. 1982. *Nigeria and the UN Mission to the Democratic Republic of the Congo: A Case Study of the Formative Stages of Nigeria's Foreign Policy*, Tampa: University of South Florida.

O'Toole, Thomas. 1986. *The Central African Republic: The Continent's Hidden Heart*, Boulder: Westview.

Paranjpe, Shirkant, and Raju G.C. Thomas. 1991. "India and South Asia: Resolving Problems of Regional Dominance and Diversity," in David J. Myers, ed., *Regional Hegemons: Threat Perception and Strategic Response*, pp. 161–189. Boulder: Westview.

Phillips, Jr., Claude S. 1964. *The Development of Nigerian Foreign Policy*, Chicago: Northwestern University Press.

Potholm, Christian P. 1970. *Four African Political Systems*. Englewood Cliffs, NJ: Prentice-Hall.

Radu, Michael S., and Keith Sommerville. 1989. *The Congo*, London: Pinter.

Riviere, Claude. 1977. *Guinea: Mobilization of a People,* trans. Virginia Thompson and Richard Adloff. Ithaca: Cornell University Press.

Schatzberg, Michael G. 1991. *Mobutu or Chaos: The United States and Zaire, 1960–1990.* Lanham, MD: University Press of America.

Schwab, Peter. 1971. *Biafra,* New York: Facts on File.

Shaw, Timothy. 1976. "The Foreign Policy of Zambia: Ideology and Interests." *Journal of Modern African Studies* 14 (1): 79–106.

Smock, David R, and Audrey C, Smock. 1975. *The Politics of Pluralism: A Comparative Study of Lebanon and Ghana.* New York: Elsevier.

Spaak, Paul-Henri. 1971. *The Continuing Battle: Memoirs of a European, 1936–1966.* Boston: Little, Brown.

Spiro, Herbert. 1963. "The Rhodesias and Nyasaland." In Gwendolen M. Carter, ed., *Five African States: Responses to Diversity,* pp. 361–470. Ithaca: Cornell University.

Stremlau, John J. 1977. *The International Politics of the Nigerian Civil War, 1967–1970.* Princeton: Princeton University Press.

Thompson, Joseph E. 1977. *American Foreign Policy Toward Nigeria.* Catholic University: Dissertation.

Thompson, Virginia. 1962. "The Ivory Coast." In Gwendolen M. Carter, ed., *African One-Party States,* pp. 237–324. Ithaca: Cornell University Press.

Thompson, Virginia. 1972. *West Africa's Council of the Entente.* Ithaca: Cornell University.

Thompson, Virginia. 1966. "Niger." In Gwendolen M. Carter, ed., *National Unity and Regionalism in Eight African States,* pp. 151–230. Ithaca: Cornell University Press.

Vanderlinden, Jacques, 1989. "Communities, Languages, Regions, and the Belgian Constitution, 1831–1985." In Robert A. Goldwin et al., eds., *Forging Unity Out of Diversity: The Approaches of Eight Nations,* pp, Washington, DC: American Enterprise Institute.

Wattenberg, Ben, and Ralph Lee Smith. 1963. *The New Nations of Africa.* New York: Hart.

Weinstein, Brian. 1966. *Gabon: Nation-Building on the Ogooue.* Cambridge: MIT Press.

Weiskel, Timothy. 1988. "Independence and the *Longue Duree*: The Ivory Coast Miracle Reconsidered."In Prosser Gifford and Wm. Roger Louis, eds. *Decolonization and African Independence,* pp. 347–380. New Haven: Yale University Press.

Weissman, Stephen R. 1974. *American Foreign Policy in the Congo 1960–1964.* Ithaca: Cornell University Press.

Welensky, Sir Roy. 1964. *Welensky's 4000 Days: The Life and Death of the Federation of Rhodesia and Nyasaland,* New York: Roy.

Wood, J.R.T. 1983. *The Welensky Papers: A History of the Federation of Rhodesia and Nyasaland.* Durban, South Africa: Graham,.

Young, Crawford. 1965. *Politics In The Congo; Decolonization and Independence.* Princeton: Princeton University Press.

Zartman, I. William. 1964. *Problems of New Power: Morocco.* NY: Atherton Press.

Zolberg, Aristide R. 1964. *One-Party Government in the Ivory Coast.* Princeton: Princeton University.

Yugoslavia

Allen, Beverly. 1996. *Rape Warfare: The Hidden Genocide in Bosnia-Herzegovina and Croatia.* Minneapolis: University of Minnesota Press.

Ash, Timothy Garton. 1993. *In Europe's Name: Germany and the Divided Continent.* New York: Random House.

Baker, James Addison. 1995. *The Politics of Diplomacy: Revolution, War And Peace, 1989–1992.* New York: G.P. Putnam's Sons.

Bennett, Christopher. 1995. *Yugoslavia's Bloody Collapse: Causes, Course and Consequences.* New York: New York University Press.

Bicanic, Ivo and Iva Dominis. 1993. "The Multiparty Elections in Croatia: Round Two." *Radio Free Europe/Radio Liberty Research Report* 2,19.

Bookman, Milica Z. 1992. *The Economics of Secession.* New York: St. Martin's Press.

Brown, J. F. 1993. "Turkey: Back to the Balkans." In Graham E. Fuller, et al., eds., *Turkey's New Geopolitics: From the Balkans to West China*, pp. 141–162. Boulder: Westview Press.

Brown, J.F. 1994. *Hopes and Shadows: Eastern Europe After Communism* Durham: Duke University Press.

Burg, Steven L. and Paul S. Shoup. 1999. *The War in Bosnia-Herzegovina: Ethnic Conflict and International Intervention.* Armonk, NY: M.E. Sharpe.

Clinton, William Jefferson. 1995. Address at the United States Air Force Academy Graduation. Colorado Springs, CO.

Cohen, Lenard J. 1994. "Russia and the Balkans: Pan-Slavism, Partnership, and Power." *International Journal* 49 (4): 814–845.

Cohen, Lenard J. 1995. *Broken Bonds: Yugoslavia's Disintegration and Balkan Politics in Transition*, 2nd ed. Boulder: Westview Press.

Conversi, Daniele. 1998. "German-Bashing and the Breakup of Yugoslavia." *The Donald W. Treadgold Papers in Russian, East European, and Central Asian Studies* No. 16. Seattle: Jackson School of International Studies.

Crawford, Beverly. 1995. "German Foreign Policy and European Political Cooperation: The Diplomatic Recognition of Croatia in 1991." *German Politics and Society* 13 (2): 1–33.

Crawford, Beverly. 1996. "Explaining Defection from International Cooperation: Germany's Unilateral Recognition of Croatia." *World Politics* 48 (4): 482–521.

Danchev, Alex and Thomas Halverson. 1996. Eds. *International Perspectives on the Yugoslav Conflict*. London: MacMillan.

Danforth, Loring M. 1995. *The Macedonian Conflict: Ethnic Nationalism in a Transnational World*. Princeton: Princeton University Press.

Dellenbrant, Jan Ake. 1994. "Romania: The Slow Revolution." In Sten Berglund and Jan Ake Dellenbrant, *The New Democracies in Eastern Europe: Party Systems and Political Cleavages* 2nd ed., pp. 203–218. Brookfield, VT: Edward Elgar.

Denitch, Bodgan. 1994. *Ethnic Nationalism: The Tragic Death of Yugoslavia*. Minneapolis: University of Minnesota Press.

Discovery Channel. 1995. "Yugoslavia: Death of a Nation." *Discovery Journal* (Televised December 26–30).

Djilas, Aleksa. 1995. "Germany's Policy Toward the Disintegration of Yugoslavia," In Stephen E. Hanson and Willfried Spohn, eds., *Can Europe Work? Germany and the Reconstruction of Postcommunist Societies*, pp. 151–167. Seattle: University of Washington Press.

Donia, Robert J. and John V.A. Fine, Jr. 1994. *Bosnia and Hercegovina: A Tradition Betrayed*. New York: Columbia University Press.

Durch, William J. and James A. Schear 1996. "Faultlines: UN Operations in the Former Yugoslavia." In William J. Durch, ed., *UN Peacekeeping, American Politics, and the Uncivil Wars of the 1990s*, pp. 193–274. New York: St. Martin's Press

Edemskii, Andrei. 1996. "Russian Perspectives," in Alex Danchev and Thomas Halverson, eds., *International Perspectives on the Yugoslav Conflict*, pp. 29–51. London: MacMillan.

Editors. 1992. "Interview with John Owen." *Foreign Affairs* 72 (2): 1–9.

Friedman Francine and Robin Alison Remington. 1997. "Bosnian Muslim Views of National Security" In Constantine P. Danopoulos and Kostas G. Messas, eds., *Crises in the Balkans: Views from the Participants*, 93–112. Boulder: Westview.

Gagnon, Jr., V.P. 1991. "Yugoslavia: Prospects for Stability." *Foreign Affairs* 70 (3): 17–35.

Gagnon, Jr., V.P. 1994/95. "Ethnic Nationalism and International Conflict: The Case of Serbia." International Security 19 (3): 130–166.

Gallagher, Tom Romania. 1995. *After Ceauçescu: The Politics of Intolerance*. Edinburgh: Edinburgh University Press.

Genscher, Hans-Dietrich. 1997. *Rebuilding a House Divided: A Memoir by the Architect of Germany's Reunification*, translated by Thomas Thornton. New York: Broadway Books.

Glenny, Misha. 1996. "The Macedonian Question." In Alex Danchev and Thomas

Halverson, eds., *International Perspectives on the Yugoslav Conflict*, pp. 134–147. London: MacMillan.

Goldstein Joshua S. and Jon C. Pevehouse. 1997. "Reciprocity, Bullying, and International Cooperation: Time-Series Analysis of the Bosnian Conflict," *American Political Science Review* 91 (3): 515–530.

Gompert, David C. 1996. "The United States and Yugoslavia's Wars." In Richard H. Ullman, ed., *The World and Yugoslavia's Wars*, pp. 122–144. New York: Council on Foreign Relations.

Gordon, Phillip. 1993. *A Certain Idea of France: French Security Policy and the Gaullist Legacy* Princeton: Princeton University Press

Gow James. 1997. *Triumph of the Lack of Will: International Diplomacy and the Yugoslav War* New York: Columbia University Press.

Gutman, Roy. 1993. *A Witness To Genocide*. New York: Macmillan.

Halverson, Thomas. 1996. "American Perspectives." In Alex Danchev and Thomas Halverson, eds., *International Perspectives on the Yugoslav Conflict*, pp. 1–28. London: MacMillan.

Haynes, Rebecca Ann. 1995. "Hungarian National Identity: Definition and Redefinition." In Paul Latawski, ed., *Contemporary Nationalism in East Central Europe*, pp. 87–105. New York: St. Martins.

Hirschman, Albert O. 1945. *National Power and the Structure of Foreign Trade*. Berkeley: University of California Press.

Holbrooke, Richard. 1998. *To End a War*. New York: Random House.

Honig, Jan Willem and Norbert Both. 1997. *Srebrenica: Record of a War*. New York: Penguin Books.

Howorth, Jolyon. 1994. "The Debate in France over Military Intervention in Europe" In Lawrence Freedman, ed., *Military Intervention in European Conflicts*, pp. 106–124. Oxford: Blackwell.

Junky, Ihor. 1999. "Ukraine's Balancing Act." *New York Times*. April 27.

Kristo, Jure. 1995. "The Catholic Church in a Time of Crisis." In Sabrina Petra Ramet and Ljubisa S. Adamovich, eds., *Beyond Yugoslavia: Politics, Economics, And Culture in a Shattered Community*, pp. 431–450. Boulder: Westview Press.

Karp, Regina Cowen. 1993. *Central and Eastern Europe: The Challenge of Transition*. New York: Oxford University Press.

Kramer, Stephen Phillip. 1994. *Does France Still Count? The French Role in the New Europe*. Westport, CT: Praeger.

Kun, Joseph C. 1993. *Hungarian Foreign Policy: The Experience of a New Democracy*. Westport, CN: Praeger.

Larrabee, F. Stephen. 1992. "Instability and Change in the Balkans." *Survival* 34 (2): 31–49.

Lepick, Olivier. 1996. "French Perspective." In Alex Danchev and Thomas Halverson, eds., *International Perspectives on the Yugoslav Conflict*, pp. 76–86. NY: St. Martin's Press.

Libal Michael. 1997. *Limits of Persuasion: Germany and the Yugoslav Crisis, 1991–1992*. Westport, CN: Praeger.

Lukic, Reneo and Allen Lynch. 1996. *Europe from the Balkans to the Urals: The Disintegration of Yugoslavia and the Soviet Union*. Oxford: Oxford University Press.

Maull, Hanns W. 1995–96. "Germany in the Yugoslav Crisis." *Survival* 37 (4): 99–130.

Midlarsky, Manus I. 1992. ed., *The Internationalization of Communal Strife*. London: Routledge.

Moore, Patrick. 1993. "The Widening Warfare in the Former Yugoslavia," *Radio Free Europe/Radio Liberty Research Report* 2,1.

Morgan, Roger. 1996. "German Foreign Policy and Domestic Politics," In Bertel Huerlin, ed., *Germany in Europe in the Nineties*, pp. 152–176. New York: St. Martin's Press.

Müftüler-Bac, Meltem. 1997. *Turkey's Relations with a Changing Europe*. Mancehster: Manchester University Press.

Muller, Harald. 1992. "German Foreign Policy after Unification." In Paul B. Stares, ed., *The New Germany and the New Europe*, pp. 126–176. Washington, DC: Brookings.

Nakarada, Radmila. 1991, "The Mystery of Nationalism: The Paramount Case of Yugoslavia," *Millennium*, 20 (3): 369–82.

Nedeva, Ivanka. 1993. "Democracy Building in Ethnically Diverse Societies: The Cases of Bulgaria and Romania." In Ian M. Cuthbertson and Jane Leibowitz, eds., *Minorities: The New Europe's Old Issue*, pp. 123–156. Prague: Institute for East-West Studies.

Nielsson, Gunnar P. and Angeliki Kanavou. 1996. "Dispersed Nations and Interstate Relations: A General Perspective and a Comparative Analysis of the Hungarians and the Kurds," Paper prepared for presentation at the *Annual Meeting of the International Studies Association*, San Diego, CA.

Pettifer, James. 1996. "Greek Political Culture and Foreign Policy." In Kevin Featherstone and Kostas Ifantis, eds., *Greece in a Changing Europe: Between European Integration and Balkan Disintegration?* pp. 17–23. Manchester: Manchester University Press.

Poulton, Hugh. 1991. *The Balkans: Minorities and States in Conflict*. London: Minority Rights Group.

Poulton, Hugh. 1997. "Turkey as Kin-State: Turkish Foreign Policy Towards Turkish and Muslim Communities in the Balkans." In Hugh Poulton and Suha Taji-Farouki, eds., *Muslim Identity and the Balkan State*, pp. 194–213. New York: New York University Press.

Prelec, Marko. 1997. "Franjo Tudjman's Croatia and the Balkans." In Constantine

P. Danopoulos and Kostas G. Messas, eds., *Crises in the Balkans: Views from the Participants*, pp. 75–111. Boulder: Westview.

Pusic, Vesna. 1998. "Croatia at the Crossroads." *Journal of Democracy* 9 (1): 111–124.

Ramet, Sabrina Petra. 1993. "Yugoslavia and the Two Germanys," In Dirk Verheyen and Christian S e, eds., *The Germans and Their Neighbors*, 317–338. Boulder: Westview.

Ramet, Sabrina Petra. 1995a. "Slovenia's Road to Democracy." In Sabrina Petra Ramet and Ljubisa S. Adamovich, eds., *Beyond Yugoslavia: Politics, Economics, And Culture in a Shattered Community*, pp. 189–210. Boulder: Westview Press.

Ramet, Sabrina Petra. 1995b. "The Macedonian Enigma." In Sabrina Petra Ramet and Ljubisa S. Adamovich, eds., *Beyond Yugoslavia: Politics, Economics, And Culture in a Shattered Community*, pp. 211–236. Boulder: Westview Press.

Ramet, Sabrine Petra. 1992. *Balkan Babel: Politics, Culture, and Religion in Yugoslavia*. Boulder: Westview Press.

Rezun, Miron. 1995. *Europe and the War in the Balkans: Toward a New Yugoslav Identity*. Westport, CN: Praeger.

Rieff, David. 1995. *Slaughterhouse: Bosnia and the Failure of the West*. New York: Simon & Schuster

Rosin, Hanna. 1994. "Greek Pique." *The New Republic*. June 13: 11–12.

Schoenbaum David and Elizabeth Pond. 1996. *The German Question and Other German Questions*. New York: St. Martin's Press.

Sells, Michael Anthony. 1996. *The Bridge Betrayed: Religion And Genocide In Bosnia*. Berkeley: University of California Press.

Silber, Laura and Allan Little. 1996. *Yugoslavia: Death of a Nation*. New York: Penguin.

Steinberg, James B. 1993. "International Involvement in the Yugoslavia conflict." In Lori Fisler Damrosch, ed., *Enforcing Restraint: Collective Intervention in Internal Conflicts*, pp. 27–75. New York: Council on Foreign Relations Press.

Szayna, Thomas S. 1994. *Ethnic Conflict in Central Europe and the Balkans: A Framework and U.S. Policy Options*. Santa Monica: RAND Corporation.

Tismaneanu, Vladimir. 1997. "Romanian Exceptionalism? Democracy, Ethnocracy, and Uncertain Pluralism in post-Ceauçescu Romania." In Karen Dawisha and Bruce Parrott, eds., *Politics, Power, and the Struggle for Democracy in South-East Europe*, pp. 403–450. Cambridge: Cambridge University Press.

Tupurkovski, Vasil. 1997. "The Balkan Crisis and the Republic of Macedonia." In Constantine P. Danopoulos and Kostas G. Messas, eds., *Crises in the Balkans: Views from the Participants*, 135–152. Boulder: Westview.

Ullman, Richard H. 1996. "The Wars in Yugoslavia and the International System after the Cold War." In Richard H. Ullman, ed., *The World and Yugoslavia's Wars*, pp. 9–41. New York: Council on Foreign Relations.

Urban, Laszlo K. 1997. "Trouble in the Balkans: The View from Hungary." In Constantine P. Danopoulos and Kostas G. Messas, eds., *Crises in the Balkans: Views from the Participants*, pp. 241–256. Boulder: Westview.

Watts, Larry. 1997. "Romania and the Balkan Imbroglio." In Constantine P. Danopoulos and Kostas G. Messas, eds., *Crises in the Balkans: Views from the Participants*, pp. 225–239. Boulder: Westview.

Woodward, Susan L. 1995. *Balkan Tragedy: Chaos and Dissolution After the Cold War*. Washington, D.C.: The Brookings Institution.

Zimmermann, Warren. 1995. "The Last Ambassador: A Memoir of the Collapse of Yugoslavia." *Foreign Affairs* 74 (2): 2–20.

Zimmermann, Warren. 1996. *Origins of a Catastrophe: Yugoslavia and its Destroyers—America's Last Ambassador Tells What Happened and Why*. New York: Times Books.

Index

Abkhaz, 244n8
Adoula, Cyrille, 57, 58
Africa, role in case selection, 30; role in vulnerability argument, 2, 8–9, 13–14
African-Americans, 245n26
Ahidjo, Ahmadou, see Cameroon
Albania, costs of refugees, 3; role in Yugoslav conflicts, 142, 143, 146; support of Kosovo, 1, 204, 213, 246n10
Angola, 219
Arab countries, role in Nigerian Civil War, 73, 90–91
Argentina, 216
Arkan, 246n9
Armenia, 160, 185
Ash, Timothy Garton, 128
Austria, role in Yugoslav conflict, 124, 141–142, 143, 144, 146, 153
Azerbaijan, 160, 185

Badinter Commission, 108, 123, 130, 140

Baker, James, 139
Balewa, Abubakar Tawafa, 54–55
Baltic Republics, 163
Basques, 9
Belgium, role in the Congo Crisis, 37–40, 41–46, 63, 64, 68, 155, 204, 207, 208, 209, 211
Biafra, see Nigerian Civil War
Bilirakis, Michael, 140
Bongo, Albert, see Gabon
Bosnia, 1, 113–114, 158, 163, 197, 246n9; ethnic cleansing in, 3; see also Yugoslavia
Brioni Accords, 107
Bulgaria, role in Yugoslav conflict, 114, 142, 143, 152, 207
Burundi, 219
Bush, President George, 138, 139, 140

Cameroon, role in Nigerian Civil War, 87–89, 96
Caritas, role in Nigerian Civil War, 73–74

Carment, David and Patrick James, 23, 232n86

Central African Republic, role in Congo Crisis, 60–61, 63

Chechnya, 3, 30, 32, 135, 146, 185, 247n15

Chernomyrdin, Viktor, 214

China, Republic of (PRC), 197, 207, 245n21, 245n24; role in Nigerian Civil War, 74, 75, 83, 207–208, 217

Chopra, Jarat, 5

Civic nationalism, 43, 49, 51–52, 55, 56, 68, 79, 204, 210–211, 216

Clash of Civilizations, 152, 203, 209, 246n5

Clinton, President Bill, 138–139, 140, 209

Clinton, President William, 4; impeachment and foreign policy, 6; policy towards Yugoslavia, 5, 242n149;

Collective action, logic of, 15

Communism, role in Congo Crisis; 46, 57–58, 69; role in Nigerian Civil War, 74, 81

Confederation des associations Tribales due Katanga (Conakat), 39–40

Conference on Security and Cooperation in Europe, see Organization for Security and Cooperation in Europe

Conflict management, techniques, 5, 221–222, 247n132

Congo (Zaire), 244n8, also see Congo Crisis

Congo Crisis, 6, 96, 97, 99, 103, 106, 107, 153, 155, 204, 205, 207, 208, 220, 221, 222; ambivalent and neutral states, 56–61; case selection

of, 30–31, 70, 71; ethnic politics within, 38–40; origins, 37–38; supporters of Congo, 50–56; supporters of Katanga, 41–50;

Congo-Brazzaville, 60; role in Congo Crisis, 41, 48–50, 63, 66–68, 204, 206, 209

Constituency, 22–23

Contagion, 223n14, 244n113

Conventional wisdom, see Vulnerability

Corsica, 9, 117–118, 146

Crawford, Beverly, 126, 128–129

Croatia, 123, 158, 163, 222, 239n35, 239n38, 240n80, 244n8; irredentism, 104, 112–113; see also Yugoslavia

Cuban Missile Crisis, 59, 209

Czech Republic, 158

Dacko, David, 60

David, Steven, 20

Davies, John, 5

Davis, David and Will H. Moore, 23

Dayton Accords, 108, 138–139, 205

De Gaulle, Charles, 58, 118; influence on Francophone countries, 80, 91

Diori, Hamani, see Niger

Diversionary theories of war, 6–7, 215–216, 240n76

Djilas, Aleksa, 124

Dodd, Thomas, 59

East Timor, 32

Economic Sanctions, 4, 106, 120, 221

Egypt, 244n9; role in Nigerian Civil War, 90, 96, role in Yugoslav conflict, 141

Eisenhower, President Dwight D., 57–58, 63

Eritrea, 158, 163
Ethiopia, 196; role in Congo Crisis, 55–56, 231n74, 232n90; role in Nigerian Civil War, 85–87, 96, 99, 101, 209
Ethiopia-Somalia war, 4
Ethnic Cleansing, 3
Ethnic conflict, danger of spread, 4–5, 16
Ethnic enmity, 24–25
Ethnic politics and foreign policy, 6, 8; and the Congo Crisis, 66–69; elaboration of, 22–29; ethnic ties, 23–24, 26–29; impact of heterogeneity, 25–26. 45; implications for broader academic debates, 215–219; implications of cases studies for, 208–211; and the Nigerian Civil War, 99–101; statistical summary of case studies, 155; and trends in the international relations of ethnic conflict, 163–166; and why groups receive support, 168–169, 175, 181, 212; and why states give support, 185, 212; and the Yugoslav conflicts, 149–152
Ethnologue, 171
European Community, involvement in Yugoslavia, 1, 103, 107–108, 114, 117, 122–123, 133, 136, 138, 146–148, 149, 206, 238n2, 243n8
European Union, see European Community

Falkland Islands, 216
Federation of Rhodesia and Nyasaland, role in Congo Crisis, 40, 41, 46–48, 50, 63, 64, 69, 204, 207

Former Soviet republics, 158
Former Yugoslav Republic of Macedonia (FYROM), see Macedonia
Forum-shopping, 217–218
France, 207, 245n21; role in Congo Crisis, 38, 40, 48–49, 50, 60, 207; role in Nigerian Civil War, 74, 80, 81, 82, 83, 92, 207; role in Yugoslav conflict, 1, 5, 116, 117–119, 123, 133, 139, 144, 146, 151, 152, 197, 209, 218, 229n85, 240n79
Frankfurter Allgemeine Zeitung (FAZ), 128

Gabon, role in Nigerian Civil War, 74, 82–83, 86, 92, 96, 97
Genscher, Hans Dietrich, 122, 123, 129
Georgia, 244n8
Germany, 197, 244n9, 245n21; refugees in, 3; role in Kosovo conflict, 214; role in Yugoslav conflict, 1, 116, 117, 118, 122–131, 133, 144, 148–149, 206, 207, 240n79
Ghana, 79; role in Congo Crisis, 49, 51–53, 222, 231n63
Gibbs, David, 57, 220
Gligorov, Kiro, 115; see also Macedonia
Gorbachev, Mikhail, 118, 134
Gowon, Yakubu, 71, 73
Great Britain, 207, 245n21; role in Congo Crisis, 38, 40, 47, 207, 208; role in Kosovo conflict, 214; role in Nigerian Civil War, 85, 207; role in Yugoslav conflicts, 1, 5, 117, 123, 139, 144, 146, 197, 218, 240n79

Greece, 142; conflict with Turkey 3,
140–141, 215; policies towards
Macedonia, 1, 109, 115, 116, 123,
126, 127, 130, 135–137, 143, 144,
148, 151, 152, 210, 238n11,
242n136
Greek-American lobby, 139, 140, 209
Guinea, 244n9; role in Congo Crisis,
49, 55–56
Gurr, Ted Robert, 5, 29

Haiti, recognition of Biafra, 233n2
Hammarskjold, Dag, 38
Harvey, Frank, 5
Hausa-Fulani, see Nigerian Civil
War
Henderson, Errol, 23
Heraclides, Alexis, 17–18
Herbst, Jeffrey, 14–15, 17, 69, 99
Hercegovina lobby, 112
Houpou—t-Boigny, Felix, 86; see also
Ivory Coast
Humanitarian concerns, 2–4
Hungary, relations with Romania, 121,
151; role in Yugoslav conflict, 116,
131–133, 143, 144, 146, 207, 208
Huntington, Samuel, 209; see also
Clash of Civilizations
Hutus, 245n23

Ibos, 88–89; see Nigerian Civil War
India, 79, 196, 219, 232n86, 232n87,
245n21; role in Congo Crisis, 55,
63, 205, 218, 231n74
Indigenous peoples, 219, 245n26
Indonesia, 32, 244n9
Indo-Pakistani War, 4
International norms, 7, 16
International organizations, ; role in
case selection, 31; role in ethnic
conflict, 7, 16

Iran, 114, 116, 141, 146, 197, 204,
244n8, 245n24
Iraq, 245n24
Irredentism, 104, 136, 225n2, 238n4,
238n11
Israel, 235n60; role in Nigerian Civil
War, 73, 74, 83–84, 98
Italy, 245n21; role in Yugoslav
conflicts, 141–142, 143, 144, 146,
153, 204, 206
Ivory Coast, role in Nigerian Civil
War, 74, 80–82, 86, 92, 97, 206

Jackson, Robert and Carl Rosberg, 13,
17, 69, 99
Japan, 197, 245n21
Jeszenszky, Gáza, 131

Kasavubu, Joseph, 37, 42,57; ties to
Congo-Brazzaville, 49
Katanga, 36, ethnic politics within,
38–40; role of white settlers, 39
Kaufmann, Chaim, 5
Kaunda, Kenneth, 86; see also Zambia
Kennedy, President John F., 58–59,
63, 209, 218
Kenya, role in Nigerian Civil War, 92
Keohane, Robert, 14
Kohl, Helmut, 123
Kosovo Liberation Army, 142, 213
Kosovo, 4, 30, 35, 126, 185, 203, 206,
212–215, 217, 238n11, 246n9;
supporters of Albanians, 1, 144;
threat to spillover, 140–141,
214–215, 239n53
Kurds, 245n24
Kuwait, 244n8

Labs, Eric, 21
Latin America, 234n11
Libal, Michael, 126–127, 128, 130

Libya, 246*n*42; role in Nigerian civil war, 90
Lumumba, Patrice, 37, 39, 42, 43, 51, 57, 64, 68, 210, 231*n*43; fear of, 46, 50, 207, 211, 232–2333*n*94

Maastricht Treaty, 125
Macedonia, 3, 114–115, 123, 126, 127, 130, 152, 163, 207, 238*n*11, 242*n*128, 242*n*129; role in the Kosovo conflict, 213, 239*n*53; see also Greece, Yugoslavia
Malavinas, see Falkland Islands
Malaysia, role in Yugoslav conflict, 141, 197, 244*n*8
Maull, Hans 128
Milosevic, Slobodan, 105–106, 110, 131, 134, 212, 214, 228*n*65
Minorities At Risk dataset (MAR), 29, 35, 154, 158–160, 166, 171, 211, 220, 229*n*75, 229*n*87, 229*n*87, 243*n*4, 244*n*16
Mitterand, Francois, 118–119, 209
Moldova, impact on Romania, 121, 151
Moravscsik, Andrew, 7, 217
Morgan, Clifford and Kenneth Bickers, 215–216
Morocco, role in the Congo Crisis, 55–56, 63, 232*n*90

Nagorno-Karabakh, 3
Nakarada, Radmila, 9, 16
Neoliberal Institutionalism, 7, 14, 217, 225*n*18
Netherlands, role in Nigerian Civil War, 92
Niger, role in Nigerian Civil War, 89–90, 96
Nigeria, role in Congo Crisis, 53–55, 231*n*74, 232*n*84

Nigerian Civil War, 6, 106, 153, 197, 204, 205, 207, 208, 221; ambivalent and neutral states, 91–94; case selection of, 30–31, 70–71; ethnic politics in, 72–74; origins of the conflict, 71–72; supporters of Biafra, 74–85; supporters of Nigeria, 85–91;
Nkrumah, Kwame, 49, 86, 231*n*63; see also Ghana
Nordchurchaid, role in Nigerian Civil War, 73–74
North Atlantic Treaty Organization (NATO), 42, 44; intervention in Kosovo, 1, 213–214, 215, 247*n*15; role in Yugoslav conflicts, 103, 106, 108, 109, 114, 119, 123, 124, 125, 126, 131–132, 133, 134–135, 137, 139–140, 143, 146–148, 205, 208, 217, 218, 242*n*149
Northern Ireland, 9, 146, 224*n*33
Nyerere, Julius, see Tanzania

Offensive capability, 19
Ojukwu, C. Odumegwu, 72, 73, 91
Organization for Security and Cooperation in Europe (OSCE), criticism of Croatia, 113; role in Yugoslav conflicts, 103, 108. 141
Organization of African Unity (OAU), 64; role in case selection, 30–31; role in Nigerian Civil War, 70, 72, 75, 82, 85, 86–87, 88, 92, 99, 167, 196, 205, 218role in vulnerability argument, 2, 8–9, 14;
Organization of the Islamic Conference, 137, 243*n*8
Outcomes of ethnic conflict, 2

Pakistan, 196
Pan-Africanism, 40, 47, 51–52, 56, 63, 81, 86, 204, 207, 210, 211, 217, 222

Papandreou, Andreas, 137
Policy relevance, 2–6
Political competition, assessment of, 209; coding, 33–34; implications of, 216–217
Polity dataset, 172; role in theory of ethnic politics and foreign policy, 26, 224n31, 228n69, 228n72;
Pope Paul VI, 233n8
Portugal, role in Nigerian Civil War, 74, 80, 83–84, 98, 204, 207
Power, indicator for, 169–171
Precedents, 1, 3, 9, 74, 154, 158, 160, 229n88, 240n66

Realism, 6, 7, 12, 224n34, 226n32, 226n34; and the Congo Crisis, 61–64; defensive realism, 18; expansion and elaboration of, 18–22; offensive realism 18, 20–21; implications of cases studies for, 206–208; and the Nigerian Civil War, 94–97; statistical summary of case studies, 155–158; and trends in the international relations of ethnic conflict, 163; and why groups receive support, 167–168, 182–183, 212; and why states give support, 184–185, 196–197, 198, 212; and the Yugoslav conflicts, 143–146
Refugees, 3–4, 213
Regan, Patrick, 172
Regime type, impact on why groups receive support, 183
Research design, 10, 29–35; case selection, 29–32; coding rules in the case studies, 33–35; quantitative analyses, 35; selecting observations, 32–33; see also Chapter 6

Rhodesia, role in Nigerian Civil War, 83–85, 97, 98, 101, 207
Roma, 219
Romania, costs of sanctions, 3, 4, 120; role in Yugoslavia conflict, 116, 119–122, 133, 144, 146, 151, 152, 209, 240n66
Russia, 32, 160, 196, 207, 212, 245n21; assessment of ethnic conflict, 4; role in Kosovo conflict, 213–214, 247n14, 247n15; role in Yugoslav conflicts, 1, 6, 111, 116, 123, 134–135, 144, 146, 148, 149, 151–151, 198, 204, 206, 210, 217; see also Soviet Union
Rwanda, 3, 30, 219, 229n3

Safe areas, 108
Sanwi, 81–82
Sarbanes, Paul, 140
Sardinia, 9
Saudi Arabia, 141, 197, 244n8
Schweller, Randall, 20–21
Scotland, 146
Selassie I, Haile, see Ethiopia
Self-determination, 126–127
Senegal, role in Nigerian Civil War, 91–92, 94, 99, 101, 209
Senghor, Leopold, see Senegal
Serbia, 222; history of conflict, 4; irredentism, 4, 104; Kosovo conflict, 1, 213–215; nationalism, 110–111; relations with Macedonia, 114; sanctions against, 4; see also Yugoslavia
Sierra Leone, 244n9; role in Nigerian Civil War, 92–94, 237n123
Slovakia, 158
Slovenia, 111, 123, 158, 163; see also Yugoslavia
Somalia, 196; impact of intervention in,-

139, irredentism, 13, 14, 85; role in
    Nigerian Civil War, 90–91, 96
Somaliland, 32,
South Africa, 245n23, 245n24; role in
    Congo Crisis, 40, 50, 63, 69; role
    in Nigerian Civil War, 74, 83–85,
    97, 98, 101, 204, 207
South Korea, 197, 245n21
Soviet Union, 171, 243n159; role in
    the Congo Crisis, 297; role in
    Nigerian Civil War, 85, 96, 208,
    229n85; role in Yugoslav conflicts,
    107, 118, 146, see also Russia
Spaak, Paul Henri, 42, 44, 68
Specific reciprocity, 14–15, 17,
    205–206
Srebrenica, 108
Sri Lanka, 3, 232n86
Stedman, Stephen, 5
Sudan, 185, 196; border disputes with
    Ethiopia, 85; role in Nigerian Civil
    War, 90, 96
Suhrke, Astri and Lela Garner Noble,
    13–14
Syria, 244n8

Taiwan, role in Congo Crisis, 38
Tamils, 245n23
Tanzania, role in Nigerian Civil War,
    74–78, 92, 96, 97, 99, 101, 206,
    207, 209
Tatar Republic, 244n8
Territorial Integrity, 218–219; role in
    vulnerability argument, 2, 9, 13
Toure, Sekou, 49, 86, 232n85; see also
    Guinea
Touval, Saadia, 13
Trends in the international relations of
    ethnic conflict, 158–166
Tshombe, Moise, 37, 38, 40, 41, 43, 44,
    46, 58, 64, 68, 209–210, 230n37

Tudjman, Franjo, see Croatia
Tunisia, role in Congo Crisis, 38,
    55–56, 63, 232n91; role in
    Nigerian Civil War, 91
Turkey, 197; conflict with Greece, 3,
    140–141, 215; role in Yugoslav
    conflict, 116, 137–138, 144
Tutsis, 245n21
Tyrol, 9

Uganda, 187, 229n3; role in Nigerian
    Civil War, 94, 237n123, 237n124
Ukraine, role in Kosovo conflict, 214
United Nations, 4, 30, 31, 70, 205;
    and the Congo Crisis, 36, 38, 41,
    44, 45, 46, 48, 53, 57, 65–66, 69,
    218; and the Nigerian Civil War,
    92; and Yugoslav conflicts, 103,
    107, 107–109, 116, 117, 118, 125,
    136, 137, 139–140, 141, 146–148,
    217
United States, 207, 212, 245n21; role
    in the Congo Crisis, 37, 44, 50–51,
    56–60, 63, 68, 208, 209, 217,
    232n93; role in Kosovo conflict,
    214–215; role in Yugoslav conflict,
    123, 134, 138–141, 144, 146, 148,
    149, 151, 196, 197, 198, 206, 208,
    209, 217, 242n144

Violence, impact on why groups
    receive support, 183
Vojvodina, 132–133, 240n119; see also
    Serbia, Yugoslavia
Vulnerability, and case selection, 30;
    coding, 34; and the Congo Crisis,
    64–66; elaboration, 13–17;
    implications of cases studies for,
    204–206; and the Nigerian Civil
    War, 97–99; statistical summary of
    case studies, 158; summary, 2, 8–9,

Vulnerability *(continued)*
12; testing claims about trends,
158–166, 212; and why groups
receive support, 166–167, 181–182,
211–212; and why states give
support, 184, 187, 196, 198, 211;
and to the Yugoslav conflicts,
146–149

Wachuku, Jaja, 53–55
Walt, Stephen, 9, 96; extension to
ethnic conflicts, 18–20, 61, 206,
226n36
Walter, Barbara, 5
Weiss, Thomas, 5
Welensky, Roy, 46–47, 50
Woodward, Susan, 111
World Council of Churches, role in
Nigerian Civil War, 73–74

World War I, implications for present
day, 4

Yeltsin, Boris, 6, 134, 135, 213–214
Yoruba, see Nigerian Civil War
Youlou, Fulbert, role in Congo Crisis,
48–50, 66
Yugoslavia, 1, 3, 4, 5, 6, 203, 205, 207,
210, 221, 222; case selection of,
31–32, 103–104; contact group, 5;
intervention by international
organizations, 106–109, 238n9; key
external actors, 116–142; origins of
the conflict, 105–106; separatists
within, 109–115

Zambia, role in Nigerian Civil War,
75, 78–80, 86, 92, 96, 97, 206, 207,
211